REMIXING
REGGAETÓN

REMIXING
REGGAETÓN

The Cultural Politics of Race in Puerto Rico   Petra R. Rivera-Rideau

Duke University Press   Durham and London   2015

Library of Congress Cataloging-in-Publication Data
Rivera-Rideau, Petra R., [date]
Remixing reggaetón : the cultural politics of race in Puerto Rico /
Petra R. Rivera-Rideau.
pages cm
Includes bibliographical references and index.
ISBN 978–0–8223–5945–6 (hardcover : alk. paper)
ISBN 978–0–8223–5964–7 (pbk. : alk. paper)
ISBN 978–0–8223–7525–8 (e-book)
1. Reggaetón—History and criticism. 2. Puerto Rico—Race relations. I. Title.
ML3532.5.R58 2015
781.646097295—dc23
2015008877

COVER ART: Tego Calderon; epa european pressphoto agency b.v. / Alamy

For Ryan

CONTENTS

ACKNOWLEDGMENTS

This book has benefited from the support, encouragement, constructive criticism, and love of a great many people. The ideas first percolated during the writing of my dissertation in the African Diaspora Studies department at the University of California, Berkeley. When I tell people I study reggaetón, they often respond with a polite nod and a perplexed, and sometimes skeptical, look on their faces. I am grateful for a dissertation committee that never batted an eye when I approached them with this idea. I am forever indebted to Percy Hintzen, Jocelyne Guilbault, and Leigh Raiford for their mentorship, advice, and encouragement over the years. I hope they can see how much they have shaped my thinking and molded me as a scholar when they read this book. I am thankful to have had the opportunity to learn from the rest of the faculty in the department, especially Ula Taylor, Robert Allen, Brandi Wilkins Catanese, Stephen Small, and the late VeVe Clarke. Thanks to Lindsey Herbert, who not only helped me navigate UC, Berkeley, but also is a great friend.

At UC, Berkeley, I benefited from the insight of my friends and colleagues in the Afro-Latino Working Group, including Vielka Hoy, Rebecca Bodenheimer, Ryan Rideau, Jennifer Jones, Juan Herrera, and Tianna Paschel. I also appreciate the comments and suggestions from the Center for Race and Gender Dissertation Writing Group.

I completed many of the revisions of the manuscript as a postdoctoral fellow in the Latin American and Iberian Studies Department at the

University of Richmond. I would like to thank Sharon Feldman for her support, encouragement, and mentorship. I am especially grateful to Lázaro Lima for his friendship, guidance, and support over the past few years. My amazing undergraduate students in the Afro-Latino Identities and Latin Music and Migration courses provided important feedback on various chapters in the book (even if they did not realize it at the time).

My colleagues in Africana Studies, Women's and Gender Studies, and Sociology at Virginia Tech have been a great source of support as I put the finishing touches on the manuscript. I would like to thank John Ryan and Ellington Graves for their leadership and support during my time here. Also, my senior colleagues Kwame Harrison, Laura Gillman, David Brunsma, Wornie Reed, and Anthony Peguero have been excellent models and mentors for me as I move forward with my academic career. I am blessed to be part of a great cohort of tenure-track faculty in the Sociology Department, including Sarah Ovink, Christine Labuski, and Nick Copeland. Brenda Husser and Amy Kokkinakos have tolerated my millions of questions and expertly handled all of my copy machine problems. I must give a very special thank you to Tish Glosh who helped me figure out the bureaucracy at Virginia Tech. My graduate assistants, Talitha Rose, Jose Torres, Kristin Richardson, Joy Thompson, Phil Carey, Sofia Ruhkin, and Jessica Herling, have been incredibly helpful with teaching and administrative duties, giving me the time I needed to finish the book.

It is a dream to be able to publish my first book with Duke University Press. Gisela Fosado has been an especially enthusiastic and helpful editor, and her guidance has made this manuscript the best that it could be. Lorien Olive expertly guided me through the process of preparing the final version of the manuscript. Thank you also to Willa Armstrong, Susan Albury, Christopher Robinson, and the staff at Duke University Press who made this book possible. The two anonymous reviewers made incredibly insightful and generous comments.

I am grateful for the funding that allowed me to pursue this research, including a Ford Foundation Predoctoral Fellowship, a Social Science Research Council Dissertation Proposal Development Fellowship, and a Puerto Rican Diaspora Research Grant from the Center for Puerto Rican Studies at Hunter College. At UC, Berkeley, I received funding from a Chancellor's Opportunity Fellowship, the Dean's Normative Time Fellowship, and a Tinker Summer Field Research Grant from the Center for Latin American Studies. The University of Richmond and the College of Liberal

Arts and Human Sciences at Virginia Tech also provided much needed financial support as I revised the manuscript.

I have been fortunate to present portions of this work at several conferences and symposia and would like to thank those whose comments and questions helped me refine my ideas. Daphne Brooks, David Brunsma, Christine Labuski, Manisha Sharma, Minjeong Kim, Sarah Ovink, Rachelle Brunn-Bevel, Madhavi Murty, and others have provided feedback on various parts of the manuscript. Kwame Harrison, Jasmine Johnson, Tianna Paschel, and Ryan Rideau took time out of their very busy schedules to read the entire manuscript. Raquel Z. Rivera shared many resources and suggestions with me when I was just beginning to pursue this research. Jorge Duany met with me while I was doing research in Puerto Rico and connected me to several people and resources. I must also thank the artists and fans who agreed to talk to me about their opinions, ideas, and experiences. Without them, this book would not be possible.

Thanks are also due to Miriam Jiménez Román and the late Juan Flores who have offered me tremendous support and invaluable opportunities over the years. Juan passed away while this book was in production. I first encountered Juan's work as a college student, and it helped me to imagine what kind of research could be possible. Since then, Juan has been a generous mentor and friend who encouraged me to pursue this project and to refine my ideas. I will miss him dearly.

My friends have been a constant source of support, reality-checks, fun, comfort, and happiness. Special thanks to Maryclaire Capetta, Danielle Robles, Idalia Perez, Jamie Lawrence, Carla Martin, Arya Soman, Taj Frazier, Kelley Deetz, Lia Bascomb, Jasmine Johnson, Ron Williams, Kelly Middlebrook, Arvin Lugay, Patricia Herrera, Erika Zimmermann Damer, Minjeong Kim, Melanie Kiechle, and Dennis Halpin. This academic journey would be infinitely more lonely and dull without my dear friends Tianna Paschel and Jennifer Jones. Charisse Padilla offered me a couch to sleep on when visiting New York, sent me interesting articles and leads to pursue, accompanied me to conferences, concerts, and parades, visited me wherever I've lived, and is the best friend ever.

My family is everything. My parents, Gene Rivera and Meg Weiss-Rivera, have always taught me to pursue my passions, ask lots of questions, and love music. They even read my papers and give me comments! I am incredibly lucky to have such amazing people to look up to. My sister, Carmen Andrea Rivera, is my best friend and confidant, and always keeps me grounded. Her partner, Nico Udu-Gama, has been a good friend and source of support throughout this process. My extended family is always there, even when we're far apart—shout out to my cousin Alex Arroyo for being a great roommate while I was conducting part of this research in New York. I am fortunate to have married into the very loving Rideau and LaCroix families. A very special thank you to my in-laws, Brenda, Kevin, and Ashley Rideau, for welcoming me with open arms.

Adrian arrived just days before I received the contract for this book. He keeps me busy, reminds me not to sweat the small stuff, and always finds joy in the littlest things. I'm sure Adrian will think reggaetón is old and boring by the time he is old enough to care, but I hope that this book makes him proud.

This book is dedicated to my amazing partner, Ryan Rideau, who has been there from the very beginning. Ryan encouraged me when things seemed tough, celebrated with me when things went well, attended (almost) all of my presentations, and read the entire manuscript. He put many of his own goals on hold so that I can achieve mine. And Ryan is the most caring and loving father to our precious boy. I appreciate everything more than you'll ever know. I love you a lot.

INTRODUCTION
REGGAETÓN TAKES ITS PLACE

It was a curious omission. By 2005, one could hear reggaetón's steady "boom-ch-boom-chick" dembow beat blasting from cars and windows throughout the United States and beyond. Daddy Yankee's rapid vocals on his massive hit "Gasolina" appeared to reach every corner of the globe. Radio stations dedicated exclusively to reggaetón broadcast all over the United States, and mainstream television stations like MTV included "Gasolina" in their regular rotations. And yet, not one reggaetón artist was nominated for a Latin Grammy for Album of the Year.

"Gasolina" received a nomination for Record of the Year (but lost to Alejandro Sanz's pop song, "Tú No Tienes Alma"). Besides that, only the "Best Urban Music Album" category contained any reggaetón nominees or winners (Daddy Yankee's *Barrio Fino* won that year); but, "Urban Music" was created specifically for hip-hop, rap, and reggaetón albums. And it wasn't just Daddy Yankee who was left out. Many people were shocked when the "Producer of the Year" category excluded reggaetón production duo Luny Tunes. "Producer of the Year" nominee Sebastian Krys commented, "I thought Luny Tunes should've been nominated for Producer of the Year. Their productions are changing the landscape of radio, of television, of everything."[1] The ghettoization of reggaetón within the Urban Music category prompted Kalefa Sennah of the *New York Times* to proclaim, "Luckily, exciting new genres don't typically wait for statuettes before they set about taking over the world . . . By the time reggaeton stars start winning Latin Grammys by the armload, they won't need them."[2]

Still, the Latin Grammys could not completely ignore reggaetón. Despite the absence of reggaetón in the list of nominees, the broadcast featured some reggaetón sets, including a historic performance by Los 12 Discípulos, a group of reggaetón artists convened by Eddie Dee (incidentally, one of the cowriters of "Gasolina").[3] It began with veteran artist Vico C singing his salsa-reggae inspired song "No Aguanta Pela," in which he donned a white suit and hat and performed a choreographed dance routine. After his performance, the stage went black as the sounds of the Fania All-Stars song "Quítate Tú" played over the speakers. Suddenly, the music ended, and the audience could hear Eddie Dee saying, "They were the masters, and we are the twelve disciples."[4] Beginning with spoken word artist Gallego, reggaetón artists Vico C, Eddie Dee, Tego Calderón, Voltio, Zion, Ivy Queen, Johnny Prez, Tito el Bambino, and Lennox, took the stage one-by-one to perform their verses to the dembow beat laced with the salsa sample from the Fania hit. Each of the artists wore baggy black jeans, white sneakers, a black T-shirt, and a sparkling chain. Emblazoned on the front of each shirt was a photograph of a renowned salsa artist from the 1970s, such as Héctor Lavoe, Ismael Rivera, Cheo Feliciano, Rubén Blades, Celia Cruz, and others. The verses were classic *tiraera*—a battle in which the artists boasted of their lyrical prowess. For the last thirty seconds of the performance, the artists gathered together on stage and repeated the line borrowed from Fania's original song, "¡Quítate tú pa' ponerme yo!" [Get out of the way, I'm taking your place!].

There was something powerful about the group of reggaetón stars standing on the Latin Grammys stage, repeating "¡Quítate tú pa' ponerme yo!" in unison. The T-shirts, and the Fania sample, linked reggaetón to one of Latin music's most beloved genres, salsa, despite critics' attempts to paint reggaetón as "inauthentic" and not "real" Latin music. In typical *tiraera* fashion, the performance responded to an organization that had dissed reggaetón when it excluded the genre from the most prestigious awards.

But the repeated exclamation, "¡Quítate tú pa' ponerme yo!" extends beyond the Latin Recording Academy's snubbing of reggaetón that year to respond to more insidious forms of exclusion faced by many of reggaetón's artists and fans. The artists involved in Los 12 Discípulos are from Puerto Rico, often recognized as the epicenter of reggaetón.[5] On the island, reggaetón has long been associated with working-class, urban, and nonwhite

FIGURE I.1. Eddie Dee performs "Quítate Tú Pa' Ponerme Yo" with Los 12 Discípulos at the 6th Annual Latin Grammy Awards on November 3, 2005. Note the image of salsa artist Willie Colón on his T-shirt. *Credit*: Michael Caulfield Archive/Wireimage/ Getty Images

communities. These communities have been subject to persistent racism, despite hegemonic discourses that define Puerto Rico as a "racial democracy"[6] in which everyone lives in racial harmony. Moreover, dominant definitions of Puerto Rican national identity[7] privilege whiteness and Spanish cultures as the most influential in the island's development. In this context, reggaetón has served as a space for expressing a "race-based cultural politics"[8] that both points out the continued presence of racism and devaluation of blackness in Puerto Rico, and foregrounds Puerto Rico's connections to other sites in the African diaspora. As Frances Negrón-Muntaner and Raquel Z. Rivera state, "[R]eggaetón calls attention to the centrality of black culture and the migration of peoples and ideas in (and out of) Puerto Rico, not as exotic additions but as constitutive elements. If Puerto Ricans and other Latin Americans have celebrated Spain as the 'motherland,' reggaetón redirects the gaze towards Africa's diasporas."[9] In this vein, we might understand Los 12 Discípulos' performance as part of reggaetón's larger insistence on the full recognition of those communities whose cultural practices are not only considered too "unrefined" for spaces like the Latin Grammys, but also those who are systematically excluded by racist and classist discourses that inform dominant definitions of Puerto Ricanness.

What are the possibilities reggaetón offers for countering the persistence of social inequalities such as racism and classism, not only in Puerto Rico, but also elsewhere in the Americas? What are the limits of reggaetón's contestatory politics? These questions are at the heart of this book, which examines reggaetón events and figures from the mid-1990s to the mid-2000s[10] in order to provide a window into the shifting entanglements between blackness and Puerto Rican identity. Many scholars have shown how Latin American and Caribbean popular music serves as a site for the negotiation of black identities.[11] In Puerto Rico, reggaetón builds from genres of popular music like bomba,[12] salsa, and others that unveil the contradictions within Puerto Rico's so-called racial democracy and produce new ideas about blackness and Puerto Rican identities.[13] However, reggaetón's newness is often linked to its reputation as a uniquely transnational phenomenon.[14] Transnational processes of migration and cultural exchange not only influenced reggaetón's sound, but also its aforementioned "race-based cultural politics."[15] Musically, reggaetón incorporates beats, vocal styles, and other aesthetics from several genres popular in the African diaspora in the Americas, especially hip-hop and dancehall. But beyond the musical, reggaetón artists and fans also relate to the experiences of racial exclusion often described in

Figure I.2. Los 12 Discípulos perform at the 6th Annual Latin Grammy Awards on November 3, 2005. *Credit:* Vince Bucci/Getty Images Entertainment/Getty Images

hip-hop, dancehall, and other musical genres that, in turn, provide opportunities to express connections between the island and other African diasporic sites. *Remixing Reggaetón* details how reggaetón integrates aesthetics and signifiers from other sites in the African diaspora to produce new understandings of Puerto Ricanness that center blackness and diasporic belonging, and to articulate Afro-Latino identities on the island and elsewhere.

"We Can All Say That We Are Black"

"We can all say that we are black," Adriana, a college student I met in San Juan, told me.[16] She continued, "it would be illogical to be racist against a black person, but it happens. And it's stupid. It's stupid because it doesn't make sense because we are all partially black, even if a person is white, albino, *jincho*,[17] blond with green eyes, blue eyes." Adriana's assessment of the simultaneous recognition of blackness in Puerto Rico ("we are all black") with the existence of racism on the island reveals one of the fundamental contradictions of dominant discourses[18] of racial democracy in Puerto Rico—that is, the persistence of racism on the island despite official rhetoric that purports that a history of race mixture has produced a racially harmonious society.

Dominant discourses of racial democracy and *blanqueamiento* in Puerto Rico share many characteristics with other sites in the Americas. In places where the majority of the population was classified as nonwhite, elites often deployed discourses similar to racial democracy in an effort to affiliate their respective Latin American and Caribbean countries with European modernity.[19] Although such moves attempted to unify diverse racial and ethnic populations under an all-inclusive national and/or regional identity, they were also committed to *blanqueamiento*, or whitening, which involved considerable efforts to culturally whiten populations and "Europeanize" national cultures throughout the region.[20] Ironically, discourses that proclaim a racial democracy throughout much of Latin America and the Caribbean generally reproduce racial hierarchies that devalue blackness and indigeneity and fortify structural racism that adversely affects black and indigenous communities.[21] Despite their embrace of *blanqueamiento*, it is important to recognize that discourses that promote racial democracy do not entirely eliminate blackness from their depictions of national identity. Rather, they entail the "strategic inclusion"[22] of certain constructions of blackness into their definitions of national identity while simultaneously rejecting other conceptions of blackness. This strategic inclusion furthers the racial inequality inherent to discourses of racial democracy because, often, problematic stereotypes of blackness as primitive become emblematic of the African influence within a specific place.

Historically, comparisons between race relations in the United States and Latin America have played critical roles in portraying Latin America as a "racially harmonious" region. Assumptions about the leniency of slavery in Latin America and the Caribbean as well as the absence of de jure segregation in the region served as evidence of its allegedly raceless societies. This comparison is particularly important for Puerto Rico given the island's colonial relationship with the United States since 1898. Not only does this situation hinder many overt discussions about racism, but it also frames the adoption of a black identity on the island as the influence of U.S. imperialism (e.g., see chapter 1). In this way, blackness is continuously represented as foreign and fundamentally incompatible with Puerto Ricanness, even though hegemonic depictions of Puerto Rican national identity integrate other, very specific constructions of blackness.

Representing the United States as the locus of all things racist fosters the development of a sort of historical and cultural amnesia regarding the perpetuation of racial hierarchies under Spanish colonialism and the ways that Puerto Ricans themselves have been complicit in keeping them intact. Like other places in the Americas, Puerto Rico also had slavery and, in fact, did not abolish it until 1873. Although Puerto Rico did not develop as robust a plantation economy as other Caribbean countries, the island's population still consisted primarily of people of color, including not only enslaved Africans and Afro–Puerto Ricans, but also a substantial group of free people of color from both Puerto Rico and the surrounding islands for much of the eighteenth and nineteenth centuries.[23] However, the perception of a relatively small slave economy has contributed to the idea that Puerto Rico has more "lax" race relations than the United States.[24] It also furthered popular assumptions that the Spanish were somehow more racially tolerant than other colonizers (namely the British and, subsequently, the Americans), ignoring the ways that the Spanish contributed to the production of racial hierarchies that valorized whiteness and demonized blackness.[25]

This "silencing"[26] of blackness and of racism continued after 1898, albeit in a revised way that presented the United States as the primary site of racial strife as opposed to the allegedly raceless Puerto Rico. The promotion of racial democracy discourses took on particular intensity with the writings of the *Generación de los 1930s*, a group of intellectuals whose work is central to definitions of Puerto Rican racial democracy and national identity.[27] By the 1930s, the United States had firmly established Puerto Rico as one of its colonies, with U.S.-appointed leaders (a practice that would not change until the 1940s) and economic control of crucial industries such as sugar production by U.S. corporations. As a result of the "Americanization" of the island, many elites, who felt "a loss of power, cultural and political authority, feelings of outrage at a loss of legitimacy with respect to their perceived right to lead the nation, to serve as models of civility," sought to establish a new national identity that would distinguish them from the United States while still affiliating the island with the ideals and standards of European modernity.[28] The result was a vision of Puerto Rican national identity that celebrated a whitened, Spanish heritage even as it propagated the image of Puerto Ricans as racially mixed.

Among the proponents of the racially mixed (but conceived of as white) Puerto Rico were authors such as Antonio S. Pedreira and Tomás Blanco, whose work is often considered typical of the arguments promoted by the *Generación de los 1930s*. Interestingly, Pedreira and Blanco disagreed on the impact of race mixture in Puerto Rican society: Pedreira argued that it resulted in a "con-fused" people and thus led to the perpetual colonization of the island,[29] while Blanco claimed race mixture proved Puerto Ricans' moral superiority and therefore discredited U.S. colonialism.[30] However, both men shared profoundly problematic views of blackness and valorizations of Spanish culture. Each of them identified Spanish contributions to Puerto Rico as the most important in the island's development, both culturally (such as when Pedreira declared that the Spanish brought "intelligence and planning" to Puerto Rico[31]), and biologically (for example, when Blanco proclaimed that race mixture progressively whitened Puerto Rico through the "dilution" of African blood[32]). Despite these commitments to *blanqueamiento*, both men professed that racial prejudice did not exist in Puerto Rico.[33]

Several scholars have critiqued the works by the *Generación de los 1930s*, pointing out their problematic depictions of blackness and promotion of racial stereotypes.[34] A later generation of scholars and writers, the *Generación de los 1970s*, also sought to define the racial dynamics of Puerto Rican national identity; however, they did so in part by emphasizing certain aspects of black culture and identity in Puerto Rico that had been ignored or distorted by theorists like Pedreira.[35] Two authors in particular, José Luis González and Isabelo Zenón Cruz, produced theories that upended the typical Hispanophilia of the *Generación de los 1930s*. Zenón Cruz's two-volume *Narciso descubre su trasero* presented myriad examples of persistent racism on the island and highlighted the contributions of Afro–Puerto Ricans to Puerto Rico's history and culture in order to assert that blackness was equally important in defining Puerto Rican identities.[36] José Luis González made a similar claim when he characterized Puerto Rico as racially mixed, but that of the "three roots the one that is most important for economic and social—and hence cultural reasons—is the African."[37] As members of the *Generación de los 1970s*, Zenón Cruz and González challenged the emphasis on whitening and Spanish culture in dominant discourses of racial democracy, although they remained committed to race mixture as the basis of their own understandings of Puerto Rican national identities.[38]

Since then, many scholars have discredited the dominant discourse of racial democracy in Puerto Rico.[39] Through her analysis of the island's "slippery semantics," or the ways that individuals speak about race, Isar Godreau demonstrates how ambiguity around racial identification and racism in Puerto Rico coexists with a racial binary that distinguishes blackness and whiteness.[40] Indeed, the attachment to black/white racial binaries within Puerto Rico's so-called racial democracy is not surprising given that the celebration of race mixture requires the identification of "pure," original groups that mixed together. Here, ideas about place are particularly important, for they provide another way to understand the simultaneous, and contradictory, attachment to specific stereotypical tropes of blackness and the promotion of racelessness as the basis of Puerto Rican national identities.

Mapping Blackness(es) in Puerto Rico

As scholars have documented, blackness is tied to specific places or regions within many Latin American countries that, like Puerto Rico, ascribe to discourses comparable to racial democracy.[41] Assumed to be the sites of "authentic" black life and culture, such regions serve as geographic symbols of the African component of these countries' national identities. Similar processes occur in Puerto Rico. Mapping the island's racial topography shows how multiple ideas about blackness have been emplaced within very specific and bounded places. Some constructions of blackness symbolize the African branch of Puerto Rico's racial triad, while other images of blackness are considered the complete opposite of whitened Puerto Ricanness. Although they sometimes contradict each other, understanding how these various constructions of blackness operate in relation to one another illuminates how discourses of racial democracy are kept intact in Puerto Rico and elsewhere.

I term the construction of blackness that is generally understood to represent the African branch of Puerto Rican racial democracy *folkloric blackness*. Symbolized by such cultural practices as the Afro–Puerto Rican music and dance bomba, the narratives surrounding folkloric blackness consistently depict blackness as the "least" influential element in the racial triad that comprises Puerto Rican identity by positioning blackness as a historical and almost archaic relic of the island's plantation era. Isar P. Godreau argues that this "folklorization" of blackness enables the incorporation of blackness into constructions of Puerto Rican identity while still depicting the island as "Spanish" through a process of "spatial/temporal distancing."[42] In this vein, Godreau points out that racial democracy "not only encourages, but also enables dominant, romantic representations of black communities as remnants of a by-gone era."[43] Besides relegating blackness to the past, this distancing also involves locating it within specific places in Puerto Rico (for example, the town of Loíza [see chapter 3]), imagined to be distinct from the rest of the island. Confining folkloric blackness to restricted places and times implies that blackness is irrelevant to contemporary Puerto Rican society, while simultaneously acknowledging the African heritage that is part of Puerto Rico's racially mixed identity.

However, this folkloric blackness does not account for the realities of other black populations that live throughout Puerto Rico, including in the urban areas where reggaetón developed. The mere *existence* of self-identified black populations outside of the emplacements of folkloric blackness undercuts the restriction of blackness to rural and "pre-modern" geographies. In an attempt to manage the potentially destabilizing impact of these visible black communities elsewhere, other images of blackness also circulate in Puerto Rico, including one which I term *urban blackness*. Urban blackness perpetuates common stereotypes of blackness, such as violence and hypersexuality, that are attributed to the residents of working-class, predominantly nonwhite, public housing developments called *caseríos* (see chapter 1). The emplacement of urban blackness within *caseríos* also foregrounds the intersections of race and class; for example, Zaire Dinzey-Flores demonstrates how *caseríos'* portrayal as sites of blackness coalesces with their status as low-income housing.[44] Consequently, urban blackness links blackness to stereotypes of urban poverty, violence, and hypersexuality.

Although these images circulated in both the United States and Puerto Rico throughout the twentieth century, they were cemented during the 1990s anticrime initiative known as *Mano Dura Contra el Crimen* (Iron Fist against Crime). During this time, images of young, predominantly black male *caserío* residents accused of crimes ranging from robbery and drug dealing to homicide pervaded the Puerto Rican media. *Mano Dura* thus depicted *caseríos* as sites of abjection, the loci of an urban blackness defined by various "immoral" characteristics that differentiated them from the presumably more "respectable" Puerto Rico, all while ignoring the larger structural policies that produced the adverse conditions affecting *caserío* residents. Gates constructed around the perimeters of *caseríos* that were intended to "contain" criminal activity signified both ideological and physical boundaries that distinguished urban blackness from the rest of the island, situating it only within select and limited geographic areas. As a result, urban blackness became the identifiable counterpoint to hegemonic constructions of whitened Puerto Rican identity.

Although they may appear antithetical to one another, folkloric blackness and urban blackness work together to maintain racial democracy discourses. Folkloric blackness allows for the integration of blackness into the Puerto Rican nation without compromising the image of Puerto Rico as white(ned) due to its spatial/temporal distancing. On the other hand, urban blackness supposedly encompasses those values considered to be the "opposite" of normative, respectable Puerto Ricanness. Urban blackness thus symbolizes the internal black "other" against which Puerto Ricanness can be defined as white(ned).[45]

In the eyes of many detractors, reggaetón typifies the stereotypes associated with urban blackness. Mayra Santos-Febres argues that reggaetón is associated with "rap territories," or the very same urban neighborhoods targeted by *Mano Dura*.[46] Although reggaetón sometimes appears to reinforce the stereotypes associated with urban blackness, it also exposes the contradictions within dominant discourses of racial democracy in ways that allow for new imaginings of blackness to emerge.

Reggaetón as a Cultural Practice of Diaspora

In its current iteration, reggaetón is marketed as Latin music, a category that elides the substantial differences between the musical practices it encompasses.[47] Although *Latin music* supposedly incorporates styles and practices popular among Latin Americans and U.S. Latinos, the concept is primarily a U.S. construction that is consistent with the homogenizing impulse behind the label *Latino* itself.[48] As a category that denotes an ethnoracial group in the United States, Latino includes individuals from diverse geographic and racial backgrounds. U.S. Latinos have therefore been imagined as a distinct group that is located at various points between the black/white racial binary depending on shifting political and economic contexts.[49] As a result, Latinidad becomes distanced from blackness, which is instead primarily associated with U.S. African Americans. The music industry similarly relies on discrete, "unambiguous racial and ethnic categories" considered to align with specific markets such that Latin music is tied to a "Latino" audience understood to be distinct from both "black" and "white" audiences.[50] As Deborah Pacini Hernández notes, such rigid distinctions problematically neglect the cultural hybridity of not only Latin music (which includes countless examples of cultural exchange between Latinos and African Americans, among other groups), but also popular music more generally.[51] Moreover, such classification schemes within the music industry could potentially divorce genres marketed as "Latin music" from their African diasporic connections in the popular imagination, especially given the stringent divisions between blackness and Latinidad already prevalent in the United States.

Reggaetón's commercial entrance in the United States began in 2004, with songs like Daddy Yankee's "Gasolina" and N.O.R.E.'s "Oye Mi Canto" circulating regularly on radio stations and television programs. However, unlike the crossover Latin Music Boom from the late 1990s that was affiliated with mainstream popular music, the U.S. press presented reggaetón as similar to hip-hop. Within the Latin music industry, reggaetón has been labeled *música urbana* [urban music]. The term *urbana* carries with it racial and class connotations that speak to the music's affiliations with blackness. Indeed, not only does the term *urbana* imply reggaetón's ties to urban blackness in Puerto Rico, but also ideas about urban Puerto Rican communities in the United States that historically have been linked to African Americans in the popular imagination both on the island and the mainland (see chapter 5). Therefore, while many people may consider reggaetón as yet another genre encapsulated by the Latin music category, its associations with hip-hop and urban culture bring to mind specific ties to blackness that extend beyond the race mixture that presumably forms the basis of all things "Latino."

On the one hand, some media outlets such as MTV reproduce stereotypes of blackness when representing reggaetón's connections to hip-hop. At the same time, these links are also critical to reggaetón's African diasporic aesthetics. As Marc D. Perry argues, hip-hop offers possibilities for new self-fashionings among marginalized groups around the globe precisely because of its international commodification.[52] For those individuals who also identify as black, Perry claims that hip-hop can "mobilize notions of black-self in ways that are at one time both contestive and transcendent of nationally bound, hegemonically prescriptive racial framings."[53] In contemporary Puerto Rico, reggaetón constitutes a space for Puerto Rican youth to engage in practices of self-fashioning that respond to local racial politics and express an affinity with African diasporic populations.

Of course, not all reggaetón singers identify as black. Some popular artists such as Tego Calderón and Don Omar have publicly claimed black identities. Others may identify as white or one of the other racial categories in Puerto Rico that denote a position in the middle of the black/white racial spectrum. Still, fans may identify certain artists as black, or at least nonwhite, even if the artists themselves do not identify as such (see, for example, the discussion of Ivy Queen's racial identity in chapter 4). Some artists just claim a Puerto Rican identity without ever addressing race. Considering the racial diversity within reggaetón, how exactly do these African diasporic connections manifest?

This question has implications for not only the way we study reggaetón but also the very definition of what constitutes the African diaspora. Initially, the term *diaspora* referred to the dispersal of individuals from one place to another that produced a shared longing for an imagined or real homeland. Many theorists have proposed various characteristics that define diasporas, including displacement, attachment to homelands, exclusion from host societies, establishment of a group consciousness, and feelings of connection to other diasporic groups.[54] Furthermore, diaspora as a concept can attend to both the experiences of forced dispersal as in the transatlantic slave trade, and more voluntary migrations. The problem with this conflation is that making diaspora a catch-all phrase for experiences of migration could potentially discount the very different causes and modes of dispersal as well as the unequal abilities of groups to travel or access their homelands. Still, many of the characteristics identified by theorists such as migration, development of group consciousness, experiences of marginalization in host societies, and other dynamics remain central to understanding diaspora.

Early definitions of the African diaspora emphasized the dispersal of individuals out of Africa, especially because of the transatlantic slave trade, who then recognized the African continent as their homeland. In addition, they often assumed that a unified racial consciousness linked these communities across the diaspora.[55] However, such definitions tend to position Africa as a historical and static point of origin rather than an important site for the negotiation of contemporary African diasporic identities.[56] In the

Puerto Rican context, identifying a static African origin actually supports dominant discourses of racial democracy. As I described above, folkloric blackness depends in part on the assumption that Afro–Puerto Rican cultural practices are direct transplants from Africa, a narrative that frames these traditions within a premodern, romanticized African past and denies the histories of intercultural exchange that produced them. My point is not to discount the very substantial African cultural contributions to Puerto Rican society, but rather to underscore how the concept of the African diaspora as emerging from a historical and essentialized Africa may actually further the project of racial democracy.

Several scholars have questioned the assumption that a unified consciousness connected to a static perception of Africa forms the basis of diaspora. Instead, they insist on the importance of understanding diaspora as an ever-changing process of identity negotiation that pays equal attention to differences and similarities across geographic sites.[57] Following these arguments, the status of blackness more generally as a "counterculture of modernity" produces similarities across African diasporic sites.[58] The global reach of modern European colonial projects constructed blackness as the primitive and premodern counterpoint to whiteness, and, subsequently, has conditioned the development of the African diaspora.[59] We see this process in Puerto Rico where urban blackness functions as the internal, "black" opposite to the "white(ned)" Puerto Rican population. These arguments thus connect diasporic populations via experiences of antiblack racism and misrecognition that stem from the hegemony of discourses of Western modernity.

At the same time, this understanding of diaspora also takes heed of difference across African diasporic groups. Here, attention to the local is critical. As Jacqueline Nassy Brown reminds us, diaspora is experienced in specific places.[60] How individuals perceive themselves in relation to the African diaspora depends in part on how they are positioned within their local communities. This is especially important given that different locations hold varying definitions of blackness, such that someone identified as "black" in the United States may be recognized as some other category in Puerto Rico or elsewhere. Nevertheless, although Puerto Rico and the United States appear to have starkly contrasting racial discourses, both places reproduce eerily similar and equally problematic stereotypes of blackness. This illuminates the continued salience of Western modernity across geographic boundaries even when different places hold distinct systems of race relations.

In this context, the linkages across diasporic sites occur via complex processes of "recognition" whereby individuals perceive commonalities with other black-identified communities, even if the actual parameters that define their blackness are different. Similar experiences with racial exclusion form the basis of these diasporic connections.[61] The "encounter" between groups in different locations allows for individuals to recognize new possibilities for defining blackness that would otherwise be obscured in "place-bound fixities."[62] Individuals draw from cultural practices, symbols, and icons from other African diasporic sites, what Jacqueline Nassy Brown terms *diasporic resources*, to produce alternative definitions of blackness that respond to their localized experiences of racial exclusion.[63] In this way, diaspora is a dynamic process that is always in flux and distinctly articulated across sites. It also acknowledges the differences that exist within the African diaspora even though these communities are all affected by the problematic consequences of Western modernity. Reggaetón exemplifies this process by integrating diasporic resources from various African diasporic cultural practices in the Americas—especially U.S.-based hip-hop and Jamaican dancehall—to create new understandings of Puerto Rican identities that center blackness.

Reggaetón is also indebted to the long histories of migrations throughout the Americas. Despite the debate about reggaetón's origins, it is undeniable that reggaetón is supremely transnational, emerging from multiple streams of migration and cultural exchange. Indeed, reggaetón is a prime example of circum-Caribbean music characterized by the "shared history of colonization, diasporic movement, and immigration" in the Caribbean basin.[64] For example, the (im)migration of Puerto Ricans, West Indians, Panamanians, and Dominicans (among others) to the United States was essential to reggaetón's development, as were other streams of migration, such as when West Indians moved to Panama or Dominicans to Puerto Rico. In fact, part of reggaetón's shift to a pan-Latino audience resulted from the ways that the music resonated with Latino youth understood to be immigrants or the children of immigrants in the United States, and the subsequent push from record companies to market products to these communities (see chapter 5).

But beyond thrusting reggaetón into larger commercial markets, these patterns of migration also introduced new opportunities for cultural exchange that familiarized communities with diverse musical practices and ideas about blackness. Juan Flores proposes the term *cultural remittances* to account for "the ensemble of ideas, values, and expressive forms intro-duced into societies of origin by remigrants and their families as they return 'home,' sometimes for the first time, for temporary visits or permanent re-settlement, and as transmitted through the increasingly pervasive means of telecommunication."[65] In his analysis of Puerto Rican, Dominican, and Cuban migration, Flores points out that cultural remittances have resulted in the dissemination of both cultural practices like hip-hop as well as new forms of "black consciousness" in the Spanish Caribbean.[66] In particular, the embrace of Afro-Latino identities evident in these cultural remittances—either in the self-stylings and identities of return migrants or in the forms of cultural expression that travel to the islands via recordings, Internet, and other avenues—often jar with the dominant definitions of national identities in the Spanish Caribbean.[67] Indeed, fears and anxieties regard-ing reggaetón's embrace of diasporic blackness underlay the Puerto Rican government's multiple attempts to censor the music (see chapters 1 and 2). Therefore, understanding the emergence and significance of reggaetón re-quires attention to the ways that Puerto Rican and other Latino diasporas' cultural remittances are integral to reggaetón's diasporic blackness.

Reggaetón thus developed in Puerto Rico as a cultural practice of di-aspora. Here, the term *diaspora* addresses both the histories of migration that are crucial to reggaetón, and reggaetón's articulation of diasporic links across different sites, particularly between Puerto Rico and elsewhere in the African diaspora. As a cultural practice of diaspora, reggaetón must be understood in relation to both global and local factors—a music "routed" through various geographic sites that has become "rooted" in local commu-nities as an expression of particular understandings of race, class, gender, and national identities. In Puerto Rico, reggaetón significantly departs from dominant discourses of racial democracy because it *centers* African dia-sporic belonging in the construction of Puerto Rican identities. Blackness becomes reconfigured as essential to contemporary Puerto Rican life, re-futing both the stereotypical tropes of urban blackness and the premodern characteristics of folkloric blackness. As part of this broader aim, reggaetón includes a critique of the inconsistencies within Puerto Rico's so-called ra-cial democracy, not the least of which are persistent racial inequalities.

The development of this critique is not a uniform or linear process. The racial diversity of reggaetón artists and fans results in different configura-tions of diasporic resources within reggaetón. For example, self-identified black artists integrate African diasporic aesthetics to articulate a uniquely

Afro–Puerto Rican identity, positioning themselves as members of the broader African diaspora. On the other hand, artists and fans who may not identify or be identified by others as black, per se, may incorporate these same resources as a way to express solidarity or affinity with African diasporic populations despite embracing a racially mixed or even white identity. Likewise, female reggaetón artists or fans may select alternative diasporic resources than their male counterparts that speak to their specific gendered experiences, even when they destabilize similar structures of racial inequality. Although the results may not always be the same, what reggaetón offers to all of these groups is a set of cultural practices that can be manipulated in ways that shed light on the materialities of poor, urban, and predominantly nonwhite Puerto Rican communities. In a place where racism purportedly does not exist, reggaetón provides a language, sometimes verbal, sometimes visual, and oftentimes aural, to speak about the "unspeakable" black presence on the island.[68] And as a result, reggaetón offers an opportunity to express new understandings of Puerto Ricanness and Afro-Latinidad.[69]

While reggaetón may challenge the racist underpinnings of hegemonic discourses of racial democracy, it also reinforces some problematic hierarchies, particularly regarding gender and sexuality. Many of reggaetón's critics have maligned the music because of its misogynistic lyrics and representations. I will show how, sometimes, these criticisms of reggaetón conceal racist presumptions of an inherent black hypersexuality. However, sometimes such criticisms point out significantly troublesome elements of the reggaetón scene that must be addressed in order to imagine a truly inclusive reconfiguration of Puerto Rican identities. At the same time, it is important to remember that reggaetón is not the first popular music in Puerto Rico (or elsewhere) to have a vexed relationship with questions of gender and sexuality. One needs only look at salsa, one of the most beloved national musics of Puerto Rico, to see how patriarchal and heteronormative structures inform cultural practices from both dominant and subaltern positions throughout the island and the diaspora. Thus, reggaetón, like other forms of popular music, is best thought of as what George Lipsitz has termed a "dangerous crossroad,"[70] one that simultaneously contests and reaffirms different hierarchical structures at different times and in different places.

Of course, reggaetón is above all a commercial music, and at this point a thriving, multimillion-dollar industry. But, rather than assume that reggaetón's marketability renders it devoid of "political" messages, I follow the work of scholars such as George Lipsitz and Jocelyne Guilbault, who posit that while popular music may appear fleeting, it develops from entrenched historical processes and produces spaces for social transformation.[71] In spite of frequent declarations by its critics that reggaetón is a mere fad destined to end in the near future, reggaetón has evolved, with new artists springing up throughout Latin America, mixing the dembow with other forms of music and producing innovative recordings that have become tremendously popular. Most important, whether reggaetón continues to be popular or not, it presents a specific moment in history where racial and national identities could be reconfigured in new and imaginative ways. By focusing on significant historical moments and figures in reggaetón, the chapters that follow reveal the various strategies reggaetón artists and fans use not only to criticize dominant discourses of racial democracy, but also to call for the realization of its promise of full equality for all Puerto Ricans. Reggaetón makes meaningful and critical interventions that center the African diaspora in redefinitions of Puerto Rican identities, a process that, while often slippery and by no means perfect, has consequences for understanding constructions of blackness throughout the Americas.

Structure of the Book

What are the possibilities and limits that reggaetón offers for reconsidering blackness in Puerto Rico? What are the challenges it presents to hegemonic discourses of racial democracy on the island, and how have these challenges been managed? How do the different gender and racial positionalities of reggaetón artists and fans impact their constructions of Puerto Rican identities? How has the emergence of reggaetón scenes in the United States impacted the music's relationship to blackness, Puerto Ricanness, or Latinidad (if at all)? As a cultural practice of diaspora, how does reggaetón intervene in the cultural politics of blackness in Puerto Rico, and what does this reveal about the contradictions of Puerto Rican racial democracy and similar discourses elsewhere in Latin America and the Caribbean? The following chapters address these questions in order to interrogate the cultural politics of race and diaspora in Puerto Rican reggaetón.

The first chapter, "Iron Fist against Rap," examines the development of underground, the precursor to reggaetón. This chapter takes into account a detailed discussion of both the global processes of cultural exchange and migration that led to reggaetón's development, and the local conditions on the island that sparked its emergence. Relying on newspaper articles, song lyrics, and music videos, I examine how underground artists employed diasporic resources as part of a broader critique of persistent racism and classism on the part of Puerto Rican elites, especially government officials. These arguments expressed connections with African diasporic politics that directly countered the problematic images of urban blackness that had been attributed to underground rappers during anticrime initiatives at the time. This chapter examines the multiple arguments from both supporters and detractors of underground as an example of one way in which engagement with African diasporic aesthetics intervenes in broader debates about race and national identity in Puerto Rico.

By 2002, underground had shifted to reggaetón and made inroads into the Puerto Rican mainstream. Chapter 2, "The Perils of Perreo," focuses on the Anti-Pornography Campaign initiated by Senator Velda González to eliminate pornographic content in Puerto Rican media. However, the campaign targeted reggaetón music videos. More specifically, González focused on representations of women in music videos, especially the impact of overt displays of female sexuality on the "moral education" of Puerto Rican youth. I argue that the Anti-Pornography Campaign reproduced problematic stereotypes of black female hypersexuality in an attempt to secure the hegemony of racial democracy in the face of reggaetón's insertions of ideas about blackness into Puerto Rican society.

The following two chapters address the work of specific reggaetón artists who engage with African diasporic resources to produce new understandings of Puerto Rican identities. In "Loíza," I analyze the music and persona of Tego Calderón, whose first album received critical acclaim shortly after the completion of the Anti-Pornography Campaign. While Calderón is often attributed with making reggaetón mainstream in Puerto Rico, he also embodies a distinct Afro–Puerto Rican identity and routinely discusses racism in Puerto Rico in his music and interviews. This chapter examines this provocative contradiction—that is, why would the very same elites who were so invested in racial democracy discourses readily embrace one of their staunchest critics? Using his music, media coverage of his career, and interviews, I argue that Tego Calderón's use of diasporic resources enables him to revise Afro–Puerto Rican signifiers such as the folkloric music bomba into new expressions of a unique Afro–Puerto Rican identity.

Another artist who troubles dominant discourses of racial democracy is Ivy Queen, arguably the most widely recognized woman in reggaetón.

In "Fingernails con Feeling," I demonstrate how Ivy Queen disrupts the associations between whiteness and respectability that undergird Puerto Rican national identities. I contend that the two aspects of her celebrity that have given her the most notoriety—her shift in her appearance and her lyrics about suffering and vengeance—discredit the assumptions of black inferiority that are part and parcel of racial democracy. Instead, Ivy Queen carves a space for groups normally cast out of Puerto Rico's so-called racial democracy to produce a more inclusive understanding of Puerto Rican identities.

In the final chapter, "Enter the Hurbans," I explore the racialization of reggaetón once it entered the U.S. market in 2004 with the backing of major record labels.[72] I argue that the identification of a supposedly new Hispanic urban audience (called *Hurban*) situated reggaetón within the Latin music market by distinguishing it from blackness. At the same time, Hurban identity was also linked to blackness via the reiteration of historical stereotypes of Puerto Rican and African American urban communities as violent, hypersexual, and enmeshed in a culture of poverty. And yet, some artists could still use reggaetón as a space to express unique Afro-Latino identities that contest the dominant divisions of blackness and Latinidad in the United States.

These chapters demonstrate that reggaetón's incorporation of African diasporic resources produces new ways of understanding Puerto Rican identity that depart from the Eurocentric foundations of hegemonic discourses of racial democracy. At the same time, I caution the impulse to consider an overarching, unitary expression of Puerto Rican identity in reggaetón. Rather, the various racial, class, and gender identities occupied by reggaetón's artists and fans condition these contestations to racial democracy. Reggaetón thus encompasses a set of cultural practices that engages with African diasporic aesthetics in ways that challenge the dominant discourses of racial democracy and, in the process, produce new understandings of Puerto Rican identities that center blackness and African diasporic belonging.

CHAPTER ONE
IRON FIST AGAINST RAP

In the 1980s, Luis Armando Lozada Cruz, more popularly known as Vico C, began listening to hip-hop. Born in Brooklyn, New York, Vico relocated to the Puerta de Tierra *caserío* in San Juan with his family as a young child. Vico C had enrolled in acting classes, and after honing his public speaking skills, began to experiment with rap. He related to the stories about "ghetto life" in songs by African American hip-hop artists such as Run DMC, Sugar Hill Gang, LL Cool J, Slick Rick, and KRS-One. Around 1985, Vico C won fifteen dollars in a hip-hop contest where he met DJ Negro, a young DJ who had been mixing hip-hop records.[1] The two began to record mixtapes on cassettes. DJ Negro would borrow beats from popular U.S. hip-hop songs and Vico C would rap original lyrics over them. The songs ranged from party anthems to social and political commentary about issues facing marginalized youth in Puerto Rico's *caseríos*, or public housing developments. They would make about twenty or thirty copies of each tape and sell them in the *caseríos* between San Juan and Carolina, and eventually created a name for themselves in urban Puerto Rico.

Vico C is often described as a rapper rather than a reggaetonero; however, his music is also credited for paving the way for reggaetón.[2] Vico C's popularity in the late 1980s and early 1990s occurred with the development of Puerto Rican underground. The music's name referred to the literal distribution of cassettes in the economic "underground," or the informal economy.[3] Musically, underground shares similar vocal styles and the consistent "boom-ch-boom-chick" rhythm with contemporary reggaetón; however, underground did not have the same slick productions and techno, pop, and R&B sounds of contemporary reggaetón.[4] Rather, underground DJs pieced together samples from the popular Jamaican dancehall and U.S. American hip-hop songs of the time while rappers performed over them. Wayne Marshall argues that as underground became more commercialized in the late 1990s, the music grew increasingly "synthesized" when DJs began composing more original beats, relying on fewer direct dancehall and hip-hop samples.[5] Lyrical themes centered more explicitly on sex and parties.[6] During this time, new recordings by DJ Nelson (who is often credited with coining the term reggaetón) and DJ Blass popularized the term reggaetón to refer to their music.[7] Although it is difficult to pinpoint the precise date when underground shifted to what we now know as reggaetón,[8] underground music is often widely recognized as one of its precursors.[9] Underground thus refers to the rap-dancehall fusions that developed and circulated within Puerto Rico's working class, urban barrios and caseríos from the 1980s until the 1990s without the backing of large record companies.[10]

In addition to referring to music, the term underground also connotes a space that exists outside of the "mainstream." As something that is spatially located "below," one can think of the underground as the foundation for the things that exist above it. This idea of "underground" mirrors many of the arguments concerning the position of blackness as the counterpoint to whiteness within constructions of Western modernity. In Puerto Rico, underground is affiliated with an urban blackness understood to represent the opposite of white(ned) Puerto Rican identity in the popular imagination. In many ways, then, we might think of urban blackness as part of the symbolic "underground" of racial democracy, the image against which hegemonic constructions of Puerto Rican identities are founded.

This construction of urban blackness is located in specific places, namely the caseríos, where many underground artists and fans resided. Indeed, just as bomba became a cultural marker for folkloric blackness, underground and, later, reggaetón signified urban blackness in the eyes of many detractors. Many critics viewed underground as detached from Puerto Rican culture. In some cases, denunciations of underground represented the music as "foreign" because of its associations with U.S. rap. At other times, critics charged that underground promoted values and morals that departed from the "mainstream." Ultimately, such criticisms reinforced the alleged relationship between caseríos, urban blackness, and underground.

The power of underground, however, was not that it actually caused individuals to act out violently (as critics of the music claimed), but that underground artists and fans exposed the contradictions of dominant discourses of racial democracy. Although most underground was essentially party music, underground artists also addressed the racist and classist policies adversely affecting *caseríos* and other working-class and nonwhite communities in their songs. Moreover, underground incorporated a whole host of cultural practices, including fashion, hairstyles, and language, that reflected connections between the music's artists and fans and working-class, black communities elsewhere in the African diaspora. Indeed, underground may have responded to very local issues and places, but it did so by integrating global markers of blackness and engaging in larger diasporic politics. The diasporic nature of underground disrupted the very insular definitions of Puerto Rican national identity that emphasized Spanish heritage and devalued the contributions to the island of Afro–Puerto Ricans and Puerto Ricans living in the United States. Instead, it enabled underground artists and fans to express connections to Puerto Ricanness and the African diaspora simultaneously.

Underground thus exemplifies the ways that diasporic resources circulate across geographic sites and become incorporated into a cultural practice that developed in part out of experiences with racism on the local level. Several scholars including Mayra Santos-Febres, Jorge Giovannetti, and Raquel Z. Rivera have discussed the development of underground in Puerto Rico, including its creation as a youth culture, expression of life in the *caseríos,* and the impact that the *Mano Dura Contra el Crimen* campaign, a government-led anticrime initiative, had on its development.[11] In this chapter, I do not intend to rehash the history of underground in Puerto Rico. Instead, I am interested in using underground to think about how diasporic resources work in local contexts. To fully grasp underground's interventions into Puerto Rican racial politics, it is necessary to examine both the music's ties to local places and its relationship to the broader African diaspora. I first explore the diasporic connections to hip-hop in the United States and dancehall in Jamaica, both of which not only serve as important musical influences on underground, but also developed from disenfranchised communities that faced similar circumstances as underground artists and fans in Puerto Rico. Then, I provide a brief overview of the ways that 1990s anticrime initiatives cemented stereotypes of urban blackness that underground artists addressed. Finally, I examine the debates surrounding underground from both supporters and detractors of the music. Considering the integral relationship between the global and the local in underground sheds light on the ways that diasporic linkages are forged and maintained.

Hip-Hop, Dancehall, and New Diasporic Affiliations

Underground is a typical cultural practice of diaspora. Musically, underground combines aesthetics from various genres and traditions from throughout the African diaspora in the Americas, particularly the Caribbean basin. Such combinations would not be possible without the long histories of cultural exchange and (im)migration throughout the region. Therefore, the very existence of underground is linked to the larger African diaspora both musically and aesthetically. Underground's status as a cultural practice of diaspora signals the music's African diasporic aesthetics as well as the impact of the global circulation of ideas about blackness on local communities.

These African diasporic connections manifested in underground's response to local dynamics of race, class, and national identity in Puerto Rico. As Jacqueline Nassy Brown suggests, local conditions motivate individuals to utilize diasporic resources as they develop new understandings of blackness that speak to their specific circumstances.[12] What results is an expression of blackness that draws from African diasporic influences from elsewhere in order to address local circumstances facing urban black communities in Puerto Rico.

This process is particularly important in Puerto Rico, where African diasporic connections and the long histories of Puerto Rican migration between the island and the U.S. mainland significantly challenge the insular, dominant portrayal of Puerto Rican identity, especially its fraught relationship with blackness. First, situating contemporary Puerto Rico within the larger African diaspora rejects the assumptions that a historic and static "Africa" symbolized by folkloric blackness comprises the only type of black identity compatible with the Puerto Rican nation. Rather, underground's links to Jamaican dancehall, Panamanian reggae en español, and U.S. hip-hop (among other musical practices) foreground experiences with comparable systems of antiblack racism across the Americas as the basis for articulating African diasporic connections. Demonstrating the continued existence of racism in Puerto Rico directly refutes assumptions of racelessness that are integral to discourses of racial democracy. Furthermore, identifying contemporary Puerto Rico as part of the African diaspora also de-emphasizes Spain as the cornerstone of Puerto Rican identity. From this perspective, Puerto Rico's connections to the African diaspora are ongoing and continuous (as opposed to the limited, parochial, and historical perceptions of hegemonic folkloric blackness), offering opportunities to imagine blackness and Puerto Rican identities in alternative ways.

Underground's diasporic connections also bring to the fore experiences of Puerto Rican communities in the United States. Puerto Ricans have migrated to the United States since the nineteenth century; however, the granting of U.S. citizenship to Puerto Ricans in 1917 and the subsequent growth of labor recruitment programs on the island spawned a dramatic increase in the number of Puerto Ricans living in the United States. Scholars such as Jorge Duany and Juan Flores argue that definitions of the Puerto Rican nation must incorporate U.S. Puerto Rican communities that have maintained connections to the island and have made substantial contributions to Puerto Rico's culture and politics.[13] However, the insular nature of dominant definitions of Puerto Rican identity often excludes the community in the United States. This is particularly evident in the stories of U.S. Puerto Ricans, and, especially, Nuyoricans,[14] who return to Puerto Rico only to find their claims to Puerto Ricanness questioned by many island Puerto Ricans who consider them "inauthentic" or too Americanized.[15] In many instances, Nuyoricans' racial identities and perceived connections to blackness (especially U.S. African American culture) become the primary source of contention regarding their incorporation into the island.[16] Nuyoricans' role in hip-hop furthered assumptions that they were "inauthentic" Puerto Ricans due in part to the ways that hip-hop's expressions of blackness departed from hegemonic definitions of Afro–Puerto Rican identities. Consequently, underground's connections to Nuyorican identities, particularly in relation to hip-hop, not only demonstrate the music's diasporic orientation, but also contest the limited associations between Puerto Rican national identity and blackness.

The dominant narrative of reggaetón describes the music as the marriage of U.S.-based hip-hop and Panamanian reggae en español by urban Puerto Rican DJs. Generally, this story focuses on Puerto Ricans' involvement in the genre at the expense of acknowledging the multiple layers of migration that inform the music.[17] Moreover, limiting reggaetón to Puerto Rico marks the music as "Latin" or "tropical" in ways that reinforce the restrictive marketing classifications of the music industry while "overlook[ing] its stronger connections to hip-hop and reggae, connections crucial because of their links with a cultural politics based more around race and class and transnational linkages than national or pan-Latin identities."[18] In the rest of this section, I discuss the social moorings and musical elements of U.S. hip-hop, Jamaican dancehall, Panamanian reggae en español, and reggaetón in Puerto Rico in order to elaborate the diasporic links between them.[19] As Mayra Santos-Febres writes, "It is because of these connections with African American and Jamaican exiles, since its beginnings, that the Boricua rap territories cover locations that are regional and global at the same time."[20] In order to fully grasp how underground operates as a cultural practice of diaspora, it is first necessary to briefly explain the circuits of exchange in hip-hop and dancehall that inform it.

THE HIP-HOP CONNECTION

In the popular history of reggaetón, Vico C plays a prominent role as one of the first artists on the scene in Puerto Rico; in fact, many reggaetón artists identify him as one of their primary influences. But, aesthetically, Vico C's music sounds much more like rap than reggaetón, particularly in his vocal delivery and the beats he used. Still, Vico's importance in the reggaetón narrative demonstrates the broader significance of hip-hop in the music's development. In addition, Vico C's personal history of moving from Brooklyn to Puerto Rico exemplifies the importance of migration between the island and the mainland to the development of underground and reggaetón. Indeed, Nuyoricans played a critical role in both the creation of hip-hop and its introduction to Puerto Rico since many return migrants brought the music and stories of their encounters with new forms of racialization in the United States with them back to the island.

Although Puerto Ricans settled throughout the United States, New York City received the majority of migrants. In fact, the city's Puerto Rican population soared from about 245,000 in 1950 to over 700,000 in 1970.[21] Puerto Ricans settled in neighborhoods throughout New York City, but, by the 1960s, most lived in the Bronx.[22] While New York has declined as the primary destination for Puerto Rican migrants, a substantial community of Puerto Ricans continues to reside there, and, until relatively recently, constituted its largest Latino population.[23]

Once in New York, Puerto Ricans were often racialized as distinct from both whites and blacks. Because many Puerto Ricans are racially mixed, they did not fit easily within the "black/white" binary that structures U.S.

race relations.[24] As a result, "Puerto Rican" became a distinct racial category in New York.[25] Puerto Ricans were portrayed as racialized others who were subordinate to whites and distinct from, but akin to, African Americans. Several scholars point out that Nuyoricans and African Americans share similar processes of racialization that result from larger histories of colonization and persistent racial inequalities in the United States.[26] However, these systemic inequalities are often ignored in common representations of both African Americans and Puerto Ricans that portray them as delinquent, violent, and hypersexual, among other stereotypes.[27]

Of course, not all Puerto Ricans welcomed these connections with African Americans in the popular imagination, often because some Puerto Rican migrants harbored antiblack sentiment as a result of their exposure to the whitening bias of hegemonic discourses of racial democracy on the island.[28] Afro–Puerto Ricans in the United States have detailed their encounters with racism on the part of U.S. Americans and other Latinos.[29] In addition, individuals' racial backgrounds condition their experiences of migration such that Afro–Puerto Ricans face different issues than Puerto Ricans considered white or racially mixed in the United States. Nevertheless, within the system of racial classification in the United States, Puerto Ricans have been racialized as nonwhite, and similar to African Americans—that is, on the "blacker" end of the U.S. racial binary. As Juan Flores describes, for many Puerto Ricans, migration to the United States thus constitutes a "lesson in blackness."[30] The subjection of African Americans, Puerto Ricans, and other African diasporic populations in New York to similar (though not necessarily equivalent) systems of racial exclusion produced the conditions of possibility for these groups to forge new political, social, and cultural alliances that contested this marginalization.

Historically, musical collaborations between Nuyoricans and African Americans have been important sites where affinities between the two groups manifested, evident in the development of new musical styles such as Latin soul and boogaloo that appealed to both audiences.[31] Likewise, hip-hop also emerged from cross-cultural exchanges between West Indians, African Americans, and Nuyoricans in the South Bronx neighborhood of New York City.[32] Hip-hop thus comprises yet another cultural practice of diaspora—in this case, both because of the myriad African diasporic musical practices that influence it, and in the social aspects of the music that speak to African American, Latino, and West Indian communities' experiences with disenfranchisement, racism, and poverty.

This aspect of hip-hop is critical for the development of underground since it was in these spaces that many Nuyoricans negotiated their racial identities, especially in relation to blackness.[33] Several Nuyoricans played critical roles in the formation of hip-hop culture. For example, DJ Charlie Chase belonged to one of the pioneering hip-hop groups, the Cold Crush Brothers. Nuyorican dancers like Popmaster Fabel and Crazy Legs of the Rock Steady Crew created innovative breaking styles that became central elements of hip-hop culture. As producers, consumers, and practitioners of hip-hop, Nuyoricans were intimately involved in the creation of diasporic links with other African diasporic populations in New York at the time. Consequently, for some Nuyoricans, participation in hip-hop enabled them to celebrate blackness as part of Puerto Rican identity, and something that linked them with other marginalized, urban, and black-identified youth.

It is precisely these "lessons in blackness"[34] that, along with the popular beats and music, helped to make hip-hop attractive for some youth in Puerto Rico's *caseríos* who related to the experiences of marginalization expressed by rappers in the United States.[35] Wayne Marshall claims that underground in mid-1990s Puerto Rico "supported a youth- and class-inflected cultural politics of blackness and did so, significantly, by embracing (if not amplifying) the Nuyorican dimension of Puerto Rican popular culture."[36] Indeed, Raquel Z. Rivera argues that, although underground incorporated many influences from U.S. hip-hop, it also "islandized" hip-hop culture in order to address the specific issues facing Puerto Rican youth.[37] As a result, underground "provoked new sensibilities on issues of sex, gender, and race, while [its] social moorings among the urban poor raised uncomfortable problems of class and social inequality virtually absent in other forms of popular music and typically ignored by the cultural elite" in Puerto Rico.[38] These "new sensibilities" include alternative ideas about the role of blackness in Puerto Rican identities that resulted from encounters with other African diasporic populations in New York. In the process, they destabilized the narrow definitions of Puerto Rican national identity that promoted racelessness, neglected to address Puerto Rico's contemporary ties to the African diaspora, and ignored Puerto Rican communities living in the United States.

Understanding the development of underground in Puerto Rico thus requires careful attention to what Jocelyne Guilbault has termed the "audible entanglements" of the music that "assemble social relations, cultural experiences, and political formations."[39] When one listens to the hip-hop samples and rap vocal stylings of underground, one can also hear the multiple layers of diasporic connections at work that not only produce innovative sounds and beats but also create the conditions of possibility to develop important links between Puerto Rican youth and others in the African diaspora. However, these connections became even more complex when DJs started mixing another important element into underground: dancehall.

THE DANCEHALL/REGGAE EN ESPAÑOL CONNECTION

The rapid vocals and riddims of dancehall music found their way into reggaetón through complex and overlapping circuits of migration throughout the circum-Caribbean, including Jamaica, Panama, and the United States. The audible connections between dancehall and reggaetón are notable— in fact, Tego Calderón stated that, initially, he dismissed reggaetón in part because he considered it an exact copy of Jamaican music.[40] Some artists' rapid vocal delivery sounds much more like dancehall than U.S.-based rap. Beyond that, however, the central "boom-ch-boom-chick" beat that dominates many reggaetón recordings is often understood to come from Jamaican dancehall. Although there are some questions about the location and specific recording from which reggaetón's dembow beat derived, what is certain is "that without Jamaican dancehall reggae there would be no reggaeton."[41]

Like hip-hop, dancehall's similarities to reggaetón extend beyond its beats to the social conditions in which it developed. After Jamaica gained independence in 1962, elites constructed a "creole" definition of Jamaican nationhood that, like Puerto Rican "racial democracy," emphasized the island's ties to Western modernity but also celebrated African-based folklore as symbolic of the island's African heritage.[42] On the other hand, the cultural practices of urban, poor, and predominantly black youth were ridiculed and, in some cases, marked as incompatible with Jamaican national identity.[43] Similar to the youth living in caseríos, these communities in Jamaica also suffered disproportionately from violence, poverty, and other social issues.[44]

Dancehall emerged out of this context to speak to the experiences of poor, black, urban youth. Norman Stolzoff notes that it is difficult to determine the exact date when contemporary dancehall music began, especially since the space of the dancehall has been a critical site of musical production for black, urban Jamaican youth since slavery.[45] However, he points out that "deejaying" (or "rapping" in the U.S. hip-hop context) became popular in the 1980s,[46] along with the resurfacing of the soundsystem[47] and the "selector" who would select beats or riddims over which deejays would perform.[48] Riddims became identifying characteristics of individual songs, with multiple deejays performing on the same riddim.

As dancehall music grew popular, it became associated with a broader set of cultural practices, including fashion. These cultural practices expressed a distinct identity that embraced "pride in the ghetto, in black identity, and of African culture"—elements that jarred with the understandings of Western modernity and respectability to which Jamaican creole national identity aspired.[49] Indeed, dancehall artists and fans have been subject to several criticisms from "uptown" (or elite) segments of Jamaican society based on concerns about the music's morality, particularly in relation to sexuality and violence.[50] Still, for many Jamaican youth, dancehall became an "attempt to deal with the endemic patterns of poverty, racism, and violence" through the expression of an "oppositional position within Jamaica's race-class hierarchy."[51] Like reggaetón in Puerto Rico, dancehall chronicled the social conditions and marginalization facing black urban communities in ways that conflicted with dominant ideas about Jamaican national identity.

Similar to reggaetón, transnational migration also plays a critical role in dancehall. As Deborah Thomas describes, ideas about transnational migration influence Jamaicans' understandings of national identities and belonging.[52] Moreover, Jamaicans bring dancehall and other cultural practices with them when they settle in places like New York City; in fact, the establishment of West Indian communities produced a commercial market for dancehall music in U.S. cities such as Miami, Hartford, and New York. Puerto Ricans living in New York and other cities with substantial West Indian populations in the 1990s would likely have heard dancehall at parties or on hip-hop radio stations, especially since these groups often lived near each other. But Puerto Ricans also heard dancehall, albeit a modified version, from another critical node of Jamaican migration: Panama.

The presence of West Indians in Central America stretches back to the nineteenth century. Caribbean men and women from Barbados, Trinidad, Jamaica, and elsewhere arrived in Costa Rica, Panama, Cuba, and other sites in Latin America as industrial and agricultural laborers.[53] Still, the construction of the Panama Canal, particularly under the direction of the United States, sparked the rapid settlement of English-speaking Caribbean laborers in Panama.[54] Conditions for these workers were abhorrent. Caribbean migrants endured inadequate housing, poor wages, and deplorable living conditions when they arrived in urban areas such as Colón.[55] Furthermore, as black subjects, these immigrants faced a precarious position vis-à-vis the construction of Panamanian nationhood, especially due to the passage of several laws restricting citizenship rights of Caribbean migrants and their descendants.[56] Such laws impressed upon the broader Panamanian community that West Indian blacks were "perpetual foreigners beholden to the British and the Americans, . . . ungrateful 'guests' who were reluctant to embrace Hispanic culture, and . . . foreign to the body politic, and, hence, unpatriotic and undesirable."[57]

Tying blackness to foreignness bolstered dominant constructions of Panamanian national identity as a *crisol de razas*, a discourse very similar to Puerto Rican racial democracy that defines Panamanians as racially mixed.[58] Within this system, black communities who had arrived in Panama as slaves (known as *negros coloniales*) fused into the *crisol de razas*, but, similar to Puerto Rican constructions of folkloric blackness, were marked as "premodern."[59] On the other hand, West Indians and their descendants (sometimes called *antillanos*) were supposedly unable to integrate into the racially mixed Panamanian nation because of both their foreignness and their blackness.[60] As a result, throughout the twentieth century, West Indians suffered from segregation (both the Jim Crow segregation imposed on the canal zone by the United States as well as later de facto segregation), and from unemployment and high poverty rates.[61] Like their counterparts in Jamaica, Puerto Rico, and the United States, black, urban youth in Panama were therefore disenfranchised and rejected from the Panamanian nation.

It is in this context that reggae en español surfaced. By the 1980s, West Indians had established themselves in Panama for several generations, and their communities continued to have access to Caribbean cultural practices. As youth, many Panamanian reggae artists did not actually travel to the Caribbean but rather encountered Caribbean music from places like Jamaica, Haiti, and Trinidad and Tobago through records and traveling performers.[62] Still, Jamaican music heavily influenced Panamanian popular music, in part because Jamaican styles dominate the Americas more generally.[63] Wayne Marshall argues that the popularity of Jamaican dancehall in Panama in particular "not only demonstrates the maintenance of family and cultural ties to the island, but it also provides a telling set of examples of how the meanings of Jamaican reggae continue to resonate in Panama, even after translation into Spanish."[64]

In the early 1980s, young Panamanians received Jamaican recordings and began to rap over them, mimicking the vocal style of dancehall artists.[65]

In some cases, Panamanian artists composed their own lyrics, and at other times they performed direct Spanish translations of Jamaican dancehall.[66] While most songs focused on partying, many artists also talked about the racism they experienced.[67] Similar to Puerto Rican underground, Panamanian artists distributed their recordings informally, selling cassettes to bus drivers who would play them throughout the day.[68] As the music grew popular, reggae en español artists began to record professionally.

Some artists such as Renato had several hits in Panama and elsewhere in Latin America; however, others, most notably Edgardo Franco, better known as "El General," established themselves in New York City. After performing as a background singer for Renato, El General relocated to New York City where he pursued a degree in business administration in 1985. While there, he also hosted parties and performed as an opening act during hip-hop and dancehall concerts in the city.[69] El General became so popular that he recorded several hits that circulated across the Americas and the Caribbean, including to Puerto Rico, where DJs and artists became influenced by El General's sound.[70]

Taking a cue from the popularity of dancehall and, especially, reggae en español, Puerto Ricans began mixing dancehall with the hip-hop that had already infiltrated the island and grown popular with artists such as Vico C. Dancehall is audible in many reggaetón artists' vocal styles, the incorporation of popular dancehall phrases into reggaetón performance, and, of course, reggaetón's beats and samplings. The most obvious example of the integration of dancehall aesthetics into reggaetón is its ubiquitous "dembow" beat. Although Robin Moore argues that similar rhythms can be found throughout the Caribbean,[71] stories about reggaetón's origins generally attribute the dembow to dancehall's influence on the genre. The most common assumption is that Puerto Rican underground DJs culled dembow from Jamaican dancehall artist Shabba Ranks's song "Dem Bow" from 1990.[72] However, Wayne Marshall has recently identified a pair of recordings by Panamanian artist Nando Boom, "Ellos Benia" and "Pensión," that sound most like the dembow of Puerto Rican reggaetón.[73] Jamaican producer Dennis "the Menace" Thompson used the dembow rhythm on these tracks, working with Panamanian producer Ramón "Pucho" Busta-mante, who added timbales to the dembow in order to create a more "tropical" sound.[74] Importantly, this new version of the dembow was produced not in Jamaica, nor in Panama, but in Long Island, New York, in the HC&F reggae studios.[75] According to Wayne Marshall, the New York–based,

Panamanian/Jamaican collaboration became the riddim that Puerto Rican producers applied to their hip-hop samples, looping it to form the basis of underground and, later, reggaetón. These multiple narratives of dembow's origins illustrate the importance of dancehall, whether by way of Jamaica or Panama (or both), in the development of contemporary reggaetón. They also make clear that reggaetón's emergence relied on the multiple paths of migration between Jamaica, Panama, and New York, along with transnational circuits of cultural and musical exchange across the circum-Caribbean.

In many ways, underground is an exemplary circum-Caribbean music, incorporating diasporic resources from hip-hop and dancehall (among other musical practices in the Americas) to produce a new sound. However, underground's links to these musics extend beyond the sonic to foreground the comparable ways that colonialism and racism shaped the experiences of working-class, urban, and predominantly black communities in New York, Kingston, Panama City, and San Juan. Underground draws from these diasporic connections in ways that "localiz[ed] the foreign-but-familiar" to produce a distinct expression of Puerto Rican identity informed by underground artists' experiences growing up in the working-class urban neighborhoods of Puerto Rico.[76] Underground illustrates how different ideas about blackness that circulate across geographic borders help to foster the elaboration of local responses to antiblack racism. As a cultural practice of diaspora, underground thus reflects Puerto Rico's social and cultural connections to other African diasporic sites in the Americas.

Mano Dura Contra el Caserío

Before delving into a discussion of precisely how these diasporic connections manifested in underground, it is first necessary to understand the specific, local conditions in which underground developed. Indeed, the local was particularly important to many underground artists and fans, who identified closely with their local neighborhoods.[77] Caseríos figured prominently in the development of underground as sites of the music's production, consumption, and creative inspiration. Underground artists thus integrated the ideas about blackness that they gleaned from hip-hop and dancehall into their responses to the marginalization and racism they faced, especially in relation to state-sponsored anti-crime initiatives that targeted caseríos. In 1993, the Puerto Rican government began Operation Centurion, popularly referred to as *Mano Dura Contra el Crimen* (Iron Fist against Crime), which identified *caseríos* as ground zero for criminal activity. Considered an effort to "protect" the island and its citizens from crime, *Mano Dura* ultimately stigmatized *caseríos* as not only criminal spaces, but also as sites of urban blackness marked by violence, delinquency, and hypersexuality. *Mano Dura* characterized *caseríos* and the people and cultural practices associated with them as different from the rest of the island.

The *Mano Dura* campaign built on older processes of the racialization of *caseríos*. Since their inception, what José Fusté terms "discourses of (b)ordering" distinguished working-class, racialized *caserío* residents from the rest of Puerto Rico.[78] In the early twentieth century, migration to Puerto Rico's urban centers led to the establishment of large shantytowns in places like San Juan, so much so that they constituted the majority of residential growth on the island.[79] To address the problem, and to serve as a test case for future New Deal policies of the 1930s, the Puerto Rican and U.S. governments built housing developments that they hoped would eliminate shantytowns and encourage working-class Puerto Ricans to adopt more "modern" values.[80] A series of requirements that residents had to meet in order to live in the housing projects, such as being healthy with no contagious diseases, not having a criminal record, and preferably being married with children, emphasized these values.[81] Furthermore, these housing developments were located near middle-class neighborhoods not only to encourage integration across socioeconomic lines, but also because authorities assumed that exposure to the upper classes would teach working-class *caserío* residents "appropriate" values.[82] Although framed as a question of socioeconomic class, Zaire Dinzey-Flores notes that such policies ultimately reproduced racial segregation, providing fodder for the image of *caseríos* as sites of blackness while the middle- and upper-class areas surrounding them were considered to be white(r).[83] Consequently, housing developments became marked as "pre-modern" places that contained nonwhite, working-class subjects who, with the appropriate direction, could eventually become "modern" Puerto Rican subjects.

However, frequent depictions in Puerto Rican newspapers of *caserío* residents' allegedly inappropriate and "primitive" behavior surfaced regularly, and by the 1960s, *caseríos* were considered to be ill-conceived.[84] As crime rates increased in the twentieth century, the media represented *caseríos* as the main centers of criminal activity. No longer thought to have the potential to become modern Puerto Rican spaces, *caseríos* became affiliated with an urban blackness marked by violence, delinquency, and inappropriate, uncouth, and even dangerous behaviors.

It is certainly the case that criminal activity in Puerto Rico rose dramatically in the later decades of the twentieth century. In the 1970s, drug-related crimes increased substantially with growing substance abuse on the island.[85] In addition, both the Puerto Rican and U.S. governments maintained that the island increasingly served as an entry point for drugs from South America and the rest of the Caribbean arriving in the United States.[86] The increased presence of drugs coincided with crime rates that continued to rise after the 1970s.[87] Between 1980 and 1990, the homicide rate in Puerto Rico increased by 129 percent.[88] By 1994, San Juan held the dubious distinction of being one of the cities with the highest homicide rate in the United States.[89]

Kelvin Santiago-Valles notes that this increase in crime in Puerto Rico must also be considered in relation to unemployment in the island's urban centers. He argues that, throughout the twentieth century, Puerto Rico developed a racialized division of labor with descendants of wealthy Europeans and "light *mulatos*" constituting the upper classes, and black and "dark *mulatos*" comprising the lower classes.[90] Rapid industrialization of the island led to massive migration to urban areas in the mid-twentieth century; however, by the 1970s, factory jobs declined, and unemployment, especially among young men of color, rose.[91] The high unemployment rate combined with a political system that benefited the upper classes created feelings of disenfranchisement among the urban, predominantly black poor.[92] On the other hand, from the 1970s through the 1990s, the informal economy grew steadily, with earnings estimated to be between 3.5 and 4 million dollars by the early 1980s.[93] The informal economy employed a large percentage of urban Puerto Ricans, including the young nonwhite men of the working classes.

Media coverage of the burgeoning criminal activity during the 1970s, 1980s, and, especially, 1990s often ignored the socioeconomic issues that impacted the crime rate. Instead, sensationalized reports presented *caseríos*, particularly those in San Juan, as chaotic epicenters of criminal activity perpetrated by young, predominantly black men.[94] Such depictions supposedly "justified" the intense focus of anticrime policing in housing projects and poor urban neighborhoods.[95] Ultimately, these images created explicit connections between blackness, working-class communities, and criminal activity in the popular imagination.

Mano Dura served as the culmination of the process of racializing crime and criminalizing *caseríos* in the 1990s. During his election campaign, Governor Pedro Rosselló promised to eradicate crime on the island. In 1993, he selected Pedro Toledo, a former FBI agent, to head the Puerto Rican police department and implement *Mano Dura*. Toledo suggested the involvement of the National Guard as a tremendous show of force that would assert the authority of the police, who, until that time, had a reputation as relatively powerless and defunct.[96] *Mano Dura* consisted of three phases: rescue, restore, and reempower. The rescue phase included the actual raids of housing projects, during which the National Guard guarded the periphery of the *caserío* while police entered apartments and arrested individuals identified in prior investigations as suspects of drug-related crimes.[97] A few hours after midnight on June 4, 1993, National Guard soldiers and Puerto Rican police officers stormed the Villa España housing projects in San Juan, arriving in helicopters and military vehicles to search for drugs, weapons, and other contraband in apartments that supposedly had been staked out earlier by undercover police.[98] The raid on Villa España was the first of seventy-four raids by the National Guard and Puerto Rican police department over the course of three years.[99] Police continued to occupy the *caseríos* until 1999.[100] Initially, the National Guard's presence was meant to prevent brutality against *caserío* residents by Puerto Rican police; however, the raids, which sometimes involved as many as four hundred police officers and soldiers within one *caserío*, resulted in a dramatic display where "apartments were searched, doors knocked down, and residents searched and sometimes beaten."[101] In the end, half of the *caseríos* targeted by *Mano Dura* were located in the San Juan metropolitan area, with the majority in San Juan proper.[102]

Once the raids were complete, the government constructed gates and guard towers around *caseríos*, and established police stations within them.[103] The next phase, called restore, involved repairing structural damage that had plagued the developments for years.[104] Finally, the reempower phase implemented several social service programs by a "Quality of Life Congress" that included government agencies such as the Office of Youth Affairs and the Aqueduct and Sewer Administration.[105]

Puerto Rican media outlets reported that the raids had decreased crime, and that the increased police presence led to more criminal arrests and the overall protection of *caserío* residents.[106] Headlines about the "occupation" and "conquering" of *caseríos*, often described as "warzones," emphasized that the raids successfully restored order and safeguarded the public.[107]

However, while some crimes were reduced after *Mano Dura*, the homicide rate remained unchanged, and in some cases even slightly increased.[108] Police confiscated fewer drug paraphernalia and weapons than expected during the initial raids, and even less with each subsequent raid.[109] Furthermore, *caserío* residents complained that police stationed in the *caseríos* often targeted innocent people during inspections while known drug dealers openly sold their products nearby.[110] In general, many people saw *Mano Dura* as merely a political "spectacle" to assert state power and control.[111] As Zaire Dinzey-Flores describes,

> The upbeat titles of the stages of Operation Centurion—"Rescue,"
> "Restore," "Reempower"—were a charade. Residents had not sought
> "rescue." Nothing had been "restored." There was no empowerment
> of the poor, let alone "reempowerment." Indeed, when the National
> Guard and the police force occupied . . . projects the areas were stig-
> matized as sites of criminality.[112]

In fact, *Mano Dura* reiterated old assumptions that *caserío* residents needed monitoring in order to be productive citizens, from the literal surveillance of their neighborhoods by police to the implementation of programs that reinforced normative, supposedly more "modern" values. The images and headlines in Puerto Rican media outlets strengthened stereotypes of working class, nonwhite *caserío* residents, which, in turn, were fortified by the gates that visually marked *caseríos* as sites of racial difference.[113] Consequently, *Mano Dura* successfully promoted the popular perception of *caseríos* as sites of "violence, chaos, insecurity, poverty, lack of education, lack of control, multiple-family dwellings, gates and blackness."[114] In this way, *Mano Dura* helped to naturalize the stereotypes associated with urban blackness and emplace them within the *caseríos*, reproducing old impressions of *caserío* residents as black "others" who did not belong to the white(ned) Puerto Rican nation. This intensified race and class segregation on the island, which, in turn, had very real consequences for the everyday lives of people living in *caseríos*, who faced severe unemployment, police brutality, poor access to resources, racial profiling, and a host of other issues that stem from their associations with urban blackness.[115] It was in this context that underground proliferated. Artists addressed these issues in their music, refuting the problematic images of urban blackness that, in the minds of many Puerto Ricans, supposedly justified the continued marginalization and disenfranchisement of *caseríos*.

Underground

The diasporic resources from hip-hop and dancehall provided fodder for many underground artists' and fans' responses to their experiences in *caseríos* and other urban *barrios*. While, at times, underground reinforced certain stereotypes associated with urban blackness, it also provided a space to insist on the recognition of the realities of persistent antiblack racism that impacted the lives of *caserío* residents. This disrupted the dominant, stereotypical portrayals of urban blackness that did not consider how larger social and economic conditions of inequality produced urban blight, violence, and poverty. The adoption and adaptation of fashion, music, or performance styles from hip-hop and dancehall may not necessarily appear "political" on the surface; however, the integration of these practices into underground fostered important opportunities to reimagine Puerto Rican connections to blackness and the larger African diaspora.

Fashion trends and monikers adopted by underground artists often expressed affiliations with black identities in the Americas. For example, the visual art included on underground mixtapes' packaging reflected a working-class black identity. DJ Playero's series of mixtapes from the mid-1990s featured urban landscapes, graffiti, and "lots of images of stylish, and often dark-skinned, denizens of the underground" on their covers.[116] Clothing and hairstyles borrowed from popular hip-hop and dancehall fashion also dominated the underground scene of the 1990s.[117] Many of these styles included overt signifiers of blackness, such as dreadlock hairstyles, pendants emblazoned with the continent of Africa, and Rastafarian-colored (i.e., red, yellow, and green) hats, shirts, and jewelry.[118] These fashion trends served as important physical representations of affiliations with other African diasporic populations for Puerto Rican underground artists and fans. Likewise, the vocabulary used to describe underground and its artists emphasized the music's connections with blackness. Many underground rappers chose monikers that indicated their self-identifications with blackness, such as OG Black, DJ Negro, and Prieto M.C.[119] Furthermore, frequent references to underground as *melaza* [molasses] and *música negra* [black music] stressed the music's connections to blackness.[120] Taken together, the musical aesthetics, popular fashions, and vocabulary affiliated with underground music exemplified the impact global signifiers of blackness had on local constructions of black Puerto Rican identities.

Several artists also included important social and political critiques of the issues affecting their communities in their songs. Vico C's first hit, "La Recta Final" [The Final Stretch] (1989) described violence, drug addiction, sexual abuse, and the prevalence of AIDS in Puerto Rico's poor communities. Other songs by Vico C include "Xplosión" [Explosion] (1993) about violence and the drug trade in *caseríos,* and "Tony Presidio" (1990), which tells the story of a young assassin who works for drug lords. Another key theme in underground was the routine discrimination that rappers faced. For example, in the 1992 recording "Somos raperos pero no delincuentes" [We are rappers but not delinquents], Ivy Queen rapped that "Us rappers are victims of discrimination / We are also put in jail / Just for being who we are."[121] Eddie Dee has also produced several songs addressing the stigma and discrimination against rappers in Puerto Rico, including more contemporary recordings such as "En Peligro de Extinción" [In Danger of Extinction] included in his 2000 album *El Terrorista de la Lírica* [The Lyrical Terrorist], and "Censurarme por Ser Rapero" [Censor Me for Being a Rapper] on his 2004 *Doce Discípulos* [Twelve Disciples] album.

One of Eddie Dee's popular underground hits, "Señor Oficial" [Mr. Officer], illustrates the type of criticism that underground artists made against the discrimination they faced, in this case regarding police brutality. Although he had performed the song since 1995, Eddie Dee received a nomination in the best lyrics category of a national Rap and Reggae competition for the second Día Nacional del Rap y Reggae [National Day of Rap and Reggae] in November of 1997. *El Nuevo Día* published the lyrics to the popular song, which the reporter described as "a call for understanding that the rapper directs toward his enemy, the police."[122]

Eddie Dee stated that the song reflected "my life, my experiences in the street with my friends."[123] "Señor Oficial" describes the hypocrisy of government officials who harass rappers and their fans despite the fact that most rappers just want to party, meet girls, and, in Eddie Dee's case, help his mother financially. Eddie Dee lists a series of activities that he does in his everyday life, including playing the stereo in his car, talking on his cell phone, driving in the streets, or going to a *caserío.* And yet, while doing such mundane activities, officers stop him, assuming that he is buying drugs, robbing people, or engaging in other types of delinquent, or even criminal, behavior.

Beyond a simple depiction of the everyday reality of police harassment that rappers endure, Eddie Dee also presents an important critique of the presumed divisions between *caserío* residents (as embodied by underground artists) and the rest of Puerto Rico. Throughout the song, he stresses the commonalities between underground artists and authorities. For example, in response to the charges that underground encouraged drug use and violence, Eddie Dee raps that the level of drug use and homicide in Puerto Rico also disturbs him, but he angrily rejects the notion that rappers are to blame. Such lyrics point out that rappers are just like everyone else, including police, and that they also hope for the end of violence in Puerto Rico's *caseríos*. Eddie Dee continues in this vein when he sings that rappers' activities are no different than those of other youth, including the officer's own behavior as a teenager. Throughout the song, the officer represents the authorities who implemented *Mano Dura* and helped to propagate stereotypes of urban blackness. By highlighting the commonalities between rappers and officers, then, Eddie Dee erases the perceived boundaries between the *caseríos* and the rest of the island.

Eddie Dee also calls for the recognition of rappers' humanity and equality to other Puerto Ricans. Throughout the song, he pointedly asks, "¿por qué?" [why?], questioning why officers assume that he will buy drugs if he is on the corner, or why they stop him when he drives in his car. In the chorus, Eddie Dee continues to address the officer directly, declaring, "déjeme cantar mi canción" [let me sing my song] and "déjeme ser como yo soy" [let me be who I am]. By outing the authorities' hypocrisy, requesting an explanation for their aggression toward Eddie Dee and the communities he represents, and insisting on being accepted for who he is, Eddie Dee demands the full recognition of rappers and, by extension, *caserío* residents, as equal citizens of Puerto Rico, dismantling the perceived distinctions between urban blackness and the rest of the island.

The accompanying music video for "Señor Oficial" emphasizes this call for recognition through incorporating visual signifiers of blackness that make clear the racist underpinnings of the police's harassment of underground artists and fans. The video begins when Eddie Dee emerges from his dark SUV to meet up with some friends on the corner. The young men are dressed in "hip-hop" style, with baggy jean shorts, oversized T-shirts, and sneakers; some wear baseball caps. Eddie Dee's friends have short haircuts and appear racially ambiguous. Eddie Dee is black and wears shoulder-length dreadlocks. As he greets his friends, a group of police officers approaches the young men, guns drawn. They throw Eddie Dee and his friends on the ground, handcuff, and search them. Then, Eddie Dee, the

FIGURE 1.1. Eddie Dee participates in a police lineup in his music video for "Señor Oficial."

only black youth with dreadlocks in the group, is arrested and driven to the station.

Once there, Eddie Dee participates in a police lineup with three other men who are also young, black, and wear dreadlocks. The camera pans across the men holding their identification numbers as if the viewer were the person identifying someone in the lineup. Then, the men leave the room, Eddie Dee and the first two men smiling with relief. The final man stares into the camera, shakes his head, and throws his paper with his number on it at the camera, as if he were disgusted with being considered a suspect.

Afterward, Eddie Dee appears at a press conference wearing a black suit and tie. He stands at a podium where he says he will address underground's critics, who fault rappers for the problems in Puerto Rican society. Eddie Dee raps about the discrimination he faces because of his "look," which includes "hip-hop" clothing, earrings, and natural hairstyles such as dreadlocks. He relates the criticisms he receives for his hairstyle and earrings, and, more troubling, the way he is prevented from entering certain establishments because people assume he is a criminal. Although he does not explicitly discuss race here, the association between his hairstyle, his fashion choices, and African diasporic aesthetics make evident that the discrimination Eddie Dee faces as a result of his "look" is fundamentally linked to the racist assumptions about blackness, and urban blackness in particular, on the island.

Indeed, "Señor Oficial" rejects the stigmatization of urban blackness upon which dominant portrayals of *caseríos* and their residents (including underground artists) rely. Eddie Dee exposes the hypocrisy of Puerto Rico's so-called racial democracy, discrediting claims of a raceless society by depicting young black male youth's everyday experiences with racial profiling and police brutality. In the process, Eddie Dee both embraces a black identity that incorporates influences from other African diasporic sites and argues for equal rights for working-class and black Puerto Ricans marginalized by dominant discourses of racial democracy.

Because of the close associations between underground and the same working-class black communities targeted by *Mano Dura* policies, the music itself also became the focus of anticrime and antidrug campaigns. In the mid-1990s, record stores in popular locations like the Plaza de las Américas mall began selling underground recordings, ending their circulation via informal channels.[124] In 1995, the Drugs and Vice Control Bureau of the police department raided six record stores to confiscate underground cassettes and CDs.[125] The raids ignited a debate about the alleged "obscenity" of underground. However, as Eddie Dee's video implies, underlying these debates were anxieties regarding new conceptualizations of blackness that the music inserted into Puerto Rican society, ideas that could disrupt the hegemony of dominant constructions of racial democracy. Underground had become out of place via its distribution in more "mainstream" channels, and therefore had to be contained once more within the *caseríos*. Critics attempted to do so by reinforcing the strict parameters around Puerto Ricanness, and once again casting the urban blackness that underground supposedly represented outside of this definition.

"Rap: Soy Boricua pa' que tú lo Sepas"

On March 15, 1995, approximately one month after the raids on record stores, the newspaper *El Nuevo Día* published an article detailing the activities of the Task Force of the Drug- and Gun-Free School Zones Program. Officials entered schools in Arecibo, Humacao, Loíza, Caguas, San Juan, and Luquillo to look for drug paraphernalia. The article listed items that the Task Force considered indicative of drug use and subject to confiscation: "Marijuana, syringes and envelopes with suspected drugs, bottles of alcohol, *underground music*, beepers and cell phones."[126] The inclusion of underground recordings among the contraband items seized at schools reveals the extent to which underground had been criminalized within Puerto Rican society.[127] The popular association between drug use, crime, and underground persisted even though a judge had dismissed the charges against the owners of the stores targeted by the raids.

Antidrug initiatives like the school raids that connected underground to drugs and other activities associated with *caseríos* reinforced the problematic stereotypes of urban blackness that circulated during *Mano Dura*. If *Mano Dura* ultimately reinforced racial and class segregation on the island, discussions about underground also served to reemplace ideas about blackness within the *caseríos*—that is, outside of the mainstream. As Mayra Santos-Febres writes:

> The invasion of *caseríos* and poor neighborhoods as part of Pedro Rosselló's "*Mano Dura contra el Crimen*" initiative and the invasion of nightclubs and schools to eradicate rap is not a pure coincidence . . . Part of the master plan is also the channeling and limiting of rap territories, i.e. the communities where it originated and where (preferably) the influence of rap is supposed to be contained. In this way, they propose to stop rap from colonizing other social territories. Needless to say, the border between legal Puerto Rico and rap territories is marked by a police barrier.[128]

Both the attempts to censor underground and *Mano Dura*'s policing of *caseríos* sought to reinforce a perception of Puerto Rican identity as whitened by creating discursive and physical boundaries between the urban blackness of the *caseríos* and the rest of the island. In the case of *Mano Dura*, the gates and towers constructed around the housing projects marked the alleged difference between them and the rest of white(ned) Puerto Rico. Likewise, critics of underground developed metaphorical boundaries that defined underground, and the blackness it represented, as absolutely *not* Puerto Rican.

One result of the salience of discourses of racial democracy on the island is the displacement of racism elsewhere—that is, the assumption that racism only exists outside of Puerto Rico's supposed "racial democracy." Oftentimes, that elsewhere is the United States, where histories of de jure segregation in the twentieth century are offered as evidence of the "uniquely" racist United States. Following this logic, to talk about racism or to embrace blackness is understood as the result of "foreign," and, more specifically, "American," influence in relation to the supposedly more race-less Puerto Rico. This context is crucial for understanding critics who described underground as a form of "cultural imperialism" from the United States that displaced other, more "authentic" Puerto Rican traditions.[129] Indeed, these critics latched onto the diasporic resources, especially hip-hop, that underground artists infused into their performances as evidence of this supposed "cultural imperialism." However, such critiques reinforced assumptions that blackness was inherently foreign and existed outside of both the geographic and moral boundaries of Puerto Rican identity.

Fernando Clemente published an editorial in the periodical *Claridad* that exemplifies the "cultural imperialism" critique.[130] Clemente considers rap to be one of many U.S. cultural phenomena imported into Puerto Rico, similar to the Hula-Hoops, miniskirts, and psychedelic clothing of his youth. Throughout the editorial, he depicts these previous cultural fads as relatively benign and the unfortunate results of broader processes of globalization and capitalism. However, he identifies rap as a particularly insufferable and damaging cultural import. Clemente begins his assault on rap by describing young men piercing their ears and noses; he claims that in his time, the only men wearing earrings were "pirates and gypsies in the movies; and only bulls had hoops inlaid in their noses." For Clemente, piercings form part of a "rapper-look" that is detrimental to Puerto Rican society: "And who benefits from this 'rapper-look' and—even worse—the 'rapper conduct'? Puerto Rican culture? Definitely NOT! What it does, whether we like it or not, is perpetuate our colonial condition and the vulgar economic power of the United States." Raquel Z. Rivera states that Clemente's criticism of rap typifies the cultural imperialism argument that considers the presence of rap on the island as the result of U.S. colonialism, "as if rap were not already an integral part of Puerto Rican culture."[131]

Beyond the cultural imperialism argument, however, Clemente's editorial employs racialized language and imagery that also distinguishes blackness from Puerto Rican identity. Considering Clemente's relatively dismissive attitude toward cultural practices that are associated with "mainstream" (read "white") U.S. American culture (i.e., Hula-Hoops and "make love not war" T-shirts), his virulent admonishing of "rapper-looks" and "rapper conduct" implies that it is rap's associations with blackness that makes the music and anything associated with it so "damaging" to Puerto Rican soci-

FIGURE 1.2. Caricature of an underground artist that accompanied Fernando Clemente's editorial, "Entrando por la Salida" published in *Claridad*, February 18–24, 1994. Note the figure's hair and facial features that suggest he is of African descent, as well as the hand gesture that is reminiscent of a gang sign.

ety. The visual image accompanying the editorial emphasizes the presumed connections between rap and urban blackness. Located in the center of the text is a black and white drawing of a man with a goatee and long hair. The wide nose and curly hair signify that the man is of African descent. He wears large hoop earrings, a patterned jacket and belt, and makes a hand gesture that resembles a gang sign. This caricature of a young, black, male rap fan reinscribes notions that it is rap's association with blackness that informs "rapper conduct" (including criminal behavior suggested by the gang sign) and supposedly "threatens" Puerto Rican society.

One year later, *Claridad* published another frequently cited editorial regarding underground's "foreign" roots titled "Rapeo sobre el rap en Ciales" [I'm rapping about rap in Ciales] by Edwin Reyes.[132] Reyes described his participation in a school function celebrating the founding of Puerto Rico in the town of Ciales. After screening a brief documentary about poet Luis Palés Matos to the students, Reyes followed them into the auditorium of the school to find, to his horror, a rap concert. Throughout his editorial, Reyes admonishes school officials for inviting rappers to the celebration of

Puerto Rican culture because, in his estimation, not only is rap associated with "drug subculture and gang street violence," but it is also not Puerto Rican. He notes that rap began in the "black and Hispanic ghettos of North America" as a "primitive form of musical expression that lends itself perfectly to broadcasting the most primordial forms of emotion." Reyes's reference to the "black and Hispanic ghettos of North America" underscores hip-hop's origins in the United States, but also in areas that have been racialized as "black" (or at least nonwhite). Even if he mentions "Hispanic[s]," his condescending tone mimics common representations of Nuyoricans as "African Americanized" and "inauthentic" Puerto Ricans that circulate on the island.[133] Not only does Reyes locate hip-hop outside of Puerto Rico, but his problematic depictions of it as "primitive," "primordial," and "violent" connect rap to stereotypes of blackness rooted in assumptions that it represents the "uncivilized" counterpoint to whiteness.

Rather than the "stupidity of rap," Reyes advocates that Puerto Rican youth should listen to "our music, sophisticated and popular, varied, beautiful, irreducible . . . the sublime music of Puerto Ricanness." Of course, Reyes implies the inclusion of Luis Palés Matos, a poet from the 1930s, in his definition of "sublime" Puerto Rican culture. This juxtaposition of Palés Matos and rap is especially important for interrogating the racial implications of Reyes's argument. A widely revered literary figure on the island, Luis Palés Matos is best known for his poetry that celebrates blackness and Afro-Caribbean identity. As a contemporary of the *Generación de los 1930s*, Palés Matos put forth an important perspective that situated Puerto Rico in relation to the Afro-Caribbean at a time when other writers like Antonio Pedreira sought to assert the island's ties to Spain. However, critics have argued that Palés Matos's poetry maintains perceptions of blackness as "primitive" and "mythologized" consistent with dominant tropes of folkloric blackness.[134] Indeed, Reyes's comparison of the "sublime" Puerto Rican poetry of Palés Matos with allegedly "foreign" rap replicates the dichotomy between folkloric blackness and urban blackness that sustains racial democracy. As a result, Reyes strengthens the associations between underground and "foreign" blackness, while at the same time reinforcing the perception that the only blackness compatible with a white(ned) Puerto Ricanness is one that exists in the past.

For Reyes and Clemente, underground could corrupt Puerto Rican national culture with its unapologetic embrace of "foreign" (black) American cultural aesthetics. But for other critics, the potential consequences of underground's growing popularity on the island were far worse. These included the perceived danger of underground to the moral and physical health of Puerto Rican youth—indeed, for these critics, the very future of the island was at stake. Shortly after the raids, Yolanda Rosaly published an editorial in *El Nuevo Día* about the potentially negative effects of underground on Puerto Rican youth.[135] Rosaly argued that readers should protect children from underground, or what she termed the "underworld," in order to "help improve the quality of life in Puerto Rico 100 percent." To combat underground, Rosaly urged adults to talk to children about the music, and "insist that promoting this type of music does not help the healthy and positive development of their generation at all, the generation that we are all proud of and that we hope will do great things. And, even more important, present them with alternatives for better and more creative ways to distract themselves."

Another columnist, Mateo Mateo, published an essay a few weeks later that praised the police raids on record stores.[136] Like Rosaly, Mateo argued that underground negatively impacted youth, exposing them to the "three disgraces": sex, drugs, and violence. He warned that underground was a "contagion" among Puerto Rican youth that caused them to engage in immoral and unhealthy activities. In fact, Mateo considered underground's "sinful" lyrics so destructive that he labeled it "AIDS for the soul of our children and adolescents."

The moral panic surrounding underground caused many of its critics to reproach the Puerto Rican government for inadequately protecting youth from the music, especially after the judge dismissed the obscenity charges against record store owners. Quoting Milton Picón, the president of the advocacy group Morality in the Media, Rosaly claimed that allowing the proliferation of underground recordings weakened the impact of the government's antidrug policies and *Mano Dura* because, in her estimation, underground encouraged drug use and promiscuity.[137] Mateo concurred, arguing that he thought it would be "sufficient to listen to these lyrics in order to angrily bang the mallet on the table and find guilty everyone who has contributed to creating and propagating this contagious sin." Shocked that such "obscene" lyrics would not constitute illegality in the eyes of the court, Mateo asked, "are we starting to legislate the *assassination* of conscience and immorality?"[138] Such language represented underground as especially violent, and called for government intervention in ways that mirrored the demands for policing of *caseríos* during *Mano Dura*.

Although critics often did not explicitly mention blackness in their condemnation of underground, the visual imagery and language used in their arguments connoted racist stereotypes of urban blackness. The anxieties about the social ills that underground would promote replicated assumptions that the difference between "modern" Puerto Ricans and more "primitive" *caserío* residents was predicated on racial distinctions. Mayra Santos-Febres argues that

> We should not forget that the rapper identity is defined by society as pertaining to a group of identities that are three-fold criminal. Because of his or her gender, race, and class position, the rapper is from the start a gangsta [*sic*]. If not in reality, then potentially. And it is precisely as a result of falling into this social position thrice criminalized by the state that the rapper develops responses, some rhetorical, others real, to establish himself or herself and confront his or her marginalization.[139]

As Raquel Z. Rivera writes, during *Mano Dura* and the censorship campaigns about underground, "class and racial boundaries were being strictly policed given a discourse that assigned blame and polluting qualities along class and racial lines and reinforced a sharp 'us vs. them' attitude."[140] Both the cultural imperialism and morality arguments established ideological distinctions that positioned urban blackness as fundamentally distinct from Puerto Rican identities, couching these racial hierarchies within a discourse of "morality."

Underground artists responded to these criticisms in their songs and in newspaper interviews. Soon after the raids, the *San Juan Star* published an interview with an "up-and-coming" underground group called Nizze.[141] Although Nizze's interview took place in the notorious Lloréns Torres *caserío*, the group's profile differed from the stereotypes of underground artists because its members attended universities, indicating a more middle-class position (or, at least, the potential to improve their socioeconomic status through a university education). Still, Nizze criticized the government for unfairly targeting rappers, arguing that underground conveyed "real" life and struggles in the impoverished urban neighborhoods of Puerto Rico. They claimed that morality groups were "hypocrites" who expressed opinions about *caseríos* without ever having experienced urban life. While not explicitly stated, Nizze's interview implied that it was race and class bias rather than any serious concern for the public that motivated anti-underground sentiment.

Likewise, several academics and cultural critics published editorials in newspapers arguing that underground revealed the lives of marginalized sectors of Puerto Rican society and therefore should be taken as legitimate social commentaries rather than glorifications of violence or drug use.[142] Many editorialists countered the morality arguments by maintaining that underground's hypersexual and violent lyrics, while problematic, did not necessarily reflect the everyday lives and activities of the singers who composed them.[143] These arguments directly countered the assumption of an inherently "primitive" blackness, instead emphasizing that economic policies, as well as institutionalized racism and classism, produced the violence and other issues impacting *caseríos.*

Others argued that rap was in fact a Puerto Rican phenomenon, thus refuting the notion that underground—and, by extension, blackness—were "foreign" to Puerto Rico.[144] In direct response to Edwin Reyes's editorial, Rafael Bernabe published an article entitled, "Rap: Soy Boricua pa' que tú lo Sepas" [Rap: I'm Puerto Rican just so you know], also in *Claridad.*[145] Bernabe accused Reyes of treating rap in a way that resembled a colonizer attempting to control and assimilate the colonized. He considered Reyes's descriptions of rap as "monotonous, elementary, primitive, subculture, underground" similar to Joseph Conrad's portrayal of Africa as the "Heart of Darkness." For Bernabe, the comparable language in Conrad's work and Reyes's editorial presented the ghettos of the United States as "primitive" spaces, thus revealing Reyes's classism, racism, and narrow, elitist conceptualization of Puerto Rican national culture. In the end, Bernabe asserted that rap's presence in Puerto Rico revealed a need to create more "inclusive" and "dynamic" understandings of Puerto Rican culture that took into account diverse experiences, including those of black Puerto Ricans on the island and Nuyoricans in the United States.

The backlash against underground in the mid-1990s elucidates the extent to which underground's expressions of urban, working-class, and black subjectivities were perceived as threatening to dominant constructions of Puerto Rican identity. Although underground circulated in Puerto Rico for several years prior to this controversy, the moral panic surrounding the music did not surface until it entered more mainstream markets on the island. That critics pushed for underground's censorship once the music moved into more mainstream channels makes evident that the primary issue was the expansion of underground outside of the *caseríos,* and the expression of new understandings of Puerto Ricanness that challenged discourses of racial democracy by centering blackness and African diasporic belonging. Despite the attempts to censor underground, however, the music continued to resonate with Puerto Rican youth who sought an outlet to express their experiences of marginalization, to contest the racism and classism that adversely affected their communities, and to articulate their affinities for blackness.

IT IS DIFFICULT to pinpoint exactly when underground shifted to reggaetón. What is certain, however, is that the controversy surrounding underground in the mid-1990s exposed the music to new audiences. According to DJ Playero, one of the pioneering underground DJs, the confiscation of underground recordings provided free publicity that led many artists to realize that they could attract a much larger audience. They began producing albums with "clean lyrics" to avoid censorship, and changed their "look" and presentations to appeal to more mainstream audiences.[146] As underground became more visible, it received sponsorship from television, radio, and record companies that also sought to capitalize on the music's success. By the late 1990s, underground became more mainstream, and Puerto Ricans referred to it almost exclusively as "reggaetón."

Still, reggaetón's entrance into the mainstream did not prevent discrimination against rappers and their communities. In a 1999 interview, DJ Playero claimed that, while rappers enjoyed new airplay on television and radio, they continued to be unfairly attributed with stereotypes associated with drugs, sexuality, and violence due to their working-class roots.[147] Ten years later, many of the Puerto Rican youth whom I spoke with agreed that reggaetón is more accepted in Puerto Rican society than before, but that often rappers and reggaetón fans face discrimination. For example, Ana María, a reggaetón fan and college student, claimed that many Puerto Ricans blamed reggaetón for societal issues because of the music's lyrics even though, in her opinion, reggaetón did not differ much from rock or other popular music genres. Marcela, a hairdresser from the San Juan area, said that police targeted reggaetón fans, stating "if you're listening to reggaetón [in your car], say [the police] stop you for whatever reason, when they stop you and you're listening to reggaetón, their whole attitude changes, the way they treat you changes." Fans' everyday experiences with discrimination illustrate the extent to which the mid-1990s associations between criminality, blackness, and underground have been entrenched in Puerto Rican society even after reggaetón's success.

Despite reggaetón's global reach, it continues to impact local cultural and racial politics in Puerto Rico. The multiple migrations that inform underground and, later, reggaetón provide diasporic resources that allow for reimagining Puerto Rican identities in ways that foreground African diasporic belonging. Global and local forces converge in reggaetón's connections with blackness, making it a quintessential cultural practice of diaspora. As with their underground predecessors, reggaetón artists continue to adapt and incorporate diasporic resources in their performances in ways that question the validity of Puerto Rican racial democracy. In 2002, these challenges motivated a second censorship campaign against reggaetón that once again focused on questions about morality in order to mask fears about reggaetón's potential to expose the fallacy of Puerto Rico's "racial democracy."

CHAPTER TWO
THE PERILS OF PERREO

In May 2002, reggaetón once again took center stage in Puerto Rican newspapers. Front-page headlines like "What is behind pornographic videos" (*Primera Hora*, May 16, 2002), "The Government thwarted against pornography: Experts detail constitutional obstacles for attacking it" (*El Nuevo Día*, May 16, 2002), and "*Perreo* scandalizes the Legislature" (*Primera Hora*, May 15, 2002) appeared almost daily in the island's papers. These headlines referred to the Anti-Pornography Campaign, spearheaded by Senator Velda González, chairperson of the Special Commission for the Study of Violent and Sexual Content in Puerto Rican Radio and Television. The Anti-Pornography Campaign aimed to eliminate pornographic content from all media, including radio and television; however, González and her colleagues specifically targeted reggaetón, which they considered a "vulgar" music with "pornographic" videos that threatened to destroy Puerto Rican society's values and corrupt middle-class youth. Reporters covering the campaign wrote articles about the hearings in the Senate, exposés on the "real" behind the scenes activities on music video sets, the opinions of individuals in the reggaetón industry, and advice from social workers, educators, and psychiatrists for parents who wanted to "protect" their children from "pornographic" materials. Accompanying photos featured youth dancing in nightclubs, Senators scrutinizing music videos on a large screen, and artists surrounded by scantily clad women in compromising positions.

In many ways, the anxieties about reggaetón's impact on the morality of youth expressed in these articles seem similar to the backlash against underground in the 1990s. However, this campaign differed in two significant ways. First, rather than the independent distribution of underground in the 1990s, by 2002, reggaetón had become more mainstream in Puerto Rico, attracting young audiences from all socioeconomic classes. Artists performed regularly in nightclubs, and reggaetón album sales began making significant inroads into the Puerto Rican market. The music had emerged from the "underground," poised to expand not only within Puerto Rico but also internationally. Reggaetón had transcended the *caseríos'* gates into globalized technoscapes and mediascapes that provided platforms for reggaetón to spread to wider audiences. This context influenced the goal of the campaign; if in the 1990s, would-be censors sought to prevent the spread of underground in Puerto Rico, by 2002, the concern was how to deal with reggaetón's omnipresence and potential international expansion.

To address these concerns, the Anti-Pornography Campaign sought to accommodate reggaetón into Puerto Rican national space, transforming reggaetón from a signifier of blackness to one of Puerto Ricanness. Rather than censorship, González advocated for more "clean" reggaetón lyrics and representations of women in music videos. As Senator González described,

> What I am trying to avoid is that [rap and reggaetón] fall prey to those who, because of economic interests, their mediocrity and the inability to produce good music and quality presentations, resort to denigrating expressions of the genre [reggaetón] and the degradation of women in order to make money at the expense of the emotional and social health of our people. Now it is time to clean up the name of rap and reggae and other musical genres and the youth that follow them . . . It is time to eliminate the merchants of pornography and indecency in the media . . . for the education and healthy amusement of our people.[1]

In addition to media representations, Senator González was also concerned with *perreo*, the dance associated with reggaetón. *Perreo* typically involves a woman standing back-to-front with a man as she gyrates her hips provocatively against his; the name *perreo* derived from the Spanish word *perro*, or dog, as the dance presumably simulated the sexual act between dogs. González not only considered *perreo* inappropriate for television, but also a dangerous dance that led to improper sexual behavior and provoked violent altercations in nightclubs. She argued that reggaetón had a danceable rhythm that "could be danced another way, without having to do obscene movements."[2]

González's championing of the need to "clean up" reggaetón demonstrates that, ultimately, the goal was to situate reggaetón within the ideals of Puerto Rican racial democracy rather than to censor it altogether. The Anti-Pornography Campaign also differed from previous censorship attempts because it focused specifically on the role of women as music video dancers, as well as the potential effect of videos on young women's self-esteem and opinions about sexuality. Indeed, reggaetón music videos at once destabilized the dominant constructions of "respectability" that underpinned Puerto Rican national identity and reproduced stereotypical images of black, working-class, female sexuality. During this time period, the dancers featured in music videos came from a variety of racial backgrounds ranging from white to black, although the majority of them were on the whiter end of the racial spectrum.[3] These women were frequently filmed wearing thong underwear, gyrating in front of men or next to poles as if in strip clubs, and sometimes positioned as if they were performing sex acts. Certainly, these videos can be read as reinforcing heteropatriarchal gender hierarchies. However, women's participation in these videos requires analysis of the complex and often contradictory structures that shape the possibilities of women artists and dancers to exert their agency within reggaetón. As Jillian Báez contends, although these videos "can rightly be accused of being misogynistic and homophobic, reggaetón should not be considered monolithic."[4] Moreover, reggaetón is not unique in its representations of women, since other musical genres popular in Puerto Rico, such as salsa, have similar types of representations.[5]

The emphasis on female sexuality that pervaded the Anti-Pornography Campaign sheds light on the intersections of gender, sexuality, and race in the construction of Puerto Rico's so-called racial democracy. Attributing characteristics such as hypersexuality or respectability to the sexualities associated with different racial groups contributes to larger processes of racialization and has implications for how these groups are included or not within a specific society or nation. In many places (including Puerto Rico), respectability relied upon a female sexuality that conformed to particular heteropatriarchal gender norms such as maintaining the nuclear family and avoiding overt displays of sexuality, attributes often associated with upper-class white women. Hypersexuality, on the other hand, emphasized promiscuity and immorality, characteristics generally considered to be embodied by black women.[6] Thus, differentiating sexualities is central to processes of racialization that locate individuals within the racial hierarchy intrinsic to discourses of racial democracy.

In this context, the overt displays of female sexuality in reggaetón music videos became especially threatening to the continued hegemony of racial democracy since they symbolized an aspect of urban blackness that troubled the perception of Puerto Rico as a "white(ned)" society, igniting a moral panic among several sectors of the Puerto Rican population.[7] On the one hand, women involved in reggaetón were sometimes portrayed as victims of a misogynistic, opportunistic, and male-dominated music industry; on the other, female dancers were also considered hypersexual women who did not conform to the "moral" standards of Puerto Rican society. These women generally expressed a certain "erotic autonomy" in their video performances that was particularly upsetting to the status quo. Erotic autonomy defies the assumption that sexuality should only serve the purposes of the state through, for example, the perpetuation of the nuclear family.[8] Embodied by figures such as the prostitute (who engages in sexual activity without the expectation of procreation), erotic autonomy threatens to "corrupt, it signals a danger to respectability."[9] On the surface, the arguments deployed during the Anti-Pornography Campaign expressed deep concern for the well-being of the women dancing in music videos; however, embedded within this discussion was an understanding that these women posed a serious threat to the respectability that was a defining feature of dominant constructions of Puerto Rican national identity. Reggaetón thus became identified as "a social and political problem, a problem that had to be rectified in order to restore a moral social order" and to secure the hegemony of racial democracy.[10] To do so, the Anti-Pornography Campaign engaged in a "politics of respectability" that "emphasized reform of individual behavior and attitudes," particularly for female reggaetón dancers and young Puerto Rican women who watched them.[11]

To combat the "indecency" of reggaetón and *perreo*, the Anti-Pornography Campaign involved multiple Senate hearings regarding the impact of reggaetón on Puerto Rican society. Senators watched reggaetón music videos to assess their pornographic content, and questioned sociologists, social workers, and psychiatrists about the potentially disastrous effects of these videos on the moral and psychological health of Puerto Rican youth. Some artists appeared before the Senate to defend their use of certain images in their videos. In the end, González and her colleagues recommended a five-part legislation that would regulate pornographic content in the media. The plan included the creation of the Office of the Monitor against Obscenity and Pornography in Media and Communications, under the auspices of the Department of Consumer Affairs, which would educate people on the "dangers of pornography" and how to prevent exposure to youth; the Citizens' Bill of Rights against Obscenity and Pornography, which imposed legal repercussions for the distribution of pornographic content; a law requiring televisions to have a V-chip that would allow parents to block programs they deemed inappropriate for their children; a law that ordered movie theaters and video rental businesses to inform consumers of pornographic and violent content in movies; and a law prohibiting government agencies from engaging with any media outlets that contained pornographic content.[12] The Puerto Rican Senate approved these recommendations on June 14, 2002, which were signed into law in August of that year.

My concern is not with the representations of women in reggaetón music videos as much as it is with the government's *response* to these videos and the debate that ensued. Close examination of the multiple arguments both in favor of and against reggaetón music videos reveals the racial, class, and gendered dynamics of racial democracy discourses. In particular, they illuminate the ambiguous position of black female sexuality as critical to the formation of the Puerto Rican nation and yet continuously left out of contemporary representations of Puerto Ricanness. At the same time, the Anti-Pornography Campaign reveals how government officials, cultural critics, reggaetón artists and producers, dancers, and fans negotiated their social positions in relation to the intersections of race, gender, and class within discourses of racial democracy. In the final analysis, these debates demonstrate how reggaetón's perceived connections to urban blackness were construed as a real threat to Puerto Rico's racial democracy.

Constructing Puerto Rican Identity through Women's Racialized Bodies

In her autoethnography about living in Puerto Rico and the United States, Maritza Quiñones Rivera describes being "visibly invisible" as a black woman in Puerto Rico. Writing about her experiences growing up in Carolina,[13] Quiñones Rivera states, "On the one hand, I am nation. On the other hand, I am race, and erased. The latter is ambiguously silenced, not necessarily by the self but by the eyes of the others."[14] Quiñones Rivera is "nation" as a Puerto Rican woman; however, as a black woman, Quiñones Rivera's race "erases" her from the whitened Puerto Rican nation, even though her blackness makes others hyperconscious of her presence, especially with respect to her "always sexually enticing" black female body.[15]

The "visibly invisible" black female body exemplifies the ambiguous position of black women vis-à-vis Puerto Rican national identity. Histories of slavery in Puerto Rico often identify interracial sexual relationships between Spanish men and Taíno and, especially, African women as the basis for the racially mixed population. For example, in his textbook about Puerto Rican history from the conquest through the sixteenth century, Ricardo Alegría describes race mixture as the foundation of Puerto Rican society: "From the beginning, the Spaniards mixed racially with the support and encouragement of the crown and the church, marrying the Indian woman in the early years and, in the later years, the African slave woman, thus creating a mixed population which received its language, social, and religious customs and way of being from Spanish culture."[16]

Likewise, in his classic text, *Historia de la esclavitud negra en Puerto Rico*, Luis Díaz Soler describes the small numbers of Spanish women relative to men during the colonial period as part of the catalyst that created Puerto Rico's racially mixed population: "These circumstances, in addition to the fact that the Spanish were willingly intimate with women of other races, made *mestización* an American reality.[17] When the Indian disappeared from the Antilles, the Spaniard found in the African woman a substitute to satisfy his sexual appetite."[18]

These accounts portray black women as essential to the creation of the Puerto Rican nation since they birthed the racially mixed population. At the same time, however, they do not attribute black female ancestors with the respectability often associated with the founding and maintenance of modern nations. Rather, such descriptions represent black female sexuality as an always available option for Spanish men seeking to "satisfy [their] sexual appetites" when not presented with any other recourse (i.e., white or indigenous women). By singling out elite Spanish men as the primary and most valuable actors in the creation of the Puerto Rican nation, these narratives perpetuate hierarchies of race, class, gender, and sexuality that locate black women on the bottom, equating them with hypersexuality and primitivity.

Despite these histories that paint black women as foundational to the "birth" of the Puerto Rican nation, the contemporary preservation of the nation now relies on white(ned) Puerto Rican women. As scholars like Ann Laura Stoler and Anne McClintock have shown, nationalist projects that attempted to unify multiple racial groups within a particular nation-state usually regarded the figure of the white woman to personify the nation while simultaneously reinforcing racial boundaries through emphasizing white female purity.[19] As discourses of racial democracy took hold, however, "pure" whiteness became unattainable since all individuals were presumed to be racially mixed.[20] Nevertheless, particular tropes that had been associated with "pure" whiteness, including "respectability," were made attributes of national identities, thus allowing for a simultaneous valorization of whiteness and recognition of racial mixture.[21]

Respectability's associations with whiteness were defined relationally, such that in Puerto Rico "wealthy white women's [respectability] was also premised on the disreputability of poor and Afro-Puerto Rican women."[22] In this context, intersections of race, class, gender, and sexuality remained fluid, at times allowing individuals to move toward the whiter end of the racial spectrum. For example, in specific circumstances, nonwhite women of higher socioeconomic class backgrounds might be divorced from stereotypes of black female hypersexuality, provided that they conform to ideals of respectability represented by whiteness.[23] Likewise, white women of lower socioeconomic backgrounds may be associated with stereotypes of black women's sexuality.[24] Women actively managed these classifications through policing each other's behavior, advocating certain standards of respectability, and asserting their own individual positions vis-à-vis other women.[25] Ironically, the relational aspect of defining respectability and hypersexuality maintains the essentialist nature of racial categories, portraying working-class black women as "sexual deviants" in relation to both white women and upper-class, nonwhite women.

Because of their associations with stereotypes of sexual deviance, working-class black Puerto Rican women have become "visible" as racialized and gendered "others" on the island. Consequently, they have been subject to various forms of surveillance and policies that stigmatized black womanhood as inherently hypersexual. At times, this involved literal surveillance, such as the nineteenth- and twentieth-century medical "inspections" targeting working-class, nonwhite women suspected of prostitution.[26] These antiprostitution campaigns also circulated images of poor and black women that reinforced assumptions of their allegedly inherent hypersexuality.[27] Often, language employed in these campaigns did not address race outright; however, "racial labels were conjured up indirectly in Puerto Rico by referring to other, racially loaded characteristics such as 'disreputability,' 'respectability,' and 'honor.'"[28] As Eileen Findlay demonstrates, these discourses played a critical role in connecting respectable whiteness with Puerto Rican national identity through the continuous repudiation of black women as degenerate, disreputable, and "outside the community of moral citizens."[29]

The 2002 Anti-Pornography Campaign's representations of reggaetón music video dancers recycled the same stereotypes of black women as "uncontrollable" sexual "deviants" that circulated during (and since) the nineteenth-century antiprostitution efforts. Media coverage of reggaetón music video dancers routinely depicted them as strippers or prostitutes who did not value education or develop monogamous sexual or close-knit family relationships. In the end, supporters of the Anti-Pornography Campaign, including cultural critics, social scientists, health professionals, and politicians—many of them also women—perpetuated these problematic images of black female sexuality in an attempt to "justify" government policing of reggaetón.

"Protecting the Puerto Rican Family"

Women dancing in music videos became hypervisible in the debates about morality and respectability that permeated the Anti-Pornography Campaign. Supporters used "respectability" and "hypersexuality" as racial code words that signified Puerto Ricanness and blackness, respectively, implying that there was a fundamental difference between *caserío* residents and the rest of Puerto Rican society. Because of reggaetón's associations with urban blackness, the female "hypersexuality" expressed in reggaetón was construed as a moral "threat" to Puerto Rican youth, and, more insidiously, the foundations of Puerto Rican identity. The Anti-Pornography Campaign's supporters contrasted "hypersexual blackness" with "respectable Puerto Ricanness" in an attempt to reinforce the racial hierarchies intrinsic to hegemonic discourses of racial democracy.

Many Puerto Ricans supported Senator González's efforts, publishing editorials almost daily in the island's newspapers. A few letter-writers expressed that they liked reggaetón, but opposed certain artists' lyrics; however, the majority of these letters argued that music videos severely hindered the moral education of Puerto Rican youth. One person wrote,

"Truthfully, it is sad that many people support the right to free speech in order to demoralize the minds of our children, youth, and adults. It is time to exalt the values that dignify us as human beings."[30] Another called on Puerto Ricans to "raise our voice in protest against this degeneration," arguing that music videos were "offensive to human dignity."[31] A group of local Pentecostal churches claimed that reggaetón music videos could dissolve the unity of the Puerto Rican people, stating, "We are living in a critical time in terms of the moral health of our people. Marriage and the family, indisputable pillars of our social structure, are being undermined and the entire structure is coming down on us with unprecedented repercussions that threaten the existence of our collectivity, our people."[32] Government officials supporting González's campaign made similar arguments regarding the government's responsibility to protect Puerto Ricans from such "extreme obscenity." Governor Sila M. Calderón stated, "It seems positive to me that Congress and specifically Senator Velda González are tackling an important problem and social preoccupation in Puerto Rico, especially when we have to protect the Puerto Rican family in all aspects."[33]

Several government agencies came together to support Senator González, including the Office of Youth Affairs, the Office for Drug Control, the Office of Consumer Affairs, and the Office of the Procurator of Women.[34] Some government officials vowed to use their departments' resources to ensure the safe and "clean" production of music videos and thus do their part to ameliorate the threat that reggaetón supposedly posed to society at large. Director of the Department of Family Services, Yolanda Zayas, argued that reggaetón music videos not only encouraged immoral behavior, but also violated minors' rights.[35] Zayas promised that the Department of Family Services would investigate any music video where it appeared that a minor *may* have participated, including the mere presence of artists' children on music video sets.[36] The secretary of the Department of Work and Human Resources, Victor Rivera, offered the support of his officers, who would intervene at random on music video sets suspected of employing minors. Since individuals who participated in videos without pay could not be subject to the regulations of the Department of Work and Human Resources, the Department of Family Services, Department of Justice, and Police would work together to monitor music video sets.[37] While officials from many of these agencies cautioned that González's measures must not violate rights to free speech, they all generally agreed that pornography, and reggaetón music videos in particular, required constant surveillance and intervention from government agencies in order to repress whatever corrupting influences emerged from these videos.

Some of the alleged "justification" for government intervention derived from the solicitation of expert opinions from sociologists and psychologists about the impact of reggaetón on youth's behavior. Senator González contended that reggaetón promoted drug use, violence, and sexual promiscuity.[38] Many supporters concurred. Psychologist Mercedes Rodríguez testified before the Senate that all violence is "interconnected." She identified the employment of minors in music videos as a type of violence, implying that youth's exposure to reggaetón could lead them to commit other forms of "violence" in the future. Moreover, Dr. Rodríguez stated that *perreo* degraded all human beings who participated in it, not just women.[39] Social worker Sally López affirmed in a newspaper interview that, "Unfortunately, access to pornographic material can have harmful, long-term effects. Exposed children can imitate inappropriate conduct that is often aggressive."[40] Special commentaries published by professionals who worked in areas such as domestic violence or youth development maintained that reggaetón music videos would negatively influence girls' self-esteem by encouraging them to measure their self-worth in terms of sexuality, and would send young boys the message that violence against women was acceptable.[41] In general, many of these experts publicly declared that reggaetón was more than simple party music—rather, it inhibited healthy and "normal" youth development.

One particular incident exemplified the potential consequences of reggaetón's impact on Puerto Rican youth for many of the Anti-Pornography Campaign's supporters. On May 27, 2002, a group of teenagers stopped one hundred kilometers of traffic along Highway 2 in Aguadilla to protest the Anti-Pornography Campaign. Although protest organizers had assured the transit authorities that they would not act "disorderly" in public, passers-by reported that protesters shouted obscenities and made provocative gestures at them. One witness described the scene: "There were youth on the tops of cars, yelling vulgar words. There were young girls who took off their bras and poured beer on their sweaters."[42] The radio operator for the transit authorities reported, "They were out of control, many were drunk, and the women in very disgraceful positions. Some women lowered the bottom half of their bathing suits."[43] Once transit authorities arrived at the scene, protesters fled without causing any accidents or damage; however, the sexual exhibitionism, alcohol use, and vandalism described by witnesses of the protest illustrated the potential effects that experts had testified could result if youth listened to reggaetón.

The accounts of the protest on Highway 2 also shed light on the ways that coverage of the Anti-Pornography Campaign centered on women. While undoubtedly men and women participated in the protest, the article only detailed women's actions. These women allegedly engaged in hypersexual acts by removing their bras and/or underwear and pouring alcohol all over their bodies—actions that seemed similar to those in some reggaetón music videos. This behavior departed dramatically from the respectability that formed the basis of dominant constructions of Puerto Rican womanhood. Through an obsession with the potentially disastrous effects of women's erotic autonomy, the Anti-Pornography Campaign reinscribed stereotypes of reggaetón artists and fans (and urban blackness) as inherently hypersexual and therefore not Puerto Rican. However, not everyone viewed reggaetón as absolutely divorced from Puerto Rican identity.

"Bomba Was the Rap of Today"

While supporters of the Anti-Pornography Campaign attempted to distinguish reggaetón from the values associated with Puerto Ricanness, some critics of the campaign argued that reggaetón could be integrated into Puerto Rican identities as a "black" cultural practice that existed within the island's racial triad. These arguments described reggaetón's blackness as an offshoot of the folkloric blackness of bomba and other Afro–Puerto Rican cultural practices that were already widely accepted as part of Puerto Rico's heritage. Nevertheless, they shared with the Anti-Pornography Campaign's supporters the maintenance of racial hierarchies inherent to dominant discourses of Puerto Rican racial democracy through reproducing the assumptions that folkloric blackness was inherently "primitive" and "pre-modern."

On May 16, 2002, *Primera Hora* published an article entitled "*La bomba fue el rap de hoy*" [Bomba was the rap of today]. The article began,

> Puerto Ricans have rhythm in their blood . . . [*sic*] and sensuality, too. Since the first days of the conquest, the 'islanders' gave in to the dances with a passion not matched [elsewhere] and, since then, dance has been one way to represent the grace and sensual rhythm of Latinos.

The majority of the dances in Puerto Rico began in poor neighborhoods, not the large salons of the aristocrats. Because of their popular character and, many times, erotic overtones, they were criticized and prohibited by the governments of the time.[44]

Reporter Nieve Vásquez then described bomba as one such dance, interviewing Modesto Cepeda, the son of Puerto Rico's "patriarch" of bomba, Rafael Cepeda, about government bans of bomba in the eighteenth and nineteenth centuries. Cepeda also mentioned that the now national folkloric music included lyrics historically considered "erotic" and inappropriate by many elites. Next to the article, a dialogue box featured a drawing of a faceless white couple, the man seductively dipping a woman wearing a tight dress with a long slit. The box described three other Latin American dances historically stigmatized for erotic content, including merengue, tango, and the lambada, stating, "True or not, the fact is that in many dances, sexual overtones are clearly evident."[45]

Although writer Nieve Vásquez did not explicitly mention *perreo*, through the title's comparison of bomba and rap, the article presented a genealogy that situated *perreo* as the most recent manifestation of "sensual" dances in Puerto Rico and Latin America more generally. Shared histories of their emergence out of marginalized communities and their persecution by authorities insinuated connections between bomba and reggaetón. Sexuality (referred to via the tropes of "sensuality" and "passion") and place (specifically "poor neighborhoods") became signifiers of an unspoken blackness that linked these musical practices together. Implicit in the description of these connections was a critique of González's campaign, for if *perreo* were just the latest manifestation of national folklore, then the sexuality associated with the dance could not be especially threatening. The sexuality of dances like bomba or *perreo* became domesticated, folded into the folkloric blackness that forms a constitutive element of Puerto Rican national identity (albeit in ways that reproduced notions of black primitivity). This line of reasoning presumed that, while *perreo* might not necessarily be "respectable," it also could not be especially "damaging" to Puerto Rico because the sexuality displayed in *perreo* correlated with a particular segment of the population that supposedly had more African ancestry than the rest of the island. Following this logic, it would be impossible to eliminate blackness from the island since all Puerto Ricans were already assumed to be mixed. Instead, these critics focused on the need to effectively manage overt expressions of black hypersexuality in order to maintain the island's white(ned) identity.

In a more explicit critique of González's campaign, one writer for *Primera Hora*, Adria Cruz, argued that the Anti-Pornography Campaign did not address the major problem of women's low self-esteem.[46] Cruz claimed that girls participating in reggaetón music videos sought to replace feelings of unworthiness and lack of love by seeking attention in music videos that ultimately degraded them. Sexuality and race become intimately tied together as Cruz distinguished between sensual dances and sexual ones that influenced girls' self-esteem: "*Perreo* does not try to be a sensual dance, but rather a sexual one. Tango is sensual, bomba is sexual."[47]

Like Vásquez's article, Cruz's descriptions of bomba and tango draw on racialized signifiers that connect sexuality and blackness. Although tango traces its origins to Afro-Argentinean communities, contemporary images of the dance bring to mind a white couple dressed elegantly and dancing in subtle yet suggestive ways;[48] such perceptions are reinforced by tango's popularity in ballroom dance competitions or international tourism. Alternatively, bomba's position as a metonym for blackness in Puerto Rico attributes it with particular stereotypes associated with blackness, including a virulent sexuality signified by bomba's historical associations with eroticism and its movements that center on the hips and buttocks. For Cruz, bomba and *perreo* shared a black hypersexuality. Although Cruz considered the sexuality of *perreo* to be a serious concern, she opposed moves to prohibit dancing, arguing that this would cause further problems. Instead, she encouraged the establishment of programs targeting young girls that focused on self-esteem and "positive" love relationships to draw them away from reggaetón. To that end, Cruz described *perreo* as an inevitable consequence of an inherited blackness that must be managed so as not to harm the "self-esteem" of the Puerto Rican population. Discourses of racial democracy underlie Cruz's argument in two ways: first, it assumes that the prevalence of race mixture makes blackness an inevitable part of Puerto Rican identity; and, second, her argument reiterates problematic links between blackness and hypersexuality that form part of the basis of the racial hierarchies intrinsic to discourses of racial democracy.

Cultural critic and acclaimed author Ana Lydia Vega also provided a serious critique of the Anti-Pornography Campaign that highlighted the "sensuality" of African-based dances in Puerto Rico. Vega pointed out that, historically, Puerto Rican dances had always been sensual:

Our *criollo* dances have always been known to consecrate the leading role of the backside, that indisputable idol of Antillean eroticism. From the uncouth swerves of the buttocks of our celebrated *rumberas* to the modest, small hip moves of our global stars, sensual hip-shaking continues to be one of the essential key factors of Puerto Rican dance. How astonishing, therefore, the moralistic rage that has been unleashed at the latest manifestation of this ancestral tendency. As though they had returned to the times of ecclesiastical prohibition of the *bembés* of the slaves![49]

Bembés were gatherings where people danced bomba; prior to abolition in Puerto Rico, concerns that *bembés* could be opportunities for the organization of slave revolts combined with general portrayals of bomba as "immoral" prompted government efforts to ban the music and gatherings where it was played. In comparing the Anti-Pornography Campaign to the prohibition of *bembés*, Vega portrayed González and her supporters as absurdly moving back to the times of slavery. Vega implied a racist bias on the part of supporters of the Anti-Pornography Campaign, pointing out that not only did they rely on irrelevant concerns regarding morality to "justify" their campaign, but also they unfairly targeted predominantly nonwhite communities.

Vega emphasized this point by arguing that the Anti-Pornography Campaign erroneously blamed many societal ills on these communities. She argued that it is not morality, but rather socioeconomic inequalities that produced adverse conditions in impoverished communities and that have motivated artists to pursue reggaetón. Vega writes, "Poverty, inequality, and drug addiction were not invented by rappers. Chronic abuse dulls the senses. Mediocre education strangles the imagination. Such deep deficiencies do not get settled with courses that teach 'values.'"[50] Vega therefore chastised the Anti-Pornography Campaign for ignoring the structural issues that impacted *caseríos* and other working-class communities. However, rather than advocate for a systemic approach to eradicating such inequalities, Vega proposed a solution that concentrated on individual behavior. Similar to Adria Cruz's recommendation for better social programs for young girls, Vega claimed that providing options for youth to channel their energy into other artistic pursuits would more effectively diminish the impact of reggaetón music videos on Puerto Rican society. Vega thus missed an opportunity to reframe the debate by falling back on individual behavior and surveillance to confront reggaetón's treatment of women rather than proposing solutions that would dismantle institutionalized racism, classism, and sexism.

This is not particularly surprising considering that Vega's comments generally replicate the stereotype that blackness has contributed a particular "musicality" and "sensuality" to Puerto Rican identity. Like the article by Nieve Vásquez, Vega creates a history of Puerto Rican dance that established bomba (referenced in the *bembés*), and salsa (evident in the description of *"rumberas")*—two dances associated with working-class black communities—as the predecessors of *perreo*. Certainly, these dances and the musical genres from which they derive have important similarities to reggaetón in their racial politics, musical styles, and origins. However, Vega linked them via the "ancestral tendency" for "sensual hip-shaking," emphasizing a biological, natural musicality associated with blackness. Furthermore, Vega's specific mention of *"rumberas"* singles out women as the people who make "uncouth swerves of the buttocks." The emphasis on black and *mulata* women's hip-shaking in salsa reinscribes gender and racial hierarchies; Frances Aparicio notes that "by trivializing her hips *only* as a rhythmical and musical pleasurable entity, Caribbean patriarchy can erase from the body of the mulatta [*sic*] any traces of violence and racist practices for which it has been responsible throughout history."[51] Similarly, Vega's description of *rumberas'* hips conjures up images of black women dancing, but does not adequately address how such imagery reinforces racial stereotypes of black hypersexuality.

On the other hand, Vega's reference to the "modest, small hip moves of our global stars" implies the integration of blackness into Puerto Rican identity. Specifically, her comments allude to the career of Ricky Martin, which was in full swing by 2002. During this time, Martin gained tremendous crossover success as a pop singer in the United States, and his notoriety as a skilled hip-shaker was perhaps rivaled only by Elvis.[52] Ricky Martin hails from a middle-class *urbanización*, and, according to Frances Negrón-Muntaner, made visible the white middle-class Puerto Rican (or *"blanquito"*) community to a global audience.[53] Ricky Martin's hip-shaking thrust him into international stardom, and in some cases, reified stereotypes of Latino men in the United States as hypersexual "Latin lovers";

however, within a Puerto Rican context, Ricky Martin's dance could be read as an affirmation of discourses of racial democracy. Martin's white body has become infused with the "ancestral tendency" to shake his hips because of the African heritage he automatically has as a member of the racially mixed Puerto Rican population. As Frances Negrón-Muntaner writes, "as a white Puerto Rican of middle-class origins, Ricky incorporates black rhythms in a way that already exhibits a certain degree of restraint, symptomatic of the adoption of these styles by upwardly mobile social classes."[54] Martin thus embodies "racial democracy" with his hip-shaking dance style since he appears phenotypically white, but incorporates cultural markers of blackness including sensuality and dance in his performance.

At issue, then, was not *perreo* itself, but where Puerto Ricans were located on the "black-white" spectrum of so-called racial democracy. Vega positioned dancers with "uncouth swerves of the buttocks" (i.e., bomba, salsa, *perreo*, and other black-identified dances) on the "African" side of the spectrum. As a result, Vega considered the Anti-Pornography Campaign to be misguided in its emphasis on *perreo* since the dance was simply the latest manifestation of the blackness that already formed part of Puerto Rican identity. The focus on individual behavior rather than systemic change as the solution to this issue reproduced a presumption of a "natural" link between blackness and hypersexuality. The logic is that black hypersexuality could not be eliminated since long histories of race mixture in Puerto Rico have made blackness an integral part of the island's culture; however, through careful self-discipline, individuals could move toward the whiter end of the black-white racial spectrum. Therefore, while some critics pointed out the racial bias within the Anti-Pornography Campaign, they also maintained an emphasis on whitening by reproducing racial hierarchies and discourses of *blanqueamiento*. Other critics of the Anti-Pornography Campaign included reggaetón artists, although many of them also reinforced stereotypes of black female hypersexuality.

"They Always Discriminate Against Us"

Reggaetón artists and producers responded to the criticisms of their music and videos regularly in the Puerto Rican newspapers. Reggaetón has few well-known female singers and executives, and thus most of the industry representatives interviewed in the press were men. Many of these men openly criticized the Anti-Pornography Campaign for negatively depicting *caserío* life. Instead, many male artists and industry executives depicted *caseríos* not as sites of abjection, but rather as places constrained by discriminatory policies that created scarce economic opportunities for *caserío* residents. According to these arguments, reggaetón merely expressed the frustrations with racism, classism, and other issues that (male) reggaetón artists and fans felt.

Reggaetón artists and their supporters presented the Anti-Pornography Campaign as hypocritical, pointing to government corruption as evidence of the legislators' inability to serve as suitable judges of morality. One individual wrote in a letter to *El Nuevo Día* that government corruption in Puerto Rico made it impossible for any politicians to appropriately judge issues of obscenity, since "not all indecent things are revealed without clothing."[55] Some critics argued that González's legislation directly violated first amendment rights to freedom of speech and provided a dangerous precedent for the future (one that, some argued, also could perpetuate the colonial relationship between Puerto Rico and the United States).[56] Others claimed that González's targeting of reggaetón did not adequately address the much deeper and, to them, more serious issues of women's rights and representations more generally.[57] Several editorials identified other problems, including unemployment, education, and economic issues, that they considered more detrimental to Puerto Rican society than *perreo*.[58] Likewise, many critics of the Anti-Pornography Campaign tied these issues to reggaetón itself, reiterating artists' assertions that the music reflected the "reality" of marginalized sectors of the population. For example, one editorial emphasized, "this musical genre was born out of the social reality of a sector of our culture. You can't act like this reality does not exist."[59]

Such comments mirrored the most common criticisms of the Anti-Pornography Campaign articulated by reggaetón artists who claimed that their songs recounted everyday struggles in the *caseríos* that government officials tended to ignore. According to these reggaetón artists and producers, *caserío* residents were isolated from the rest of society, and, as a result, faced many problems in their communities. Artist Polaco stated, "The fact is that we are from the *barrio* and this is what we see and what we hear."[60] Reggaetón artist Mickey Perfecto described reggaetón as an "escape valve from our problems."[61] He advocated for more education (both "academic" and sex education programs) for poor Puerto Rican youth, and for government officials to work more closely with people from the "streets, public residences, and schools" to ameliorate the problems described in reggaetón songs.[62] These arguments portrayed "authentic" reggaetón as tied to experiences of urban poverty, violence, and being from "the street." On the one hand, these images could reinforce perceptions of *caseríos* as epicenters of violence. However, such comments also discredited the emphasis on individual behavior that permeated the campaign, instead blaming systemic, discriminatory policies for producing conditions that adversely affected the urban poor.

Considering the socioeconomic and racial inequalities facing *caserío* residents, many artists and industry executives argued that reggaetón was one of very few options that urban youth had to move out of poverty. Mickey Perfecto described typical reggaetón singers as "young men who have fought to leave the *barrios*, the money they receive from music and videos is for their parents and family so they can take them out of the *barrio* in the future."[63] Record producer Buddha explained, "If you are a baseball player and make it to the major leagues, you get out of poverty. If you are a rapper, you get out of poverty."[64] These arguments criticized the government's lack of investment in resources that would allow *caserío* residents to compete for jobs and move into the middle class (resources that were supposedly part of the initial conception of the *caseríos*), making reggaetón an important option for economic advancement.

In this context, some artists directly charged that race and class bias motivated the Anti-Pornography Campaign. Several reggaetón artists pointed out that the representations of women in their music videos did not differ dramatically from those by other celebrated artists like salsa singers Marc Anthony and Celia Cruz, and pop icon Ricky Martin; therefore, they considered the campaign's emphasis on reggaetón to reflect widespread prejudice against poor, urban youth.[65] The president of a music video television station argued that the Anti-Pornography Campaign specifically singled out, and discriminated against, reggaetón rather than encompassing all aspects of the media, as Senator González claimed to do.[66] Music video producer Héctor "El Flaco" Figueroa proclaimed, "Even though they try to hide it, [the Anti-Pornography Campaign] is prejudice against rap."[67] Although these artists and producers did not explicitly mention racism, their comments regarding the pervasive discrimination against reggaetón that they saw as a motivating factor in the Anti-Pornography Campaign implied that racial and class bias persisted on the island. Artists suggested that, just as *caseríos* had been marked as sites of difference in relation to the rest of Puerto Rico, so had reggaetón been targeted as a non–Puerto Rican cultural practice because of the particular entanglements of race, place, and gender that inform it.

Still, artists' emphasis on structural inequalities did not make them immune from reproducing problematic stereotypes of black female hypersexuality. Supporters of the Anti-Pornography Campaign occasionally presented female music video dancers as the victims of a reggaetón industry characterized by a violent, aggressive hypermasculinity. However, many reggaetón artists and producers attempted to distance themselves from accusations that they were misogynistic and exploited women. For example, several artists publicly opposed the exploitation of women in music videos.[68] Moreover, many pointed out that most women who participated in music videos did so voluntarily (and minors with parental permission), so they could not be considered "exploited" people. Music video producer Héctor Figueroa added that these women were not paid for their work because dancing in videos increased their self-esteem. In fact, Figueroa argued that, as with male artists, reggaetón provided an opportunity for women to move out of poverty: "Many of the girls, after working in strip clubs with false identification, because there are also minors there, and after appearing in videos, they feel like artists, leave the club, and even get married and start their lives over."[69]

By positioning male participants in the reggaetón industry as the "rescuers" of working-class women, Figueroa attempted to counter the stereotypes of these men as exploiters of women. At the same time, he problematically reiterated the same distinctions between "respectable" and "hypersexual" women made by proponents of the Anti-Pornography Campaign. Figueroa described reggaetón artists and producers as moral agents who gave working-class women a chance to achieve certain standards of respectability (such as marriage) that would otherwise be unavailable to them. Figueroa's arguments thus assumed that the women who danced in reggaetón music videos could not actually be considered "respectable" until they married and "start[ed] their lives over." Moreover, Figueroa implied that the dancers' potential move toward respectability allegedly justified the lack of monetary compensation for their labor. Such comments comply with historically prevalent depictions of black female sexuality as readily available, commodifiable, and exploitable.

On the one hand, the criticisms of the Anti-Pornography Campaign taken up by artists and industry executives threatened the salience of dominant discourses of racial democracy in their forthright discussions of racism and classism. The fact was that the original plan for *caserío* residents to move into more middle-class areas had still not happened, and artists' criticisms of the education system, high unemployment rates, and the government's neglect to respond adequately to crime and abuse in their communities revealed that the government, not *caserío* residents or reggaetón, perpetuated these conditions. In this respect, reggaetón artists' and producers' comments were not much different from other *caserío* residents, who also viewed their communities as targets of discrimination and who considered government support to be insufficient.[70] Still, the gendered dynamics of their arguments reveal the limits of these criticisms. While they challenged some aspects of discourses of racial democracy, many male artists, producers, and executives also problematically maintained the distinctions between respectability and hypersexuality that cast black female sexuality outside dominant definitions of Puerto Ricanness. To that end, they described reggaetón as an outlet for men who suffered from discrimination and could not find other economic opportunities; in contrast, female reggaetón dancers were described as hypersexual women who required male intervention to help them achieve the standards of respectability. According to these arguments, a shift in socioeconomic policies targeting *caserío* residents would help the men involved in reggaetón improve their quality of life. Female dancers, on the other hand, would presumably benefit more from strict self-discipline and changes in individual behavior. Media coverage of the women involved in reggaetón portrayed them similarly.

Women, Perreo, and Sexual Pathologies

On May 17, 2002, the Puerto Rican newspaper *Primera Hora* released a headline that stated, "Government Gets Involved against Pornographic Videos because of Indiscriminate Use of Minors. Department of Family Services Stops the Showing of a Video that Used Two Girls under Its Custody." The newspaper then continued with an article called "Girl in Custody of DF Runs Away and Appears in a Video," charging that Héctor Figueroa and his staff knowingly included a scene with an underage girl dancing in a bikini, water streaming from a shower above, in a Wisin y Yandel music video. The girl, who the newspaper called "Cristal," allegedly escaped from the custody of the Department of Family Services one year earlier, met with Figueroa, and subsequently appeared in reggaetón videos.[71] In response, Yolanda Zayas, secretary of the Department of Family

Services, called for the prohibition of minors in all music videos, arguing that this often promoted child pornography. Figueroa claimed that Cristal had signed a release form and provided identification that declared she was of age, so he did not know she was a minor. Furthermore, following his accusations that the government neglected to deal with "real" social problems, Figueroa stated that in this case, the generally "ineffective" Department of Family Services unfairly targeted his music video to appear as if "they are doing something for youth."[72] For her part, Cristal met with reporters to say "on the record" that she was not a minor.[73]

While Cristal's age and alleged status as a ward of the state made her story unique, Puerto Rican newspapers frequently portrayed women in music videos as having similar backgrounds, assuming that these women did not grow up with what one reporter called "proper care." In general, this included living in an impoverished area, usually raised by a single mother, and having limited educational opportunities. As one typical biography published in *Primera Hora* described, "The story is repetitive. A girl of divorced parents, without love, attention, being heard or recognized. Suddenly, she meets a producer who offers to launch her into stardom. How? *Perreando.*"[74] Such narratives portrayed female reggaetón dancers as victims of male reggaetón producers who took advantage of their desperate situation to employ them in videos for practically (if not actually) free.

However, this "sympathetic" portrayal of reggaetón women became more complicated as the Anti-Pornography Campaign wore on. Most descriptions of these women reiterated stereotypes about black working-class female hypersexuality that had been prevalent long before the Anti-Pornography Campaign. Accounts of the women's "deficient" moral upbringing in "broken families" reproduced many assumptions about the culture of poverty that supposedly plagued *caseríos*. It is important to note that accounts of the culture of poverty, including Oscar Lewis's *La Vida,* depicted women as its perpetrators, allegedly passing on problematic values, including hypersexual behavior, to their children.[75] Despite stereotypes of *caseríos* as "out of control and male," female-headed households are predominant in *caseríos*.[76] Stereotypes of women *caserío* residents portray them as "devious" people who want to take advantage of public benefits.[77] Similar sentiments surfaced in the representations of reggaetón women during the Anti-Pornography Campaign. While initially portrayed as victims of a misogynist music video industry, profiles of music video dancers ultimately emphasized that they were responsible for their own circumstances.

Music video dancers' previous occupations as exotic dancers or strippers prior to dancing *perreo* served as "evidence" of their alleged hypersexuality and deviance in their biographies published in the press. Interviews with music video producers revealed that one of the most common sites for recruitment of video dancers was strip clubs. Héctor Figueroa stated that he put out casting calls on local radio stations for dancers, and occasionally contracted "professional models"; however, usually the majority of dancers in his videos came from strip clubs.[78] This kind of biographical sketch of the "typical" reggaetón dancer implies that she already engaged in "immoral" sexual behavior prior to her involvement in reggaetón. The stripper-turned-video dancer narrative ignored any structural issues that may have motivated women to seek employment as exotic dancers, instead emphasizing their inherent hypersexuality. In other words, if music video producers had identified certain women to dance in their music videos, it was supposedly because these women already exhibited hypersexual behavior in the first place.

Certain women contributed to this perception in their statements to the media. For example, one article in *Primera Hora* focused on dancer Yaniv "Tiffany" Burgos Hernández.[79] Accompanying the article was a picture of Tiffany, a young woman of mixed race photographed from behind, crouched over to emphasize her buttocks, and clad in tight jeans and a skimpy tube top. Burgos Hernández grew up in a working-class family, married and divorced at a young age, and had two children. She lived briefly in the United States, and upon returning to the island at age twenty-one, began stripping to earn money. Burgos Hernández described herself as an "exhibitionist" who enjoyed when other people watched her dance, but denounced stereotypes of reggaetón dancers as prostitutes.[80]

Burgos Hernández's profile included a description of her family relationships, especially with her mother and her six-year-old daughter. She claimed that her mother supported her career and even transported her to the strip club where she worked before becoming a video dancer. Burgos Hernández said, "My mother applauded me, she said 'That's my daughter.' She tells me that I dance well, but the two times that I took her to the club, she left crying, and now my passion [for dancing] is not as strong because I made my mother suffer."[81] Despite this suffering, Burgos Hernández repeatedly emphasized her mother's support for her career both as a stripper and as a video dancer, and described a close relationship with her. Burgos Hernández also stated that her own daughter had seen her dance in videos, but that she explained to the young girl that this is only a dance and "I am not doing anything wrong."[82] As a result, Burgos Hernández clarified, "I taught her [*perreo*] like it was in the video. She is crazy about the dance, but she does not go to the extremes that I do, I would not like that until she was of age."[83]

The intergenerational relationship between Burgos Hernández, her mother, and her daughter reinforces several stereotypes of black working-class women's sexuality. To a certain extent, Burgos Hernández's mother is portrayed in the article as one of the people responsible for Burgos Hernández's lifestyle, praising her daughter's dancing in strip clubs and music videos. Likewise, Burgos Hernández's teaching her own daughter how to *perrear* at six years old implies that the young girl will continue to *perrear* when she is "of age." These descriptions insinuate that hypersexuality had been encouraged, if not directly passed down, through the generations of the Burgos Hernández family. At the same time, Burgos Hernández's recognition of her mother's "suffering" after watching her dance, and her acknowledgment that she would not like it if her daughter danced before reaching adulthood, suggests that she "knows" that she is doing something "wrong" (despite her claims throughout the article that she is not). In the end, the profile of Burgos Hernández portrays her as both a product and a perpetrator of an "indecent" sexuality, who bears responsibility for her own situation and for promoting *perreo* to younger generations, with no acknowledgment of the broader socioeconomic circumstances that may have informed her decisions.

Newspapers featured several other interviews with reggaetón dancers who responded to the Anti-Pornography Campaign, as well. Like Burgos Hernández, a few girls stressed that they enjoyed dancing *perreo*; however, most sought to distinguish themselves from the stereotypes of reggaetón dancers. On the one hand, reggaetón dancers expressed a certain degree of erotic autonomy in these interviews, claiming that they enjoyed being "sexy" in music videos and declaring control over their own sexuality. However, many of these women distinguished between being "sexy" and dancing *perreo*. Some attempted to circumscribe their sexuality within the definition of respectability advocated by the Anti-Pornography Campaign, differentiating themselves from women such as Burgos Hernández who were perceived as inherently hypersexual.

Two main themes emerged from newspaper interviews with reggaetón dancers. First, many dancers stressed that music video sets were "respectful" and "professional" places.[84] As Burgos Hernández explained, "There is always respect in the videos, none of the artists have gone too far with me, they have given me a beautiful friendship. They only dance. They have never made any indecent proposals."[85] Such descriptions of music video sets directly countered the claims of the Anti-Pornography Campaign's supporters that they were sites of "indecency" and "immorality" that required continuous monitoring. By describing music video sets as "professional" places, Burgos Hernández and her fellow dancers deliberately located their "sexy" dances within a respectable workplace.

These claims to respectability extended to some women's descriptions of their individual dance performances. While Burgos Hernández said she enjoyed *perreo*, many of the dancers profiled in newspapers claimed that they performed other dance styles, but not *perreo*. Some girls explained that, while they "respected" the girls who danced *perreo*, they preferred not to. Dancer Vanessa Dávila stated, "I respect the dance, but I don't partake in it. I don't dance *perreo*, I am not going to dance *perreo* here, and you will never see me in a music video dancing *perreo*."[86] An eighteen-year-old dancer, Gladys Peña, told *El Nuevo Día*, "Truthfully, there is a basis for thinking that these videos are pornographic, but not all of them are the same. What I do is different because I do not wear a g-string, and I don't dance *perreo*."[87] Likewise, another dancer, Mariela Arias, said, "I dance reggaetón, but not *perreo* because I do not have the skill. I have fun . . . but we are more reserved . . . I would never dance with my back to the camera, nor would I come out in a g-string or alone with a singer in a bed. I have really high self-esteem."[88] All three women maintained that they had control over their own careers, chose what they wore, how they danced, and whom they danced with in music videos. Moreover, newspapers further distinguished Arias and Peña from other reggaetón dancers by describing their education, Peña as a high school student hoping to major in Business Administration in college, and Arias as a cosmetology student. The emphasis on their education reveals that Arias and Peña also pursued more "appropriate" channels to improve their economic status, suggesting that socioeconomic concerns rather than hypersexuality motivated these two women to participate in reggaetón (much like male reggaetoneros). Therefore, Dávila, Peña, and Arias reinforced the importance of women's *choice* to dance *perreo* or not, distinguishing themselves from girls like Burgos Hernández without making outright "moral" judgments.

Still, other dancers asserted moral arguments that stigmatized women who danced *perreo*. Another dancer, Paulette Vizcarrondo, said,

Definitely, the women who appear in these videos are damaging women's reputations. They think that they are more "women" because they do movements like if they were having sex or they appear in bed with a singer wearing a g-string, but it isn't like that. A dance is a dance and a seduction is something else, why do I have to do that in front of other people? That is what damages reggaetón. They look for me when they want refined women who project a sexy attitude.[89]

Vizcarrondo shared with her colleagues the recognition of a woman's "right" to be "sexy," but drew a fine line between the "sexiness" of dancing and the "vulgarity" of *perreo*. She blamed women like Burgos Hernández for damaging not only reggaetón's reputation, but, more specifically, that of women who danced. Regardless of whether or not dancers expressed moral judgments against other women, the distinctions produced within the music video dancer community replicated the dichotomy between hypersexuality and respectability. Women managed their own reputations through describing themselves as respectable in relation to other women of allegedly more ill repute.

No matter how these women sought to present themselves, however, virtually all music video dancers were described via stereotypes that portrayed them as nonwhite and hypersexual. For example, while Peña, Arias, and Vizcarrondo expressed the difference between themselves and girls who danced *perreo*, the location of their interview on a music video set in the nightclub Reggae Planet, and the article's accompanying photographs of young nonwhite women with long fingernails, tight jeans, and midriff-baring shirts, reinforced the stereotype of hypersexual reggaetón women. Moreover, the media's intense focus on reggaetón dancers identified the figure of the working-class, nonwhite reggaetón woman as the "corrupting" agent in Puerto Rican society. Once again, women's choices to dance *perreo* were linked to individual behavior since it was the responsibility of these women to keep their dancing in check in order to ensure that they conformed to the dominant standards of respectability. As a result, women like Burgos Hernández who expressed erotic autonomy were cast outside of the boundaries of respectability, and therefore Puerto Ricanness, even by their own peers.

If male artists and producers took advantage of the controversy surrounding the Anti-Pornography Campaign to talk about the various discriminatory policies affecting *caseríos*, female dancers were not afforded the same opportunity. Rather, the interviews and profiles of music video dancers in Puerto Rican newspapers faulted them for the moral "threat" present in reggaetón music videos, even if they were sometimes depicted as victims of a male-dominated industry. The erotic autonomy of women who danced in music videos conflicted with the respectability that provided the basis of Puerto Rican national identity. Rather than result in any social autonomy for these women (although it presumably provided some economic benefits depending on whether or not individual dancers were paid for their work), their expressions of erotic autonomy became construed as "evidence" of the alleged hypersexuality of working-class, black women, reproducing stereotypes that had circulated throughout Puerto Rico long before the Anti-Pornography Campaign. In the end, these representations reinforced the presumed distinction between black womanhood and the rest of the Puerto Rican nation.

The End of a Moral Panic?

Reggaetón continued to grow popular even after González's legislation passed in August of 2002. On the surface, it appeared that reggaetón had become accepted as a national music, and the moral panic surrounding *perreo* had subsided. Once in a while, however, incidents took place that suggested the possibility that *perreo* was still a "problem." In May of 2003, *Primera Hora* reported that one hundred underage youth cut school in order to dance *perreo* at the club Happy Times in the city of Caguas.[90] In addition, officials discovered the students drinking only bottled water, which led many authorities, including Senator González, to conclude that they must have taken the drug ecstasy while they danced.[91] In response to the crisis, *Primera Hora* published a "Special Report" on May 19, 2003, with the front page headline, "Difficult to raise children in times of *perreo*," featuring one photograph of a faceless young couple *perreando* in a nightclub, and one of reggaetonero Yandel, who appears to be dancing next to his one-year-old son Adrián Yandel. The caption read, "It is now common to see kids [*niños*] and very young adolescents [*jovencitos*] dancing in clubs where *perreo* predominates with songs full of bad words, which worries some parents. In the photo, Yandel, a known *rapero*, does not allow his son Adrián Yandel to listen to these types of songs with obscene lyrics." The "Special Report" included several articles addressing parents' various strategies to educate their children (usually daughters) about sexuality, morality, and safety. This particular report featured interviews with three reggaetón artists (including Yandel) about their children's exposure to reggaetón, in which the artists argued that parents were responsible for teaching their children good morals.[92] For many people, including Senator González, incidents such as the one at Happy Times revealed the need for constant monitoring of youth and reminded some that the threat of *perreo* was not completely abated.

Indeed, as during the Anti-Pornography Campaign, newspapers and the government occasionally solicited experts to describe the impact of *perreo* on youth. Another special report by *Primera Hora* published in September 2003 consulted a "music specialist" who argued that reggaetón could incite violence and sexual behavior, and cause physical conditions such as loss of hearing or even the destruction of cells that carry messages from the inner ear to the brain.[93] In November of 2003, another reporter interviewed psychiatrist Victor Lladó Díaz and sociologist Enrique Gelpí Mehreb who claimed that the potentially disastrous effects of *perreo* could lead to more serious problems of extreme sexual promiscuity in adolescents, lower self-esteem in young girls, and the development of "pathologies" of sexual "exhibitionism" among youth.[94] Like the incident at Happy Times, expert opinions served as "warnings" of the potential problems that could result without proper monitoring and control of reggaetón.

Senator González continued her work with the Special Commission for the Study of Violence and Sexual Content in the Media, whose meetings and activities involved repeated analysis of the impact of media on youth, especially girls. In the fall of 2002, the Commission published the results of an extensive survey regarding individuals' opinions about what changes should be made in the media. The survey found that slightly over half of the respondents supported the Anti-Pornography Campaign and considered representations of women in television to be "denigrating" and "immoral."[95] In addition to measuring parents' and other adults' attitudes, González also concentrated on the impact of media, especially reggaetón, on youth in order to determine the success of the Anti-Pornography Campaign. In December of 2003, Senator González invited students, mostly young girls, from public schools throughout the island to participate in a workshop entitled "Videos: Representation or Reality?" Much to the Commission's surprise (at least, as reported by the newspaper), many of the youth who participated in the workshop stated that they did not think that music videos necessarily reflected reality. As such, while many disagreed with the representations of women in music videos, they did not feel obligated or pressured to emulate reggaetón dancers or even dance *perreo* at all.[96]

Similar opinions were evident in a survey published in *Primera Hora* that same year, which included two hundred participants, aged fifteen to twenty-four years old, from throughout Puerto Rico. The survey found that slightly over one half of the respondents enjoyed dancing *perreo*, but, like the students interviewed by the Commission, never felt inspired by *perreo* to engage in illegal or "immoral" activity.[97] *Primera Hora* reported that only 10 percent of the youth surveyed became sexually excited by *perreo*, while 82 percent "maintained that they were not accustomed to having sexual relations after engaging in this dance."[98] Furthermore, the survey concluded that the majority of respondents did not consume illegal substances while dancing *perreo*, and the few who did were almost all at least eighteen years old. Such reports suggested that just one year after the Anti-Pornography Campaign, youth did not seem highly affected by *perreo*. More adults, especially parents, began describing their discomfort with *perreo* as a generational issue, similar to their own parents' objections to the twist or the merengue of their youth.[99] Ultimately, the monitoring of youth by both newspaper surveys and government programs suggested that youth could learn the limits of *perreo* and avoid succumbing to "immoral" activities.

The occasional crises that continued to surface around *perreo* combined with the frequent government symposia and media analyses dedicated to its impact on youth make evident reggaetón's repeated contestations to dominant discourses of racial democracy. In order to maintain the hegemony of these discourses, reggaetón's hypersexuality was repeatedly referenced as a distinct characteristic that separated it from "respectable" Puerto Rico. The surveys and symposia revealed that young people, especially girls, recognized respectability as one of the principal tropes defining Puerto Rican nationhood when they did not participate in the "immoral" behavior (such as premarital sexual relations or drug abuse) presumed to extend from *perreo*. Likewise, the "hypersexual blackness" of reggaetón supposedly served as "justification" for the consistent monitoring of activities and sites where youth danced *perreo* even after the Anti-Pornography Campaign was complete. Once again, surveillance of the spaces where people danced *perreo* in addition to an emphasis on self-discipline were considered critical to the maintenance of respectability and racial democracy.

While the Anti-Pornography Campaign may have appeared as an almost irrational response to some provocative dance moves, it involved a critical logic that sought to maintain hegemonic discourses of racial democracy that devalued blackness. What's more, it exposed the inconsistencies in the dominant definitions of Puerto Rican national identity that, from their inception, reproduced racial hierarchies while promoting race mixture. At the same time, the fact that reggaetón repeatedly provoked new "crises" on the island demonstrates that the music continues to provide a space for the articulation of alternative interpretations of the entanglements of race, class, gender, and national identity that are often considered threatening to the status quo. Indeed, as reggaetón has become more popular internationally, artists have been able to promote their new intersections of blackness and Puerto Ricanness to a wider audience.

CHAPTER THREE
LOÍZA

In 2006, MTV aired the special *My Block: Puerto Rico,* which featured MTV personality Sway traveling around the island with various reggaetón singers to learn about the music and Puerto Rican culture. He played baseball with Daddy Yankee, attended a cockfight with Don Omar, danced salsa with Ivy Queen, and rode motorcycles with Julio Voltio. Tego Calderón's segment took place in Loíza, the small town considered the epicenter of Afro–Puerto Rican life and culture on the island. The opening sequence featured images of Calderón rapping on stage before a massive, faceless audience while Sway described him as the "underdog" and "heart of Puerto Rico." To the sound of rapid bomba drumming, images of impoverished areas of Loíza, Afro–Puerto Rican youth performing bomba and playing in the streets, and Afro–Puerto Rican artifacts danced across the screen. Then, Calderón and Sway appeared in an unmarked street of Loíza where the interview began with a description of bomba, which Calderón described as the "African heritage of Puerto Rico" that exists "everywhere where Africans are." After the brief discussion of bomba, Sway asked Calderón to describe Loíza:

SWAY: Tell them exactly where we are.

CALDERÓN: We're really in a place where not even Puerto Ricans come. This is the hardest, the roughest. And this is me. This is my block, Loíza.

SWAY: Loíza, all right, and these are the people of Loíza. What is this heritage, what makes Loíza one of the unique areas of Puerto Rico?

CALDERÓN: It's been 100 percent black population where the free slaves came. They got this land. They did the best they could. The history of blacks down here, they feel ashamed of the color of their skin, you know. Constantly on TV, they're trying to make us laugh about us. You know, they paint their faces and all that shit.[1] That's why I talk about it, and I'm not down with that shit.

SWAY: You know what's like, peculiar in a sense, when you come from other places, like I live in the [United] States, you would think that when you think Puerto Rico that everybody lives under one umbrella [camera cuts to a Puerto Rican flag waving], and came from the same place so the color skin doesn't matter.

CALDERÓN: That's what they teach you in school. It's like we're a trilogy of races, black, Spanish, and Indian. It's not like that, you know, the way we are treated in society, jobs, school, blacks in Puerto Rico are inferior, in another level. And so now, having the power of doing music, I like to talk to people on Tego's point of view. This is how I see things. Hate me or love me, I really don't care. It's been hard for Loíza forever, but people down here are happy and we have a lot of fun down here.[2]

The camera cut to more bomba drumming and dancing, as Sway turned to Calderón and said, "This is a part of the African heritage that you talk about in Loíza." Calderón responded, "Yeah, that's what it is, that's what I want them to know. This is beautiful down here. This is my block, Loíza." In the end, Sway joined the bomba dance, as a large crowd surrounded Calderón and shouted, "Puerto Rico!"

Tegui "Tego" Calderón Rosario was born in 1972 in Santurce, Puerto Rico, a working-class neighborhood in San Juan. Throughout his childhood, Calderón lived in Río Grande (a town bordering Loíza), Río Piedras, and Miami, Florida. During his travels between Puerto Rico and the United States, Calderón listened to U.S. hip-hop and rap, Jamaican reggae, Puerto Rican underground, bomba and plena, and, especially, the salsa of Afro–Puerto Rican legendary singer Ismael Rivera. Calderón also formally studied percussion at the Escuela Libre de Música in Puerto Rico. His albums include *El Abayarde* (2003), *The Underdog/El Subestimado* (2006),

El Abayarde: Contra-Ataca (2007), the mixtape *El Original Gallo del País* (2012), and *El Que Sabe, Sabe* (2015). Calderón has achieved tremendous success as a reggaetón artist, and he is recognized as the first Spanish-language rapper to cross over onto hip-hop stations in New York. Calderón has received nominations for several awards including Latin Grammys and Billboard Awards. His career also involves collaborations with other artists including Aventura, Akon, 50 Cent, Wyclef Jean, and numerous reggaetón artists, and roles in movies like *Illegal Tender* (2007) and *Fast and Furious* (2009). Calderón's success has not only made him one of the most widely recognized reggaetón artists but also played a critical role in "mainstreaming" reggaetón music in Puerto Rico.

Calderón's segment on *My Block: Puerto Rico* reflects the multiple and often conflicting ways that he is positioned vis-à-vis various constructions of blackness on the island. Félix Jiménez argues that Calderón's blackness provides him a unique niche within the reggaetón scene, stating: "The reality is that the content of Calderón's lyrics follows the model of his predecessors, but his image and his flow, his Afro and his race and his *difference* are characteristics that can temporarily trump the similarities he possesses with white rappers. His personal presentation is always intimately linked to the re-racialization of Puerto Rican rap."[3]

Indeed, despite the presence of other self-identified black artists such as La Sista or Don Omar (and the associations between reggaetón and blackness more generally), fans, critics, and scholars alike tend to recognize Calderón as the quintessential black reggaetón artist. First, Calderón's inclusion of Afro–Puerto Rican folkloric traditions, such as bomba, in his music and his frequent references to Loíza in interviews establishes popular connections between him and folkloric blackness. For example, in *My Block: Puerto Rico*, Calderón was the only artist to discuss Afro–Puerto Rican life and culture.[4] That his interview took place in Loíza with references to such popular signifiers of blackness as bomba demonstrates the extent to which his music and celebrity are often understood in relation to the folkloric blackness associated with the town.

In this context, Calderón embodies a particular understanding of blackness that is easily encompassed within hegemonic representations of Puerto Rican identity. Tego Calderón's reggaetón career[5] began alongside the mainstreaming of reggaetón, shortly after the end of Senator Velda González's Anti-Pornography Campaign. The Anti-Pornography Campaign's attempt to accommodate reggaetón into Puerto Rico's so-called racial democracy served as a turning point in reggaetón's development, providing publicity for hitherto unknown artists and revealing the potentially massive commercial market for the music. As with the 1990s censorship campaign, several artists took notice, and resolved to "clean up" their lyrics and image to take advantage of this publicity. In 2002 and 2003, reggaetón record sales skyrocketed, comprising about a third of the ten most popular albums in Puerto Rico.[6] Because of this commercial success, the genre also entered the political arena, with politicians selecting reggaetón campaign songs "to show off their hipness and try to appeal to younger voters."[7] With reggaetón's increasing popularity, the music became more accepted by elites and critics who had previously opposed it.

These developments immediately preceded the release of Tego Calderón's debut studio album *El Abayarde,* which received critical acclaim, including an endorsement from Senator Velda González. Tego Calderón's entrance into the mainstream was epitomized by his March 2003 concert in San Juan's Coliseo Roberto Clemente. Newspapers covered the preparations for the highly anticipated concert in great detail, from the set list to the invited musicians to Calderón's outfits and hairstyles.[8] People of all ages and socioeconomic classes, including famous musicians and athletes, attended the concert, which also included appearances by several musicians such as salsa artist Roberto Roena and fellow reggaetón singers Yandel, Yaga, Mackie, and Eddie Dee.[9] Ultimately, the concert was lauded as a great success, prompting Laura Rivera Meléndez to write in her review for *El Nuevo Día,* "Rap is in its most important evolutionary moment, and it can break the boundaries of the audience to which it has been confined in the past few years. Tego Calderón demonstrated on Friday, before a sold out Coliseo Roberto Clemente, that any genre cultivated with time and musical care can transcend prejudices to become the voice for various generations and socioeconomic classes."[10] As Frances Negrón-Muntaner and Raquel Z. Rivera argue, Calderón's performance symbolized the newfound acceptance of reggaetón in Puerto Rican society.[11]

The favorable reviews of Tego Calderón's performance and album thrust him into the national spotlight, and allowed him to reach audiences beyond the working-class *caserío.* Part of Calderón's appeal was his fusion of salsa and other Puerto Rican musical traditions with reggaetón. Because of his incorporation of bomba and frequent comparisons with national salsa icon Ismael Rivera, the Puerto Rican mainstream could embrace Calderón as an artist "who could be trusted to carry on the nation's officially recognized

FIGURE 3.1. Tego Calderón performs in San Juan, Puerto Rico, in March 2003.
Credit: AP Photo/Tomas von Houtryve

musical traditions."[12] Indeed, as demonstrated in his segment on *My Block: Puerto Rico* and the concert in Coliseo Roberto Clemente, Calderón incorporates signifiers of folkloric blackness that have been institutionalized as symbols of the African "root" of Puerto Rican culture into his music and performances. As a result, Calderón's blackness is domesticated in such a way that it is not automatically seen as "threatening" to dominant constructions of Puerto Ricanness. Popular associations between Tego Calderón and the symbols of folkloric blackness ultimately position Calderón as a uniquely Puerto Rican artist, as opposed to other reggaetoneros who perform presumably "foreign" rap. Thus, it is a very specific construction of blackness that allows Calderón entrance into Puerto Rican national space.

And yet, Calderon's appearance on *My Block: Puerto Rico* reveals another way of considering blackness in Puerto Rico. Tricia Rose has argued that the mainstream success of rap music in the United States allowed rappers' criticisms of societal issues such as classism and racism to reach a dramatically wider audience than they would have otherwise.[13] Similarly, Calderón's success as a reggaetón artist offers him a platform to promote alternative renderings of blackness that counter the privileging of whiteness in dominant discourses of racial democracy in Puerto Rico. For example, although Calderón's interview on *My Block: Puerto Rico* involved several commonly recognized signifiers of folkloric blackness, he situated them within a broader discussion of racism in Puerto Rico. Through this process, Calderón discounts the "folklorization" of Afro–Puerto Rican cultural practices as remnants of a romanticized past.[14] Instead, Calderón portrays these practices as critiques of racial discrimination faced by contemporary Afro–Puerto Rican communities. Calderón often makes similar moves in his music, incorporating Puerto Rican musical traditions in songs that address issues such as racism, classism, and colonialism. In the process, Calderón articulates new understandings of Puerto Rican identity that center blackness, but a blackness that does not conform to either constructions of folkloric or urban blackness.

Calderón establishes links between Puerto Rico and other sites in the African diaspora as an essential element of his articulations of Puerto Rican blackness. In several of his interviews and writings, Calderón details how his own experiences traveling to the United States and other countries in Latin America introduced him to alternative ways of imagining blackness. These new understandings of blackness are based on the recognition of similar systems of racial exclusion affecting Afro–Puerto Ricans and other

African diasporic populations. In this sense, diasporic connections provided critical tools that help Calderón to simultaneously critique racism in Puerto Rico, celebrate a uniquely Afro–Puerto Rican identity, and situate Puerto Rico within the broader African diaspora.

Shalini Puri notes that discourses such as "racial democracy" simultaneously hold the potential to reinforce racial hierarchies and to provide possibilities to counter these same hierarchies.[15] This ambivalence within dominant discourses of racial democracy in Puerto Rico is revealed in the portrayal of Calderón as both representative of and resistive to the folkloric blackness consistent with hegemonic constructions of Puerto Rican identity. I begin this chapter with a discussion of the ways that Calderón's persona and music have been situated in relation to folkloric blackness, especially via the perceived connections between him and Loíza. However, Calderón revises these same signifiers to express alternative constructions of Puerto Rican identities that center blackness and African diasporic connections. Ultimately, this ambiguous positioning of Tego Calderón exposes the contradictions inherent to racial democracy discourses. Calderón's statements in interviews and the messages in many of his songs, informed by his engagement with African diasporic resources, make evident the spaces of possibility that exist within hegemonic discourses of racial democracy to challenge their whitening bias, in the process creating opportunities to express new understandings of Afro–Puerto Rican identities.

"Holding the Name of Loíza Up High"

The location of Calderón's MTV interview in Loíza reflects the common associations between the artist and the town. A small town in the northeast corner of Puerto Rico, Loíza has often been described as the center of Afro–Puerto Rican life and culture, despite the existence of substantial black populations and African-derived cultural practices throughout the island.[16] As Moira Pérez argues, Loíza has been "othered" within a "specialization of difference" in Puerto Rico in which the town represents an allegedly "pure" blackness as opposed to the rest of the presumably racially mixed (but whiter) island.[17] This is due in part to a perception that Loíza is geographically isolated from the rest of the island, and therefore maintains supposedly "pre-modern" African traditions uncorrupted by outside influences.[18] In turn, assumptions that Loíza's population is homogenously black, the direct descendants of Africans, and lives a "traditional" way of life circulate on the island.[19] Ultimately, perceptions of Loíza's isolation and difference reflect the distancing of Puerto Rican identity from blackness that undergirds racial democracy discourses.

In the 1950s, archaeologist Ricardo Alegría described Loíza's isolation in his ethnographic work on Las Fiestas de Santiago Apóstol, an annual religious festival. He wrote that Loíza is "a forgotten town, distant from the egalitarian progress of industrialized civilization, that lives a tranquil and monotonous life, maintaining ancient beliefs and customs, as if ignoring the passing of the centuries."[20] Alegría then went on to list the various traditions, costumes, and cultural practices associated with Las Fiestas de Santiago Apóstol, which he considered to be the most obvious example of African cultural retentions on the island.[21] He described Loíza's residents as a predominantly black population that practiced cultural traditions associated with a primitive past. Alegría's account of Loíza links the supposed absence of the "progress of industrialized civilization" and alleged adherence to "ancient" customs with blackness. Such depictions produce what Isar Godreau calls the "spatial/temporal distancing" of blackness in Puerto Rico, in which blackness not only becomes relegated to specific geographical boundaries but also exists in a premodern era.[22] Blackness is thus distanced from a Puerto Rican identity that is more "modern," "civilized," and, via the process of racial mixing on the island, allegedly "whiter."

The emplacement of folkloric blackness in Loíza maintains dominant discourses of racial democracy. In Puerto Rico, cultural practices such as bomba have become emblematic of the island's African heritage. Not coincidentally, it is most often the bomba of Loíza that is often considered the most "authentic" despite the fact that diverse styles of bomba flourish throughout the island.[23] Hegemonic narratives of bomba represent it as a static cultural practice that has not changed since Africans supposedly brought it with them to the island several centuries ago (a narrative that ignores the multiple diasporic influences in bomba, its development in Puerto Rico, the diversity of musical and dance styles, and musicians' use of bomba to contest racial exclusion). In fact, bomba groups perceived to maintain "authentic" African elements in their performance have received funding from the Institute of Puerto Rican Culture, the institution charged with establishing and maintaining Puerto Rican national culture (and, incidentally, directed by Ricardo Alegría for its first eighteen years). Consequently, the narrative of bomba as an antiquated and folkloric tradition fits neatly with Loíza's perceived isolation and premodern way of life. Indeed, the Institute of Puerto Rican Culture invests more money in Loíza than any other northeastern town on the island, and "officially recognizes" Loíza's African heritage.[24]

As emblems of folkloric blackness, Loíza and the cultural practices associated with it are integrated into Puerto Rican national identity without compromising racial democracy's commitment to whiteness. Beyond the town's corporate limits, its geographic boundaries also presumably contain blackness itself. Therefore, Loíza (and everything associated with it) represents an allegedly "pure" African identity.

Such depictions of Loíza are critical for understanding how Tego Calderón has been affiliated with the town in the popular imagination. For example, one letter to the editor that congratulated Calderón after his concert in Coliseo Roberto Clemente commented, "And just as [Calderón] has done until now, I hope that he lives proud of being *Boricua* wherever he goes, and holds the name of Loíza up high."[25] These connections between Tego Calderón and Loíza occur despite the fact that Calderón never actually lived in Loíza, though he attended bomba dances there frequently as a child with his father.[26] Indeed, other reggaetón artists can also make claims to Loíza based on their family backgrounds. For example, La Sista hails from Loíza, and while she is recognized as a *loiceña* and incorporates bomba in her recordings and performances, she has not achieved the same degree of international popularity as Calderón. Also, Daddy Yankee's father, Ramon "El Negro" Ayala, was a member of the Loíza-based bomba group and family, Los Hermanos Ayala.[27] Still, Tego Calderón is the artist most recognized as having connections to Loíza. As Calderón described in one interview, "They say I'm from Loíza because I feel the love of the people from there, but I really grew up in Río Grande."[28]

Musically, these connections are audible in Tego Calderón's incorporation of bomba into his songs. In several tracks on *El Abayarde*, such as "Loíza" and "Abayarde," Calderón raps over hip-hop beats infused with bomba rhythms and percussion. He also features bomba interludes in some of his albums. Calderón's fusions of bomba and reggaetón are more of an "exceptional" rather than a "typical" reggaetón sound.[29] In fact, he considered the incorporation of bomba into his music critical for exposing bomba to a wider audience, although he described this move as a "risk" that initially raised skepticism by the reggaetón community.[30] In spite of this risk, Tego

Calderón's bomba-infused reggaetón has now been widely accepted and celebrated by reggaetón fans and music critics.

Bomba and other Afro–Puerto Rican folkloric practices also play a central role in accounts of Calderón's biography. Calderón often describes Loíza as the place where he encountered African-based cultural practices. In one interview, Calderón recalled his childhood trips to Loíza, stating, "We were constantly in Loíza. My father is from a *caserío* in Río Grande. He always took us to Loíza. We went to bomba dances, the saints always mounted us.[31] It instilled this love in me."[32] Such stories about Calderón's childhood emphasize his experience, knowledge, and familiarity with the cultural practices associated with folkloric blackness. This combination of cultural expertise and experience legitimates Calderón's reputation as the embodiment of the folkloric blackness that these cultural practices represent. The point here is not to discredit Calderón's childhood experiences or his knowledge of Afro–Puerto Rican traditions, but rather to suggest that the framing of these biographical narratives advances the perceived connections between Calderón, Loíza, and folkloric blackness.

Because of the integration of folkloric blackness into Puerto Rican national identity, the associations between Calderón and Loíza present him as a Puerto Rican artist, thus distinguishing him from other reggaetón artists who are generally depicted via tropes of urban blackness. As I mentioned in previous chapters, reggaetón's associations with urban blackness prompted many critics to depict the music as fundamentally distinct from Puerto Rican culture and identity. In this context, Calderón's association with Loíza is significant because it allows him to be considered an unmistakably Puerto Rican artist in the eyes of both fans and detractors of reggaetón. For example, Ana María, a twenty-one-year-old college student and reggaetón fan from San Juan, considered Calderón one of her favorite reggaetón artists because of his integration of "*lo cultural*":

> I really like Tego because, I don't know, because his beats are different, he mixes them a lot with *lo cultural*, for example he mixes it a lot with bomba. If you go to Loíza, they have made tributes to him and everything. In fact, in some of his songs it begins with an intonation that sounds like bomba, and I've been to concerts where he incorporates—he has his dancers like everybody else, but he has a girl who dances bomba and he incorporates this as well, and I love that, be-

cause, I don't know, bomba is a cultural thing from here, and I don't identify with it a lot but I like it.

Calderón's integration of bomba, which she identifies as a "cultural thing" from Puerto Rico, is one of the main reasons why Ana María enjoys his music. Significantly, in this case, Calderón's blackness and participation in Afro–Puerto Rican cultural practices provide the basis for his Puerto Rican identity.

Similarly, Adriana, a nineteen-year-old from San Juan who generally dislikes reggaetón, distinguishes Tego Calderón from other reggaetón artists, evident in her comparison with Don Omar below. When I asked her whether or not she enjoyed Calderón's music, she answered:

> I don't like it so much. But, I'll tell you, he is so different, he has almost the same songs as Don Omar, they talk the same, but I don't know. He has something different, it's the tone of his voice, his style, you know . . . the fact that he is doing what he does, well, you have to give him credit for that.

Don Omar is another reggaetón artist widely recognized (and who recognizes himself) as black. Consequently, Adriana's comments that Calderón is "almost the same" as Don Omar, but has something "different," implies that the two artists share ties to blackness, but in different ways. Adriana's mention of Calderón's unique tone of voice and style suggests that she sees connections between Calderón and bomba. Indeed, Calderón's style of performance and his "look" are more similar to many early salsa artists than his reggaetón peers.[33] More specifically, Calderón is often compared to the acclaimed *sonero mayor* Ismael Rivera, who, along with Rafael Cortijo, popularized bomba in the 1960s. Cortijo directed Cortijo y su Combo, featuring Rivera as lead singer. The band broke several racial barriers in Puerto Rico, becoming the first black band to perform at the prestigious Hotel Condado, and the first to appear regularly on television during a time when very limited (if any) representations of blackness existed on television.[34] They also frequently addressed racism in Puerto Rico and elsewhere in their music, combining Afro–Puerto Rican musical aesthetics with lyrical themes that addressed issues in the working-class barrio of Santurce. Not only did Cortijo y su Combo leave an indelible imprint on the development of Latin music, and salsa especially, but they also intervened in Puerto Rico's racial politics by using their music to call attention to the persistence of racism on the island.

Once the group broke up in 1962, Ismael Rivera recorded several more songs, including "Las Caras Lindas" [Beautiful Faces], a salsa piece composed by Tite Curet Alonso that celebrated a "black is beautiful" refrain and has since become an anthem of sorts for Afro–Latin American communities. Although Rivera's career was mired by his battle with drug addiction, he is praised as a national icon of salsa.[35] Tego Calderón has frequently described Rivera as his idol. Likewise, Puerto Rican newspapers often depict Calderón as a present-day Ismael Rivera due to his racial politics as well as issues like their comparable intonation and vocal style.[36] Rivera's work with Cortijo y su Combo is rooted in bomba aesthetics, and both Rivera and Cortijo have been viewed as representative of Afro–Puerto Rican identity in the popular imagination even if they have not achieved the same degree of "official" institutionalization into Puerto Rican national identity as bomba. In this context, Adriana's comments regarding Calderón's style and intonation allude not only to his use of bomba, but also the perceived connections between Tego Calderón, Rafael Cortijo, and Ismael Rivera.

These connections become even more evident when Adriana emphasizes the distinctions between Tego Calderón and Don Omar, who hails from the Villa Palmeras area of Santurce.[37] Don Omar has several reggaetón songs about caseríos and urban life; Adriana claimed that one Don Omar song in particular "was inciting the caseríos . . . like, 'we are going to fight while listening to this song.'" Don Omar has been implicated in several scandals, including reportedly assaulting a waiter at a Denny's restaurant, having presumed connections to alleged drug lord José Luis "Coco" López, and being arrested for domestic violence.[38] For Adriana, Don Omar represents a "typical" reggaetón artist who embodies many of the stereotypes associated with caseríos and urban blackness. Jennifer Domino Rudolph argues that Don Omar routinely relies on tropes of blackness such as the hip-hop "nigga" in the construction of his own persona (though Rudolph points out that these moves resist the whitening bias of hegemonic Puerto Rican identities), and therefore positions himself as representative of the caserío.[39] Rudolph contends that Don Omar's blackness involves a more "potent, black masculinity" rather than the "populist" ideas about blackness associated with Tego Calderón.[40] Thus, Adriana's comparison of Tego Calderón and Don Omar can be read as an acknowledgment of the multiple discourses of blackness that circulate in Puerto Rico. Although Tego

Calderón sings reggaetón, Adriana considers him a unique artist in part because he embodies characteristics more similar to folkloric blackness (evident in his "style") than the stereotypes of urban blackness associated with other reggaetón artists like Don Omar.

Such assumptions about Calderón's uniqueness within the reggaetón scene demonstrate how folkloric blackness affords him the possibility of being accepted into the Puerto Rican mainstream since the Afro–Puerto Rican cultural practices he integrates into his music are already recognized as officially sanctioned emblems of (Afro–)Puerto Ricanness. And yet, Calderón uses his music and writings to criticize the very same constructions of folkloric blackness and racial democracy that others have attributed to him. In fact, as a highly visible artist, Tego Calderón is frequently praised for his social commentaries regarding racial inequalities in Puerto Rico and elsewhere in Latin America. Calderón's critiques thus make evident the slippages and contradictions within dominant discourses of racial democracy.

A Black Boricua: Calderón's Diasporic Interventions

If his perceived connection to Loíza affords Tego Calderón entrance into Puerto Rican national space, it is this same connection that forms the crux of Calderón's critique of Puerto Rico's so-called racial democracy. For Calderón, the town of Loíza does not symbolize the rural, antiquated folkloric blackness of Puerto Rican national identity. Rather, Loíza exposes the persistence of racism on the island, making abundantly clear the fact that Puerto Rico's racial democracy has not lived up to the promise of racial equality for all of the island's citizens.

Calderón's resignifying of Loíza as emblematic of the contradictions inherent to dominant discourses of racial democracy is particularly evident in his segment on *My Block: Puerto Rico*. Throughout the interview, Calderón depicts Loíza's isolation as the result of racist and classist policies that maintain racial hierarchies. With statements such as "It's been hard for Loíza forever" and "This is the hardest, the roughest," Calderón implies that the poor socioeconomic conditions facing Loíza (illustrated in the images of dilapidated housing, barefoot children, and unpaved roads featured in the program) result from structural and racial inequalities rather than any inherent desire to maintain a "traditional" way of life on the part of Loíza's residents. Calderón then moves his discussion beyond Loíza's city limits when he addresses racism throughout the island, claiming that "blacks in Puerto Rico are inferior, on another level." The blackness that Calderón depicts as part and parcel of Loíza is intrinsically tied to the colonial and racial projects that inform Puerto Rico's commitment to whiteness.

The segment featuring bomba in *My Block: Puerto Rico* adds to Calderón's broader effort to discredit dominant depictions of blackness. Calderón describes bomba as an "African cultural practice," but emphasizes that it exists "everywhere where Africans are." This statement refutes the common perception of Loíza as the primary site of bomba performance since Calderón acknowledges its practice throughout the island. Importantly, blackness also exists outside Loíza when Calderón states that "Africans" are "everywhere." On the one hand, the portrayal of bomba's "Africanness" seems to comply with the dominant narrative of bomba as an antiquated practice directly transplanted from Africa to Puerto Rico. However, the performance of bomba accompanying Calderón's interview presents the music as both modern and relevant to contemporary Puerto Rican life. Rather than featuring women in long, white dresses that represent romanticized views of plantation life, the bomba practitioners in Calderón's segment dress in the "hip-hop" fashion commonly associated with reggaetón and urban neighborhoods and *caseríos*. In *My Block: Puerto Rico,* young men wearing baggy shorts, New York Yankees caps, and Nike sneakers dance and play bomba as a celebration of their Afro–Puerto Rican heritage without conforming to either the stereotypical tropes of urban blackness or the problematic depictions of a premodern folkloric blackness. In this sense, bomba performance is not about any inherent tendency or preference on the part of Loíza's residents to live in the past, but rather a celebration of a uniquely Afro–Puerto Rican identity that integrates African diasporic resources (like "hip-hop" clothing) with the island's traditions.[41]

In *My Block: Puerto Rico,* Loíza provides a platform for Calderón to discuss issues of racism in Puerto Rico more broadly. He makes a similar move in his song "Loíza" included on the album, *El Abayarde* (2003). First, the beats accompanying "Loíza" combine hip-hop with bomba rhythms. Once again, Calderón unfastens bomba's ties to folkloric blackness, using musical fusions to present it as contemporary and modern. In addition to its musical arrangements, Calderón's lyrics debunk the presumption of "racelessness" in Puerto Rico's racial democracy by frequently berating the pervasive classism and racism of Puerto Rican institutions. He ridicules the injustices of the criminal justice system, the inadequate educational system, and general corruption among Puerto Rico's politicians and elite. While Calderón criticizes colonialism, he also condemns the Puerto Rican Independence Party for not adequately addressing the problems facing the Afro–Puerto Rican community. He directly calls out racial democracy as a myth that does not correspond to the realities of black people living on the island. "Loíza" thus portrays the Afro–Puerto Rican community as "forgotten" by Puerto Rican elites and institutions affiliated with all political parties on the island.

Although the title of the song and the use of bomba may seem to refer specifically to the town of Loíza, Calderón uses "Loíza" as a metaphor for blackness in Puerto Rico more generally. In the chorus of "Loíza," Calderón positions himself as an outsider within Puerto Rico because of his blackness. Calderón questions the authority of officials, asking, "¿Va a quitarme la libertad si yo no pertenezco a su sociedad?" [Are you going to take away my liberty if I don't belong to your society?]. Here, the issue of belonging becomes critically important. Calderón belies the fact that, despite racial democracy's inclusive rhetoric, he is prohibited from gaining recognition as a Puerto Rican citizen and, hence, fully belonging in Puerto Rican society. Calderón physically locates himself in Puerto Rico, but asserts that he belongs to another space beside the one structured by racial democracy, thus rejecting the authority of those institutions complicit in the establishment and maintenance of racial inequality.

Instead, for Calderón, the new space of "Loíza" offers an alternative way to imagine blackness. In this sense, the "Loíza" in Calderón's song serves as a figurative space that both recognizes and celebrates blackness as modern and beautiful. He later raps that he has little except "la capacidad de no creer en tu verdad" [the capacity to not believe in your truth]. With this line, Calderón actively rejects the "truth" of discourses of racial democracy, especially the empty rhetoric of racial equality. As a result, he not only exposes the prevalence of institutionalized racism in Puerto Rico, but he also celebrates those aspects of blackness that discourses of racial democracy generally disparage. For example, he raps that he is proud of his appearance, including his *bemba* [big lips]. The reference to *bemba* is significant given that, historically, the term has carried with it negative connotations that portray blackness as "ugly."[42] Because of the "capacity" to reject the "truth" of dominant constructions of racial democracy, Calderón chooses to embrace his African features and, as he describes it elsewhere, "black beauty" in the face of hegemonic discourses of racial democracy that valorize whiteness.[43] The song's title,

"Loíza," thus may initially connote dominant tropes of folkloric blackness for listeners familiar with Puerto Rico's "racial/spatial order";[44] however, Calderón constructs Loíza as a metaphor for an Afro–Puerto Rican identity that exists outside of the purview of Puerto Rico's so-called racial democracy and its problematic renderings of blackness.

In addition to celebrating blackness in Puerto Rico, the metaphorical "Loíza" also appreciates the comparable circumstances of racial exclusion that Afro–Puerto Ricans on the island share with other black-identified populations elsewhere in the African diaspora. In 2006, Tego Calderón participated in a VH1 special entitled *Bling: A Planet Rock*. Along with U.S. rappers Paul Wall and Raekwon, as well as former child soldier and activist Ishmael Beah, Calderón traveled to Sierra Leone to investigate the impact of the illegal diamond trade on the country. The trip greatly affected Calderón, making him more aware of the role of capitalism and colonialism on different parts of the world.[45] In addition to discussing the diamond trade, Calderón mentioned the similarities he saw between Loíza and the places he visited in Sierra Leone in one interview with *El Nuevo Día*: "I don't feel like a foreigner [in Sierra Leone], but rather that I am in Piñones, in Loíza: the same faces, the same suffering, but different countries."[46] On a 2010 trip to Quibdó, the capital of the Colombian province El Chocó, Calderón made a similar comparison with Loíza: "In Colombia we are going to Quibdó, in the region of the Chocó, that is like Loíza and Piñones, where the Afro-descendants are."[47] The Chocó is the region in Colombia most associated with blackness, much the same way that Loíza represents blackness in Puerto Rico.[48] In both instances, "Loíza" stands in for the larger black community in Puerto Rico that is adversely affected by poverty and racism. Calderón establishes connections between black Puerto Rican communities and those in other places based on similar struggles with racial and class inequalities—or, as he states, "the same suffering, but different countries."

Loíza as metaphor thus draws from diasporic resources to counter the "miseducation" and widespread "shame" about blackness that Calderón sees as endemic to Puerto Rican society.[49] Calderón claims that this shame results from "the system that we grow up with. It's handed down from generations. So then you create a situation in your mind where you feel less of a person."[50] He sees a similar process throughout Latin America, described in his widely cited *New York Post* editorial, "Black Pride," published in 2007.[51] In the article, Calderón relates his personal experiences with racism in both the United States and Latin America, especially Puerto Rico. Central to Calderón's argument is the acknowledgment of different forms of racism in Latin America and the United States while rejecting the notion that the United States is "more" racist. This point is significant given that, historically, comparisons between the two have painted Latin America as a "racial paradise" in relation to the United States. However, Calderón considers racism in Latin America to have a more covert social impact that causes Afro-Latin Americans to devalue their blackness:

> The reality of blacks in Latin America is severe, in Colombia, Venezuela, Peru, Honduras . . .
>
> Puerto Rican (and Latin American) blacks are confused because we grow up side by side with non-blacks and we are lulled into believing that things are the same. But we are treated differently . . . We are definitely treated like second-class citizens, and we are not part of the government or institutions . . . They have raised us to be ashamed of our blackness.[52]

Calderón's description of the commonalities between Puerto Rico and Latin American countries such as Honduras and Colombia recognizes similar systems of racialized exclusion that adversely affect black populations throughout the region. In turn, he creates the conditions of possibility to forge new diasporic links between Afro–Latin American communities.

These potential diasporic links extend to North America as well. As a teenager, Tego Calderón attended high school in Miami, Florida. Many Afro-Latino immigrants to the United States relate encounters with new forms of racism in the United States perpetrated by both U.S. Americans and other Latinos.[53] For Tego Calderón, living in Miami exposed him to another system of racial classification that made him feel more affiliated with the African American community than other Latino groups:

> When I lived in Miami, I was often treated like a second class Boricua. I felt like I was in the middle—Latino kids did not embrace me and African American kids were confused because here I was a black boy who spoke Spanish. But after a while, I felt more embraced by black Americans—as a brother who happens to speak Spanish— than other Latino kids did.[54]

Calderón's experience of acceptance by African American youth became an important aspect of his recognition of black solidarity across linguistic and national boundaries, particularly given the racism he felt from other Latinos.

Calderón's social integration into the local African American community in Miami also introduced him to African American cultural practices and icons that served as important resources for him to develop his own version of "Loíza." For example, Civil Rights icons such as Malcolm X became critical figures that introduced Calderón to new understandings of blackness based on a feeling of "black pride":

> When I went to Miami, I found out about [Malcolm X]. Maybe he doesn't belong to my culture, but for some reason I felt it was my culture, because I felt that you're black, whether you speak Spanish, Italian, speak whatever language. If you're black, you're black. So then I identified with the pride that black Americans have in their heritage. And so it helped me a lot to find myself, for me to have come here and learned that blacks are proud of their race. And I felt bad because us Latinos, the black Latinos, want to imitate and want to say that we are *españoles*, and we're not. We are *negros*.[55]

For Calderón, African American struggles for racial equality in the United States valued blackness in ways that, in his experience, had been denied or absent in a Puerto Rican context. In fact, Calderón has stated that in school he never learned about important black figures from Puerto Rico or the United States who could be a source of pride for Afro–Puerto Ricans.[56] Rather, his parents, especially his father, taught him about Afro–Puerto Rican culture and history, and to take pride in his black identity.[57] Calderón's experiences in Miami were crucial to his development of diasporic connections because there he witnessed the "pride" in the U.S. African American community that corroborated what he had learned from his parents. As a result, Calderón claimed his inclusion in a "black culture" that extended beyond national boundaries. These diasporic resources from African American culture helped Calderón to interpret his own experience as a "black Latino" in new ways that moved beyond the limited representations of blackness commonly found in Puerto Rico.

Calderón views African American culture as an important diasporic resource for reconsidering Afro-Latino identities more generally. In his *New York Post* editorial, Calderón argues that "Black Latinos are not respected in Latin America and we will have to get [respect] by defending our rights, much like African Americans struggled in the U.S."[58] As part of this process,

Calderón advocates the development of new institutions such as schools and media devoted to teaching the history and culture of Afro-Latino communities.[59] On the surface, this argument may appear to impose U.S. understandings of race relations onto Latin America—indeed, this could be even more problematic in the context of Puerto Rico, considering how the island has defined its racial system in opposition to the United States. However, Calderón complicates the assumption that adopting a black identity in Puerto Rico occurs only as a consequence of U.S. imperialism by underscoring the distinct yet equally insidious nature of racism in Latin America. Calderón is careful to point out the specificities of race relations in Latin America throughout his editorial, arguing that "They tell blacks in Latin America that we are better off than U.S. blacks or Africans and that we have it better here, but it's a false sense of being. Because here, it's worse."[60] In this context, acknowledging racism and claiming black identities are not necessarily capitulations to U.S. imperialism, but rather important refutations of the assumption that Latin America is a "racial paradise" that reveal how Latin America has produced its own racial hierarchies independent of the United States. The U.S. Civil Rights Movement thus comprises a diasporic resource that informs Calderón's prescription for addressing the distinct practices and consequences of racism in Puerto Rico and Latin America.

Likewise, African American culture does not dictate what it means to be Afro–Puerto Rican. Instead, Tego Calderón adapts African American signifiers into a uniquely Afro–Puerto Rican identity expressed in his music and writings. In one interview with *Source Latino*, Calderón described how he combines diasporic influences from the United States with a distinctly Puerto Rican sound:

> SOURCE LATINO: You are the only one that has fully taken the *negroide*[61] sound from Loíza, Puerto Rico, together with rap. How did you come up with that idea?

> CALDERÓN: I believe that my success came from staying who I am. I have never tried to be a black American, even though I admire and respect African American culture. They have taught me a lot, but I'm not a black American, I did not grow up listening to Marvin Gaye, I grew up listening to Ismael Rivera and Héctor Lavoe and Chamaco Rodríguez . . . It's what I am, what I like is Muñequitos de Matanzas,[62] Puerto Rican bomba, our things . . . what I am is what I am, a black Boricua.[63]

Here Calderón makes clear that while African American culture has influenced him, his "black Boricua" perspective has most informed his work. Significantly, this perspective is intrinsically diasporic, connected to the United States via a racial politics that is invested in promoting racial equality. Popular culture and political references from U.S. African American communities help to shape the strategies and resources Calderón employs in his music, which has larger consequences for the debunking of racial democracy discourses on the island. His culling from diasporic resources is also important in the context of the profoundly insular nature of folkloric blackness in Puerto Rico. That is, Calderón's use of diasporic resources helps to reimagine Puerto Rican blackness as tied to contemporary diasporic politics and continued processes of exchange rather than historical blackness connected to a static and premodern Africa.

For Tego Calderón, music is a critical site where these diasporic connections across the Americas come together. Calderón sees music more generally as a space to express diasporic connections;[64] however, hip-hop is a particularly critical diasporic resource for Calderón's reimaginings of Afro–Puerto Rican identity. Among the musical practices he encountered in Miami, he heard hip-hop by artists such as Public Enemy, KRS-One, NWA, Notorious B.I.G. and others. He recalls,

> When I started listening to NWA, that anger—and, of course, Biggie—it just fit my situation so well that there was no turning back . . . when I got to Miami it made sense what my father told me [about black consciousness] because I heard Biggie talking about it, Chuck D, all these people talking about this *afro* consciousness, be conscious of your African heritage. And I grew up like that.[65]

Calderón thus makes clear that he was not only attracted to hip-hop's musical aesthetics, but also the messages he heard criticizing racism and emphasizing black pride. Listening to groups like Public Enemy reinforced the lessons Calderón learned from his father about being Afro–Puerto Rican. Hip-hop served as a critical diasporic resource that both validated Calderón's experiences with racism on the island and his feelings of pride in his blackness. It also became a vehicle through which Calderón established diasporic links with African American communities because he related to rappers' discussions of racism in their music.

Diasporic resources and local Puerto Rican traditions converge in Calderón's construction of an Afro–Puerto Rican identity rooted in the metaphorical space of Loíza. To that end, Calderón resignifies Loíza as a product of the extreme contradictions inherent in dominant discourses of racial democracy, especially the maintenance of racial hierarchies despite rhetoric of racial harmony. Beyond its local critique, however, Calderón's metaphorical "Loíza" extends globally through an embrace of an antiracist politics situated within the larger African diaspora. These diasporic connections thus locate Puerto Rico within the African diaspora not as a result of "antiquated" folkloric practices supposedly found on the island, but rather through foregrounding racial politics that actively resist the devaluing of blackness within Puerto Rico's racial democracy.

WHAT IS ESPECIALLY interesting about Tego Calderón is the way that symbols of Puerto Rican blackness, especially those that have been emplaced in Loíza, have caused many individuals to accept him as a Puerto Rican artist. And yet, Calderón's work ultimately redefines these same signifiers to denounce the definition of Puerto Rico as a racial democracy. Calderón continues to perform and compose songs that discredit the relevance of discourses of racial democracy in Puerto Rico. For example, "Chango Blanco," a salsa song with a "black is beautiful" refrain composed by Luis López Cabán recorded on Calderón's second album, *The Underdog/El Subestimado*, references many of the salsa traditions that originally were associated with working-class, predominantly black communities (including the vocal style of artists like Ismael Rivera) but have since become integrated into Puerto Rican national culture. The song illustrates how Calderón takes nationally recognized signifiers of blackness and mobilizes them as part of a broader antiracist project to celebrate blackness as modern and essential to Puerto Rican identities. Such moves bring to light the fundamental contradictions of dominant discourses of racial democracy, particularly their incorporation of problematic constructions of folkloric blackness in ways that maintain racial hierarchies while simultaneously making claims to racelessness.

A second and equally important element of Calderón's work is his integration of broader African diasporic resources with local signifiers of blackness in his articulation of a distinct Afro–Puerto Rican identity. While Calderón does not dismiss the African cultural influences that inform Puerto Rican culture, the crux of the diasporic connections he sees between the island and other sites centers socioeconomic and political factors—namely, the impact of racial exclusion on black communities. As a result, diasporic resources are critical tools that help to uncover the contradictions of racial democracy discourses.

This particular understanding of diaspora underscores the interconnections between global and local signifiers of blackness in expressions of Afro–Puerto Rican identities. The blackness produced via these diasporic links is not a mere copy of cultural practices from other sites in the African diaspora. Instead, these practices serve as critical resources for the creation of new understandings of blackness that relate to local issues. Therefore, Calderón can integrate ideas about blackness from elsewhere, such as the U.S. Civil Rights Movement, into his constructions of Afro–Puerto Rican identity without losing its local significance. In this case, Calderón establishes links between Puerto Rico and the rest of the Americas, and uses diasporic resources, particularly from the United States, in a way that illuminates the problems with dominant discourses of racial democracy.

Certainly, Tego Calderón's music is rife with contradictions, not the least of which is the ways that being marketed as a black artist has thrust him into the mainstream. If being black has allowed Calderón to carve a niche for himself within the reggaetón scene, as Félix Jiménez suggests, it is also true that this move into the mainstream may reify some of the same problematic images of blackness that Tego Calderón contests.[66] This is particularly evident in gender politics, for while Calderón often employs black women to model and/or dance in his music videos, their visual representations tend to follow general formats of reggaetón videos in which women appear to be objectified as voiceless, hypersexual figures. Given the pervasive preference for featuring white(ned) women in reggaetón videos, the casting of predominantly black women in many of Calderón's music videos may seem progressive. At the same time, the historical association of black women with hypersexuality means that such representations can also reinforce gender and racial hierarchies.

In other instances, Calderón himself becomes conscripted within problematic stereotypes of blackness. For example, in 2005, Calderón participated in an advertising campaign for a mortgage company in Puerto Rico. The story line for the campaign focused on a white woman who breaks into a mansion that Calderón supposedly purchased with a 1First Mortgage loan. The print ads accompanying the campaign featured the woman in Calderón's "blinged out" shower, her gazing at Calderón with skepticism as he holds up his keys to the new house, and a photo of Calderón surrounded by boxes of *blin blin* (or "bling bling," the sparkly jewelry associated with rappers) and folkloric items like drums and masks.[67] Irmary Reyes-Santos argues that the "racial humor" in the campaign reinforced assumptions that blackness is unsophisticated via the accompanying visuals that represent Calderón and his possessions as unrefined.[68] Thus, while the advertisement appears to celebrate blackness through depictions of Calderón's success, it also reproduces racial inequality through framing this success as implausible.[69]

Like all popular culture, the music and celebrity of Tego Calderón potentially reifies the same problems it seeks to address. Calderón's blackness (like blackness more generally) constitutes a "mark of difference *inside* popular culture."[70] Indeed, the popular perception that Calderón embodies folkloric blackness is predicated on his purported difference and uniqueness as the quintessential black Puerto Rican reggaetón artist, thus reinforcing the essentialist constructions of both folkloric blackness and urban blackness.

However, Stuart Hall argues that, despite the contradictory and oftentimes distorted representations of blackness in popular culture, "black popular culture has enabled the surfacing, inside the mixed and contradictory modes even of some mainstream popular culture, of elements of a discourse that is different—other forms of life, other traditions of representation."[71] This is particularly true for Tego Calderón, whose work offers possibilities for reimagining not only blackness, but also Puerto Rican identities. His definitions of Puerto Ricanness directly refute the fundamental tenets of racial democracy. On the most basic level, Tego Calderón points out the inconsistencies in dominant discourses of racial democracy through a forthright discussion of persistent racism on the island. But beyond a simple acknowledgment of racism, Calderón's music foregrounds an Afro–Puerto Rican identity tied to larger African diasporic politics, and that departs from both folkloric and urban blackness. He locates this blackness in the metaphorical space of Loíza, a space that integrates larger diasporic politics into strategies of resistance to the systemic racial inequality that Afro–Puerto Ricans face on the island. To that end, Tego Calderón's vision calls for racial democracy to finally realize its promise of full equality for all of Puerto Rico's citizens.

CHAPTER FOUR
FINGERNAILS CON FEELING

On June 10, 2012, Ivy Queen closed the Los Angeles Pride celebration in West Hollywood, California, with a performance at the "Latino Carnival" tent. Called the "Queen" or "Diva" of reggaetón, Martha Ivelisse Pesante grew up in Añasco, Puerto Rico, and New York City. She began her career with DJ Negro's The Noise in the mid-1990s, during the height of the criminalization of underground artists. In 1997, Ivy Queen released her first studio album titled *En mi imperio*, after which she recorded a second album, *The Original Rude Girl* (1998), that made her visible to both the U.S. hip-hop community and Universal Records, who eventually signed her to their Latin music label.[1] Since then, she has recorded several other albums, including *Diva* (2003), *Real* (2004), *Sentimiento* (2007), *Drama Queen* (2010), *Musa* (2012), and *Vendetta* (2015). Her extensive list of recordings also includes rereleases of albums such as *Sentimiento* as "Platinum Editions," and many collaborations and appearances on reggaetón compilations. Ivy Queen has enjoyed a long and successful career that has witnessed the shift from underground to reggaetón, achieving international popularity.

In West Hollywood, Ivy Queen received another honor. The city's mayor, Jeffrey Prang, and California governor, Jerry Brown, awarded Ivy Queen for her work advocating for LGBT rights with the proclamation that June 10 in West Hollywood would be "Ivy Queen Day." At the event, Ivy Queen declared her support for gay marriage, and stated, "It's a great pleasure to share this moment with my friends in the [gay] community.

You know that I love you and support you one hundred per cent."[2] Since early in her career, Ivy Queen has advocated for the gay community whom she recognizes as having been "supportive" and "loving," even receiving a GLAAD award for her efforts in 2008.[3] Indeed, at her San Juan concert promoting her 2007 album *Sentimiento*, Ivy Queen called out to her LGBT fans, and soon after embarked on a tour in gay clubs in San Juan and the United States.[4] She told the press that she did the tour because "they write to me a lot and give me much support. They imitate me, they buy my records, and they defend me."[5] Beyond acknowledging their importance as an audience, Ivy Queen has also directly criticized the persistence of homophobia in Puerto Rico, declaring that "Being gay is not a virus" and actively defending pop singer Ricky Martin against his critics when he came out in 2010.[6]

It may seem surprising that a reggaetón artist has been so celebrated for supporting LGBT rights given the genre's problematic gender and sexuality politics. However, as the self-anointed "queen" of reggaetón, Ivy Queen has troubled many of the questionable aspects of race, gender, and sexuality found not only in racial democracy, but also within reggaetón itself. In this chapter, I argue that despite her often contradictory stances, Ivy Queen carves a space for a more inclusive understanding of Puerto Ricanness, incorporating not only blackness but also LGBT communities and others normally excluded from it. In this context, her support of LGBT communities is not surprising, especially considering that queer subjectivities have been written out of hegemonic definitions of Puerto Ricanness.[7] Indeed, dominant discourses of racial democracy rely on constructs of respectability that present nonheterosexual contact as "deviant," comparable to the hegemonic portrayal of black female hypersexuality as outside the boundaries of "normal" Puerto Ricanness. While reggaetón generally provides an opportunity to imagine new understandings of blackness and African diasporic belonging in Puerto Rico, Ivy Queen expands this to create affinities with other groups also misrecognized by discourses of racial democracy.

Despite the presence of other women in reggaetón such as La Sista and Glory, it is Ivy Queen who has successfully carved a niche for herself as the recognized "voice of women" in the genre. Ivy Queen frequently describes herself as a "defender" of women; as she stated in one interview with *El Nuevo Día*, "I wanted to defend women because I realized that here [in Puerto Rico], they are getting a lot thrown at them, and I don't like that."[8] This "defense" of women must be understood in relation to both the stereotypes of reggaetón women that circulate in Puerto Rico (see chapter 2), as well as the problematic gender dynamics within reggaetón. In fact, during the 2002 Anti-Pornography Campaign, Ivy Queen criticized both the would-be government censors for unfairly targeting reggaetón, and her male reggaetón colleagues for objectifying women. She stated, "I am completely against girls taking part in [dancing provocatively in music videos] . . . I am in charge of reminding the men that they were born from a woman . . . but the same people who criticize rap videos should also say things about other genres."[9] The recognition of Ivy Queen as the "queen" of reggaetón stems not only from her success within the male-dominated genre, but also because her lyrics and statements in interviews help her to craft a persona dedicated to what she terms women's "empowerment."

Jillian M. Báez argues that Ivy Queen produces "competing discourses of agency" that "is simultaneously transgressive and conservative, and as such, can neither be interpreted as subversive nor compliant with dominant ideologies, but instead remains complex, problematic, and ultimately hybrid."[10] For Báez, Ivy Queen asserts ideas about female empowerment while simultaneously adhering to industry norms that eroticize women's bodies and promote anglicized standards of beauty. Here, Báez refers to a shift in Ivy Queen's "look" over the course of her career, from a "tomboy" with baggy pants, braided dark hair, puffy jackets, and sneakers to a "diva" with straight, yellow-blond hair, augmented breasts, skimpy clothes, and high heels. Báez also notes that, while Ivy Queen promotes independence for women, early in her career, she also routinely discussed her marriage to El Gran Omar in an attempt to align herself with dominant tropes of respectability that privilege heterosexuality and monogamy.[11] Báez's argument is useful for considering Ivy Queen as a contradictory figure. Ivy's newfound blondness and frequent expressions of desire for a heterosexual, monogamous relationship might be understood as an attempt to mold herself into the particular ideals of Puerto Rican womanhood as defined by whiteness, modesty, and the promotion of the nuclear family—that is, the tropes associated with respectability that undergird hegemonic discourses of racial democracy.

On the other hand, I contend that an alternative reading of Ivy Queen's look, music, and performance is possible, similar to the ways in which Alexandra Vazquez argues that Ivy "takes reggaetón aside."[12] Vazquez focuses her analysis on the aspects of reggaetón performance that sometimes are overlooked, such as the spoken interlude during a concert. Attention to these moments "broaden[s]" what "the terms of the musical can make possible," extending reggaetón's reach beyond the expected.[13] Although Vazquez centers what she describes as "unnoticed" aspects of reggaetón, my analysis emphasizes some of the most hypervisible elements of Ivy Queen's performance, namely, her lyrics and physical appearance. I argue that taking these elements "aside" allows for a productive reading of the ways in which they point out the commitment to static and essentializing constructions of race, gender, and sexuality within discourses of racial democracy. Therefore, I riff off Vazquez's suggestion to think about reggaetón's "asides" by considering how these elements push the boundaries of reggaetón in unexpected ways to produce more inclusive notions of Puerto Ricanness.

To that end, this chapter focuses on two of Ivy Queen's characteristics that are usually dismissed as insignificant, or overtly criticized: what one reporter described as her "aggressive, ghetto-fabulous style and take-no-crap lyrics,"[14] or the shift in her look and her songs about romance and suffering. While much has been made of Ivy Queen's new, hypersexualized look, there is one body part that remains intact: her ornately manicured, long acrylic nails.[15] As excessive representations of what would otherwise be signifiers of a normative, heterosexist femininity, her fingernails trouble the boundaries between respectability and disreputability, femininity and masculinity, and modesty and aggression. I argue that the artificiality of these nails ultimately calls attention to the equally artificial constructions of racial hierarchies that privilege whiteness at the expense of recognizing black humanity. In addition, Ivy Queen's fingernails become central to her performance of songs that employ suffering as a marker of her humanity. This suffering entails an outright rejection of the foreclosure of black bodies and subjectivities in dominant discourses of racial democracy. Her suffering is violent, angry, and uncomfortable for those who witness it. It is through this discomfort that Ivy Queen establishes an alternative space where not only she can be recognized as human, but also where other people who do not conform to the standards of respectability in Puerto Rico's racial democracy can, too. Both Ivy Queen's physical metamorphosis and emphasis on suffering remain contradictory, in part because she is located within larger "regimes of power" that can constrain these moves and force her to operate within static binaries in ways that sometimes result in her "being implicated in the very regimes of power that [she] opposes."[16] And yet, rather than dismiss her work because of this instability, I would like to think about how these contradictions can be productive, disrupting binaries while, at times, problematically reinforcing them. In this way, I read Ivy Queen's fingernails as fingernails *con* feeling, tools used to create an alternative space that defies the problematic qualifications and requirements of belonging of Puerto Rico's so-called racial democracy, and, instead, offers opportunities to imagine more inclusive understandings of Puerto Ricanness.

Central to the alternative space that Ivy Queen develops is the denaturalization of the connections between white womanhood and respectability that serve as markers of belonging to the Puerto Rican cultural nation. This is of special importance in the case of black women, who, as mentioned in chapter 2, are both critical to the establishment of Puerto Rico's racial democracy and cast out of it. Marta Cruz-Jansen argues that black women in Puerto Rico remain "desired women" because of their perceived sexiness, yet "undesirable mothers, daughters, sisters, and wives" because this very same hypersexuality precludes them from achieving respectability.[17] Dominant constructions of black womanhood thus rely on the objectification of the black female body—something that is simultaneously desirable and reviled because it defies the (white) "norm." Since black women are depicted as the bearers of the island's population in narratives that describe Puerto Rico's histories of race mixture, Puerto Rican racial democracy requires a continuous renunciation of the humanity of black womanhood in order to distance the population from this blackness, and to sustain the association between Puerto Ricanness and whiteness. As a result, reducing the black woman to an object—that is, not human—negates her capacity for not only reason, but also any emotions or feelings beyond the instinctual, rendering her the opposite of the notions of respectability that underlie dominant constructions of Puerto Rican identity. In contrast, Ivy Queen demands respect and recognition for all people through her music and performance, thus exposing these inconsistencies within dominant discourses of racial democracy that simultaneously promote racial harmony while circumscribing belonging to those who, as Miriam Jiménez Román describes, are "ostensibly 'white' enough."[18]

Still, Ivy Queen's engagement with these processes is also contradictory given that she often eschews racial classification, describing herself as Puerto Rican.[19] However, Ivy Queen's "physicality marks her as at least of a mixed heritage, and she is dark enough to be read as non-white."[20] Indeed, many individuals whom I spoke with described Ivy Queen with euphemisms that situated her on the "blacker" end of Puerto Rico's racial spectrum, especially the term *cafre*. *Cafre* refers to someone who is "unrefined," but also connotes negative stereotypes of blackness and working-class status;[21] in addition, the term describes people who allegedly have "no taste in clothing . . . and style."[22] Guillermo Rebollo-Gil argues that while many Puerto Ricans claim that the qualities associated with *cafre* people have to do with individual characteristics (e.g., one's behavior, one's criminal past, or one's clothing choices), "notions of a culture of poverty, of extreme social backwardness and of an irremediable Blackness envelop [the *cafre*] figure."[23] *Cafre* identity is intimately tied to many of the stereotypes associated with urban blackness, including hypersexuality, inappropriate and/or aggressive behavior, ugly fashion choices, and attachment to urban black-identified cultural practices such as reggaetón and hip-hop.[24] *Cafre* thus serves as a racial code word that marks blackness without acknowledging outright the racist assumptions that it contains. While Ivy Queen does not identify herself as "black," she is often identified by others as *cafre* due to her participation in reggaetón (a genre often considered emblematic of *cafre* identity), her allegedly "inappropriate" behavior (for example, when she criticized the American Academy of Recording Arts and Sciences for awarding a Latin Grammy to group Calle 13 in 2007 rather than to a "real" reggaetón artist such as herself), and, of course, her fashion sense. In fact, in 2007, Ivy Queen appeared on the Puerto Rican television show *Ahora Podemos Hablar* to refute accusations that she was "ugly, aggressive, and *cafre*."[25] Given its racial connotations, the frequent descriptions of Ivy as *cafre* situate her in relation to common stereotypes of urban blackness. Likewise, her participation in reggaetón, a genre linked to both local constructions of blackness and African diasporic practices, furthers her affiliations with blackness. These associations between Ivy Queen and blackness thus place her performance in conversation with larger dialogues about blackness and Puerto Rican racial democracy even if she herself does not identify as black.

In this context, I read the construction of Ivy Queen's "diva" persona as one that troubles dominant constructions of race, class, gender, and national identity in Puerto Rico. I say she "troubles" these distinctions to underscore the contradictory nature of her performances. As Alexander Doty notes, divas defy static categories, instead "troubling and breaking their 'proper' culturally assigned sex, gender, sexuality, class, national, ethnic, and racial spaces."[26] It is through this "break" that Ivy Queen makes clear the exclusionary practices inherent to racial democracy discourses. She often disrupts the many binaries that structure Puerto Rican racial democracy (despite its emphasis on fluidity), such as male/female, straight/gay, black/white, or *cafre*/respectable. Similar to Jillian Báez's discussion of Ivy

Queen's agency, I argue that these moves are contradictory, and not always easily categorized as either "conformist" or "subversive." Still, this instability is productive because it provides opportunities for those prevented from claiming full citizenship in Puerto Rico to insist on the recognition of their humanity through a celebration of self-love and demand for respect. In this way, Ivy Queen's music is comparable to Tego Calderón's diasporic interventions since both artists discredit hegemonic definitions of Puerto Rican identity.

In the rest of this chapter, I offer a detailed analysis of Ivy Queen's interventions with a focus on her shift from "tomboy" to "diva" and her lyrics on suffering. While many scholars and cultural critics have discussed Ivy's new look, few have paid attention to the importance of her fingernails. Rather than symbols of Ivy Queen's allegedly *cafre* fashion sense, I contend that her fingernails offer new possibilities to discredit the privileging of whiteness and respectability that are integral to discourses of racial democracy. Second, I examine lyrics from Ivy Queen's repertoire, focusing primarily on her 2007 album, *Sentimiento* (translated to "feeling" or "emotion"), which was marketed as a "different" kind of reggaetón that emphasized feelings, and particularly suffering, when romantic love goes awry. Through a close reading of lyrics and her music video performance, I show how Ivy Queen's recounting of suffering criticizes the exclusionary practices intrinsic to Puerto Rico's racial democracy, and demands the recognition of the humanity of those normally cast out of it. Therefore, I provide an alternative reading of Ivy Queen's repertoire to consider the opportunities it presents for reimagining more inclusive notions of Puerto Ricanness.

A Sophisticated, Fashionable Woman

By the time that Ivy Queen released *Sentimiento,* she had already received much attention from journalists and scholars alike, often because of the new look that she adopted after signing with a major record label. Ivy Queen describes her shift in her look as motivated by her own desires and choices to look a certain way, particularly given that as a working-class youth she could not afford such accoutrements.[27] Nevertheless, Jillian Báez also points out that beauty standards in the record industry cannot be ignored since Ivy Queen "remains located within the symbolic and political economy of a media industry in which women of color are forced to whiten, thin, and hypersexualize their bodies."[28] Likewise, Félix Jiménez argues that Ivy

Queen's change in look prepared her for "corporate consumption."[29] He describes this shift as a reaction to the criticisms Ivy Queen had received for her fashion choices. In the process, Jiménez states, "Sans grittiness and with obvious glee, Ivy Queen shed the legendary physical prowess and freedom of the Caballota[30] of her nickname and turned into a *mamisota*-for-hire."[31] The whitening of Ivy Queen's look follows common trends of Latina and other artists of color who transform their physiques to appeal to a larger audience; this whitening also corresponds with the discourse of *blanqueamiento* common in Puerto Rico and elsewhere in Latin America.

To be sure, Ivy Queen's new style seems similar to that of other pop stars in Latin music who have altered, and often whitened, their appearance as their popularity increased. But there is something different about Ivy Queen's transformation. When artists such as Shakira (whose own physical transformation was starkly visible in her noticeably skimpier outfits and new golden blond locks) also changed their appearance as they pursued "crossover" markets, they generally embodied stereotypes of Latina hypersexuality.[32] Ivy Queen employed similar beauty processes to achieve her new look, including hair dye, clothing, and plastic surgery; however, relative to artists such as Shakira or Jennifer López, Ivy Queen's femininity—especially as defined via hegemonic discourses that render Latina femininity as hypersexual and heteronormative—often becomes suspect. Ivy Queen has stated that many people have called her a "lesbian" or *"marimacho"* [roughly translated to "butch woman"],[33] thus questioning her sexuality because of her tomboy looks and her reputation as an "aggressive" woman. Consequently, while Ivy Queen uses many of the same beauty technologies as her Latina counterparts, her transformation has not achieved equal acceptance or praise.

This may seem surprising given that Ivy Queen performs in a male-dominated genre in which most representations of women tend to reinforce their hypersexuality and availability for men. At the same time, Ivy Queen has been represented (and sometimes represents herself) as "masculine," a trait that is often celebrated for making Ivy successful in reggaetón. For example, the Dominican online newspaper *Hoy* described Ivy Queen as a woman who "thinks, negotiates, and raps like a man" since "thinking like a woman in [the reggaetón] business isn't beneficial."[34] Likewise, Ivy Queen told BET in an interview for their 2005 *Move Your Body: A Reggaeton Special*, "This is a hard business because the guys rule this kind of job. But when I'm on stage, I'm like a man. I act like a man, I sing like a man, and I riff like a man."[35] For Ivy Queen, the adoption of a masculine stance affords her entrance into the male-dominated space of reggaetón.

In addition, Ivy's perceived masculinity stems from her particular vocal style. As she described in one interview, "The first time I got there, at the beginning of the 1990s, where everybody involved in the rap movement came together at that time, they looked me up and down but didn't say anything. As soon as I began to show them what I could do, they loved it because I sang with the same *rudeza* as they did and I wasn't there to be cute, but for my talent."[36] Indeed, Ivy Queen frequently mentions that she has a "coarse, man's voice" or "a loud, macho voice."[37] This macho voice is understood to help Ivy Queen fit in with the hypermasculine reggaetón crowd. Frances Negrón-Muntaner compares this aspect of Ivy Queen's performance with that of Afro-Cuban salsa artist Celia Cruz when she argues that Cruz's masculine voice combined with her über-feminine self-presentation (including evening gowns, fancy wigs, and high-heeled shoes) "constituted the perfect gendered arrangement" that allowed her to be accepted as a talented salsa singer.[38] Through their over-the-top fashion choices and their "masculine" voices, both Celia and Ivy could overcome their unconventional looks—that is, their perceived ugliness—not only to achieve success in their respective male-dominated genres but also to be recognized as these genres' undisputed "queens" despite the presence of other women in them.[39] Therefore, as Félix Jiménez describes: "The pretty, proper, and cultural Ivy Queen establishes a false distance from the tomboyish, ready-for-drag, no-curves starting point of her lower-class, Puerto Rican female body. Ivy Queen resurfaces as a palimpsest that acknowledges her "masculine" coded persona, a woman watermarked with her previous unglamorous self."[40] These analyses of Ivy Queen's look stress that her shift compensates for her widely recognized, more masculine persona signified by her tomboy aesthetics and macho voice that distances her from the image of the respectable Puerto Rican woman. Such readings demonstrate the ways in which Ivy Queen's persona may be constrained by hegemonic race and gender norms; that is, her presumed masculinity is meant to explain her alleged failure to achieve dominant standards of beauty despite the fairly dramatic transformation in Ivy Queen's look.

While these analyses importantly point out the continued power relations that often restrict women artists, and particularly women artists of color, they also ignore the possibilities that Ivy Queen's new look offers for thinking through the limitations of dominant discourses of racial democracy.

FIGURE 4.1. Ivy Queen shows off her long, decorated fingernails on the red carpet for the 8th Annual Latin Grammy Awards in November 2007. *Credit:* AP Photo/ Isaac Brekken

That is, the excess in Ivy Queen's look, signified by the flashy outfits, bright yellow hair color, and, above all, her incredibly long, elaborate fingernails, might be interpreted as moving beyond mimicking or achieving an impossible standard. Perhaps the power in Ivy Queen's physical transformation lies not in its replication of standards of beauty that define the feminine in relation to whiteness, but instead in the possibilities it offers to expose the problems with this ideal. Despite the problematic elements of Ivy Queen's look, I read her shift as part of a larger strategy of disidentification in which she "scrambles and reconstructs" the ideals of Puerto Rican womanhood, transforming them into "raw material for representing a disempowered politics or positionality that has been rendered unthinkable by the dominant culture."[41] Ivy Queen's new physical appearance indicates the *constructedness* of feminine ideals by disjointing the associations between whiteness, femininity, and respectability. Demonstrating that anyone can employ the services of a hairdresser, stylist, and plastic surgeon to achieve the standards of beauty associated with whiteness shows that there is nothing *natural* about them.[42] This self-presentation constitutes what Nicole Fleetwood terms "excess flesh" that works "in excess of idealized white femininity" by "turn[ing] race and gender into plasticity, highly manufactured, and purchasable goods."[43] To be sure, this commodification of body parts can be problematic, especially in relation to the long-standing objectification of black women's bodies. Nevertheless, Ivy Queen's use of artificiality brings into stark relief the very *un*naturalness of dominant constructions of race, gender, and sexuality that position whiteness as respectable and modern, and render blackness hypersexual, uncivilized, and outside of the boundaries of "real" Puerto Ricanness.

Not only does this look discredit the assumption that whiteness is always already a marker of respectability, but it also opens a new space to recognize identities normally disavowed by discourses of racial democracy through "fabricat[ing] a new sense of self that radiates a defiant sense of ownership through aesthetics."[44] Among the primary aesthetic symbols that represent this self are Ivy Queen's long, decorated fingernails, which have become one of her signature characteristics. Indeed, while the media focuses much attention on Ivy Queen's look, her nails receive equal notice as the one thing that has not changed. As one article from *El Nuevo Día* described, "Ivy Queen is a woman who always changes her look. However, her fingernails, which always appear longer and more decorated, seem to resist these changes."[45] As Ivy's hair got blonder, her nails grew longer, covered in intricate designs painted in brightly colored polish, and sometimes glinting with the shiny jewels and charms glued onto their tips. Her nails were even to be immortalized in the doll fashioned in her likeness, "Queenie," which, despite much media hype, never actually materialized. For Ivy Queen, the most important accessories that were to accompany Queenie included a device that would play remixes of her most popular songs and a box of nail polish and fake jewels that purchasers could use to design the doll's fingernails.[46]

The fingernails represent one of the more excessive aspects of Ivy Queen's style. On the one hand, they imply an upper-class status since their unusual length would prevent Ivy's participation in most forms of labor. Furthermore, their maintenance requires both time and money; at one point, Ivy Queen employed two women specifically to do her nails.[47] Still, the perceived "gaudiness" of Ivy Queen's nails, their excess, contributes to the continued impression of Ivy Queen as *cafre*. Some of the fascination with her fingernails stems from their appearance as both tawdry and luxurious, an attempt to mimic dominant standards of beauty that ultimately reinforces Ivy's *cafre* reputation precisely because their flashiness seems to exemplify her purported tastelessness. As a marker of her so-called *cafre* characteristics, Ivy's fingernails symbolize a departure from allegedly more refined styles of self-fashioning associated with more "respectable" people (that is, the whitened Puerto Rican population), and therefore situate her and the communities she represents outside of these parameters, as well.

And yet, while the fingernails represent the failure of Ivy Queen's look in the eyes of many critics, for Ivy Queen, the nails exemplify key aspects of her personality and who she "really" is. In a 2008 interview with *People en Español*, Ivy Queen responded to a question about why she has adopted a "refined and elegant" look (i.e., her "whitened" appearance) with the following:

Look, I don't care if people like or don't like my look. I like to look hip-hop because I'm a reggaetón singer. One of the dumbest criticisms I've heard about me is that I should cut my nails. I'm not Miss Universe. I'm the queen of an urban movement, and my nails represent what I like about myself . . . I can't cut them to make people happy. The people who love me have to love me as I am, and my nails don't demonstrate my talent.[48]

Here, Ivy Queen establishes her fingernails as representations of her positionality, both in describing them as "what I like about myself" and affiliating them with her status as "queen of an urban movement." This is especially relevant in Ivy's comparison with Miss Universe. International beauty pageants offer opportunities for countries to represent themselves as modern through the bodies of their beauty queens.[49] Puerto Rican Miss Universe contestants (and the few Puerto Rican Miss Universes such as Denise Quiñones) are often represented as idealized Puerto Rican women who exemplify both standards of beauty that privilege whiteness as well as the ideals of respectability that define dominant constructions of Puerto Rican womanhood.[50] By rejecting Miss Universe in favor of being the "queen of an urban movement," Ivy Queen allies herself with urban, working-class communities associated with blackness, even if she does not necessarily identify herself as black.

Moreover, Ivy Queen connects her fingernails to a broader desire to "look hip-hop," which, in turn, she links to reggaetón. Ivy Queen's reference to hip-hop is important given that it has often signified blackness (and urban blackness in particular) in Puerto Rico since the days of underground (see chapter 1). Moreover, this nod to hip-hop also acknowledges reggaetón's connections to both the African diaspora (because of the shared cultural politics between the two genres), and the Nuyorican community (due to Nuyoricans' involvement in hip-hop as well as Ivy Queen's work with U.S.-based hip-hop artists like Wyclef Jean while living in New York in the beginning of her career). In this way, Ivy Queen uses her fingernails to make an argument that at once rejects the assumptions of respectability and idealized Puerto Rican womanhood associated with Miss Universe, and simultaneously affiliates herself with local black communities who are tied to broader African diasporic cultural politics via hip-hop.

Perhaps most significant, Ivy Queen also implies that her fingernails best represent her—they are, she explains, "what I like about myself." Ivy Queen celebrates an important and widely recognized element of her style that most critics dismiss, thus recuperating those *cafre* aesthetics and, by extension, the communities with which she closely identifies. Her insistence that "people who love me have to love me as I am" is a call for the equal acceptance and recognition of the urban and diasporic communities that Ivy Queen embodies, even if they do not conform to the hegemonic ideals of racial democracy represented by figures such as Miss Universe.

Another aspect of Ivy Queen's fingernails that makes them look especially aberrant in the eyes of many critics is their allegedly menacing or threatening appearance that seems decidedly nonfeminine (at least in relation to dominant constructions of femininity). Félix Jiménez described her nails as "an emblem of danger that is not entirely sexual . . . a possible weapon."[51] Even Ivy Queen herself claimed that people do not disrespect her because "they see my nails and they're afraid."[52] In this sense, her long, decorated fingernails do not signify a demure femininity like Miss Universe, but rather one marked by violence and aggression. Furthermore, thinking of Ivy Queen's fingernails as weapons attached to her body foreground their artificiality and cyborg-like qualities. In addition to being an important part of her look, Ivy Queen's fingernails also can be implements that help defend women from injustices and, more abstractly, from being rendered nonhuman. By representing who she "really" is, Ivy Queen's artificial nails thus symbolize her humanity within a system where the raced, classed, and gendered communities she represents have been depicted as nonhuman, the counterpoint to whiteness and, by extension, Puerto Ricanness. It is no accident, then, that Ivy's fingernails have remained intact despite her broader physical transformation, for taken together, Ivy's new physique illustrates the artificiality of whiteness and racial binaries that routinely valorize whiteness over all other racial identities. But these fingernails are tied to another element of Ivy Queen's performance that emphasizes the humanity of those cast out of racial democracy discourses: her lyrical emphasis on suffering.

Suffering con *Sentimiento*

In 2007, Ivy Queen released the album, *Sentimiento*. The lyrics in *Sentimiento* described Ivy Queen's desire for love, and her ability to exact vengeance on a lover when scorned. The album included reggaetón love songs (as well as one salsa cut, and, on the platinum edition, a bachata), the majority of which Ivy Queen penned herself. In addition, she invited several guests to collaborate with her (such as her duets with Don Omar in "Robarte un beso" and Ken-Y on the "Que lloren" remix), and others like Divino and Mickey Perfecto who performed their own songs. Thematically, these songs are similar to the rest of Ivy's repertoire, which has often centered on romantic love and relationships; however, the marketing and publicity surrounding *Sentimiento* framed the album differently from her previous work. As Ivy Queen describes on the album's opening track, these songs were inspired by the boleros that Ivy grew up hearing from her parents, and the love songs her father played for her mother on his guitar. The result was, as one reporter stated, "a different reggaetón, one more for listening than for dancing" that was above all about love.[53] Importantly, for Ivy Queen, the album demonstrated to the world that she and other reggaetón singers were "artists and composers" and that, as one reporter paraphrased, "reggaetón does not have to be street one hundred percent."[54]

Univision Music Group, Ivy Queen's record label at the time, released *Sentimiento* at a time when reggaetón was supposedly on the decline. By 2007, Latin music record companies had noticed the purchasing power of female audiences of "urban Latin music" evident in the success of *bachata urbana* by groups such as Aventura, and reggaetón's *romantiqueo* duos.[55] The marketing of *Sentimiento* as a "unique" album that focused on love rather than party music perhaps conformed to this larger industry strategy to promote reggaetón to distinct audiences, particularly in light of its diminishing record sales.

That *Sentimiento* focuses on romantic love from a woman's point of view does not seem especially innovative given how pervasive such themes are in popular music, even if men dominate reggaetón. Just as the shift in her look can be read as an effort to conform to standards of beauty in the record industry, Ivy Queen's lyrics about romantic love may signify the "depoliticized" nature of contemporary reggaetón. Many critics have argued that the "mainstreaming" of reggaetón has divorced it from its "origins" in the *caseríos*, thus resulting in music that is less "political" and more "pop" (see chapter 5). Read in this way, the emphasis on romance in *Sentimiento* acquiesces to what appears to be a preference for apolitical pop music by the record industry.

However, the songs that Ivy Queen includes in the album are not simply laments that pine over lost love, but rather represent the perspective of a woman who, as one *New York Times* reporter described, "suffer[s] more dramatically and vow[s] vengeance more furiously."[56] Similar to her look, Ivy Queen's lyrical suffering and vengeance are considered "excessive." Still, they also comprise a larger political critique about the contradictory exclusions inherent to dominant discourses of racial democracy.

This critique responds to racial democracy's rendering of blackness, and black womanhood in particular, as nonhuman. Daphne Brooks argues that black female R&B artists in the United States have not received enough serious attention for the ways that their music functions as social critique; to that end, she analyzes the work of Beyoncé and Mary J. Blige in the post-Katrina era as an urgent "response of sorts to the long history of black women who have been stripped and stressed and displaced and denied" in the United States.[57] Similarly, Ivy Queen troubles the denial of nonwhite women's humanity that is part and parcel of dominant discourses of racial democracy through her lyrics that recount the suffering that ensues either from not having love—that is, not being considered loveable—or from abuse at the hands of a male partner. That this call for recognition occurs via reggaetón performance is significant given the music's associations with working-class, nonwhite communities on the island and its hypermasculine posturing. First, the desire to be seen as loveable directly refutes the problematic characterization of reggaetoneros via stereotypical tropes of urban blackness, particularly depictions of the women involved in reggaetón as hypersexual and driven by instinct. In contrast, Ivy Queen's request for love marks her as someone deserving of recognition and acceptance as both part of and equal to the rest of the Puerto Rican population—that is, someone who *should* be included in Puerto Rico's so-called racial democracy, but instead suffers from its exclusionary racist and sexist practices. Much like the ways that Brooks understands Beyoncé's music as a "distinct form of palpable sociopolitical loss and grief as well as spirited dissent and dissonance,"[58] the uncomfortable and sometimes violent nature of the suffering Ivy Queen describes in her lyrics demands the recognition of her suffering body as a human one. It is this call for recognition and for respect that transforms her lyrics from mere descriptive laments about love to ones that actively fight against the conscription of her body as nonhuman via her positioning in relation to stereotypes of black womanhood in Puerto Rico.

The concept of *feeling* is essential for establishing a space to celebrate those realities and experiences normally stigmatized by dominant constructions of urban blackness. Here, José Esteban Muñoz's conceptualization of "feeling brown" is useful. Muñoz argues that the United States has a "national affect" that centers a "racialized normativity" of whiteness. In this context, Latinos and other minority groups are considered to be "performers of excess" because they do not conform to "appropriate" modes of behavior and affect.[59] Instead, Muñoz claims that minority groups experience the "world on a different emotional register" that enables the formation of new communities that reject the distortions of their realities and experiences by the dominant culture.[60] Likewise, Ivy Queen counters the national affect of Puerto Rico as structured by discourses of racial democracy through her "excessive" performances and aesthetics. The excess in Ivy's performances is considered so disturbing and disruptive for many critics precisely because it offers alternative definitions of Puerto Ricanness that center the experiences and worldviews of those communities often rendered incompatible with the Puerto Rican nation.

Sentimiento, or feeling, thus serves as a political tool to call for the humanity of the reggaetón woman. In part, the politicization of feeling in Ivy Queen's music builds from the boleros and *filin* (a phonetic transcription of the word *feeling*) that inspired the album. Boleros grew popular internationally in the 1930s as romantic songs describing unrequited love. While several women composed and performed boleros, men dominated the bolero scene. Frances Aparicio notes that bolero performance provided a discourse about gender relations that ultimately reinforced patriarchal relations, reducing women to specific archetypes such as "the woman seductress and witch, the femme fatale, the ungrateful woman who betrays the man's love, and the 'lost woman.' "[61] Women's bodies thus play a central role in bolero performance as the "texts" upon which male artists impose their own understandings of love and desire in ways that reinforce both gender and racial hierarchies that privilege white men.[62] At the same time, however, Aparicio argues that boleros potentially expand notions of masculinity since artists articulated emotions normally considered to exist in the realm of the "feminine"; therefore, she writes, boleros provide "a language for self-disclosure and emotional healing that can be uttered only in the fictive space of the stage or in the intimate space circumscribed by the (hetero)sexual couple."[63]

One particular off-shoot of bolero, *filin*, also presents a critical referent for understanding Ivy Queen's performances of suffering. Musically, *filin* incorporated more improvisation and influence from U.S. American jazz of the 1940s and 1950s.[64] Beyond the "feeling" of improvisation and cadence of jazz, *filin* expresses feeling as emotions. *Filin* differed from the more formal, predominantly masculine nature of *bolero* as an "explicitly emotional or expressive style of singing" that included a "gestural performance style incorporating silences and pauses for dramatic effect."[65] Many women performed *filin*, including Olga Guillot and La Lupe, both of whom were known for their "excessive" performances that involved dramatic and commanding vocals as well as gestures, movements, and asides. Artists like Guillot and La Lupe demonstrate how the instability of gender relations in the bolero allow for alternative representations of women to emerge that depart from the *traicionera* depiction of many male artists and, instead, foreground the particular forms of suffering, longing, and loving of many women.[66]

Ivy Queen builds from the work of La Lupe, Guillot, and other *boleristas* and *filin* artists by using lyrics about love and suffering to make a larger call for the recognition of the humanity of reggaetón women. Still, as with her look, Ivy Queen's lyrics are contradictory, especially her commitment to heterosexual love relationships. Heterosexual encounters, particularly between black women and white men, form the basis of Puerto Rico's racial democracy (see chapter 2). In this context, Ivy Queen's calls for a male partner may reify both the sexual and racial hierarchies within dominant discourses of racial democracy; indeed, while at times Ivy Queen features black men as her love interests in her music videos, often the male protagonists embody a white(ned), "Latin" look. Furthermore, the descriptions of the suffering that men inflict upon women appear to reinscribe certain stereotypes of macho Latino and black men who mistreat their female partners. However, these stories can also be understood as serious critiques of the problematic gender politics within reggaetón that sometimes reproduce stereotypes of black women. Ultimately, the significance of Ivy Queen's lyrics lies in their demand for love on *equal* terms, a move that criticizes both the uneven gender relations within reggaetón and within Puerto Rico's racial democracy.

Ivy Queen conveyed her desire for a male romantic partner who would treat her well in many of the interviews conducted with the media surrounding *Sentimiento*'s release. In fact, she considered *Sentimiento* to be a therapeutic response to the dissolution of her first marriage, during which Ivy claimed that her ex-husband treated her poorly, causing her to suffer from much "*desamor*" [heartbreak] and "*angustia*" [anguish].[67] Ivy Queen described her ideal boyfriend as someone who was "good, caring, and attentive."[68] The main quality that Ivy Queen wanted, though, was love. She stated, "Ivy Queen has to be strong, dominant, because I am in a genre dominated by men and I have to be that way. But Ivelisse is a woman like any other that wants to be taken to the movies, brought flowers, or written a love note. Nothing extravagant that I can buy for myself. I want someone to love me."[69] She expressed similar thoughts on the song "Sentimiento" included on the album; Ivy Queen explained, "I'm a woman who needs affection, someone to open doors for me, to bring me flowers and sing to me. That's the song that best exemplifies where I am right now."[70] "Sentimiento" combines Dominican bachata, a genre that Ivy Queen identified as one of her favorites because of its romantic compositions and expressions of (male) vulnerability,[71] with reggaetón. The song begins with a verse in which Ivy Queen sings that she does not need someone famous or with fancy cars, but instead "tú sabes que una mujer como yo / necesita cariño" [you know that a woman like me / needs love]. While Ivy Queen frequently expressed her desire for a romantic partner and, eventually, children, she also declared that her focus on her career prevented her from having a relationship. For example, Ivy Queen told *El Nuevo Día*, "I'm not desperate to find someone who loves me . . . For me, the priority right now is Ivy Queen. I'm working to be a better artist, a better composer, better colleague, and better woman."[72] Along with the instances when she states that she does not need a man who brings her things that she "can buy for [her]self," Ivy Queen foregrounds love as the basis for her ideal heterosexual romantic relationship while emphasizing her economic independence in a way that renders normative gender roles that assume a male breadwinner obsolete.

On one hand, Ivy Queen's calls for love and descriptions of the difference between her star persona and the "real" Ivelisse seem like superfluous celebrity gossip. Yet, in relation to constructions of urban blackness associated with reggaetón, the desire for a respectful, loving partner insists upon recognition as someone who is *loveable*. Accepting the possibility of love for the stereotypical reggaetón woman calls into question the hegemonic narratives that represent her as always sexually available, regardless of her emotional desires. As Ivy Queen said in one *Billboard* interview, "Because people see us as reggaetón or *rap en español* artists, they think we don't have feelings and maybe can't write the way I wrote this album."[73] Here, Ivy Queen directly confronts the assumption that reggaetón artists lack basic human emotions, including longing for love, and instead underscores the importance of feeling in order to assert the humanity of reggaetón artists and fans.

Similarly, the suffering that Ivy Queen warns could result from love is intrinsically connected to questions of the human. Suffering foregrounds feelings and longings for recognition and love understood to be aspects of the human experience. This suffering, however, is not that of a submissive woman who accepts her situation; rather, Ivy Queen's lyrics and performances call for vengeance for women's suffering, sometimes in aggressive or violent ways.

The work of Afro-Cuban artist Guadalupe Victoria Yoli Raymond, better known as La Lupe, the "Queen of Latin Soul," informs Ivy Queen's performances and recounting of extreme suffering. La Lupe began her career singing boleros and *filin* in Cuba, and arrived in New York City in the early

1960s where she performed first with Mongo Santamaria, and, later, with Tito Puente. In 1968, Tito Puente ejected La Lupe from the band, replacing her with Celia Cruz. La Lupe continued to perform and record solo albums, although her career declined steadily and she died in relative obscurity in 1992.[74]

Frances Aparicio argues that La Lupe exuded a type of femininity that fundamentally disrupted the normative gender relations in Latin music.[75] La Lupe was known as much for her beautiful voice as her on-stage antics, which included screaming, kicking, punching, and removing clothing.[76] In addition, La Lupe's excess was evident not only in her gestures and movements, but also in the "excessive intensity of emotion and feeling" that marked her vocal style.[77] The excess of La Lupe's performances pushed the boundaries of race, class, and gender norms. For example, Delia Poey argues that La Lupe's performances "subver[ted] stereotypic depictions and readings of *la mulata*" and challenged the narrow racialized and gendered characteristics associated with Cubanness.[78] Likewise, Frances Aparicio claims that "La Lupe represents . . . the most feminist and radical as a performer of Afro-Caribbean music."[79] Aparicio locates La Lupe in a generation of Afro-Latina performers including Toña La Negra in Mexico, Ruth Fernández in Puerto Rico, and others who "articulat[ed] the historical visibility and agency of Caribbean women in Latina/o culture" in ways that challenged both gender and racial hierarchies.[80] As such, La Lupe's performances contested structures of race and gender that stigmatized black women, and provided a space with which groups marginalized on the basis of race, gender, sexuality, and class could identify.[81]

In addition to her unique performance style, La Lupe fostered a "feminist subjectivity" that often "contest[ed] historically negative textualizations of the feminine."[82] Typical of the boleros and *filin* that La Lupe performed, her songs spoke of "*engaño* and *des-engaño*" that deconstructed the dominant "illusions" that devalued her black and female identities.[83] As Frances Aparicio notes, although men, including the renowned salsa composer Tite Curet Alonso, wrote many of La Lupe's hits, the songs offer a reading of suffering and relationships that actively critique male dominance and patriarchy. Aparicio contends that La Lupe's performance of two of her most famous songs, "La Tirana" [The Tyrant] and "Puro Teatro" [Pure Drama] (both composed by Curet Alonso), which include lyrical asides, a sarcastic tone, and the aforementioned performance style, disrupt the masculine emphasis in most salsa and bolero performance.[84] Indeed, these songs not only tell the stories of women whose male partners have mistreated them but also actively reject the suffering that these men have caused. In this sense, La Lupe expressed an alternative gender perspective in bolero performance by emphasizing the emotion, feeling, and humanity of women and represented men as the primary culprits of women's suffering.

Ivy Queen identifies La Lupe as one of her musical influences.[85] She often incorporates specific references to some of La Lupe's hits into her own songs. For example, "Según Tú" [According to You] featured on the *Los Bandoleros* (2005) compilation album begins with a series of proclamations and vocables that lead into a few bachata bars as Ivy sings, "Según tú, yo soy la mala / según yo, esto es un drama" [According to you, I'm the bad woman / according to me, this is drama]. These lines directly cite La Lupe's "La Tirana" (which La Lupe begins with "Según tu punto de vista / yo soy la mala" (From your point of view / I am the bad woman)[86] and "Puro Teatro," which describes a relationship with a cheating lover as "theater" and a "drama."[87] Following Lupe's lead, "Según Tú" describes a tumultuous relationship in which Ivy is considered "la mala," but where her male partner is primarily responsible for its demise.

Another hit by Ivy Queen, "Te He Querido, Te He Llorado" [I've Loved You, I've Cried for You], extends from La Lupe's style of performance and disruptions of standard gender roles in bolero. Although not included on *Sentimiento*, Ivy concluded the concert performance in San Juan that accompanied the album with a drawn-out, dramatic performance of "Te He Querido, Te He Llorado."[88] On the version recorded for Luny Tunes' *Más Flow 2*, the musical aesthetics and opening lines that Ivy exclaims prior to the actual start of the lyrics establish connections between the song and romantic music like bolero or *filin*. Like "Según Tú," "Te He Querido, Te He Llorado" is a combination of bachata and reggaetón. As Deborah Pacini Hernández documents, the lyrical themes and style of playing guitar in bolero profoundly influenced bachata.[89] Ivy Queen makes these links explicit in the beginning of the song when she exclaims that some people might describe her song as *bachateo*, but she considers it *sentimiento*. *Bachateo* is a term that describes the unique combinations of bachata and reggaetón. By referring to her song as *sentimiento*, or "feeling," Ivy Queen connects it to not only her album of that title, but also the larger bolero and *filin* traditions defined in part by their displays of intense emotion.

The beginning of "Te He Querido, Te He Llorado" for *Más Flow 2* also diverges from the typical suffering in bolero and *filin* when Ivy Queen exclaims, "¡Vamos a roncar ahora!" [Let's *roncar*!] just before the lyrics begin. While in standard Spanish the verb *roncar* means "to snore," in reggaetón parlance *roncar* sometimes refers to verbally attacking one's rival, or, at other times, to bragging about one's self. In other contexts, *roncar* could mean to make noise or to make trouble, all with the purpose of demonstrating one's superiority. Jennifer Rudolph argues that in reggaetón, "the multiple meanings of *ronca* foreground the intersection of aggression and power in shifting social contexts and render aggression as a performative construct by which it is possible to tease out conflicting attempts to gain agency."[90] Though perhaps a fleeting moment in the recording, framing the song with "¡Vamos a roncar ahora!" is significant because, despite its ambiguity, all of the meanings of *roncar* in reggaetón overturn the typical portrayal of the meek or victimized woman in bolero; instead, Ivy Queen uses the word *roncar* to frame the song as an assertion of power and a demand for equal recognition.

The beginning of "Te He Querido, Te He Llorado" therefore links the song to bolero and *filin* while simultaneously disrupting normative bolero performance. The song recalls La Lupe's "Amor Gitano" (written by Hector Flores Osuna), in which La Lupe narrates seeing her lover with another woman, and then sings in the chorus that she will use a dagger (*puñal*) to slit her wrists and kill herself as a result. "Te He Querido, Te He Llorado" similarly recounts using violence to overcome the suffering caused by a cheating man. Ivy Queen begins the song by declaring her unwavering love for her partner, even though she describes him as a liar, cheater, and abuser who made her "suffer." Rather than lament the suffering she underwent, Ivy Queen plots her revenge. Ivy tells of the horrible life that awaits the man who left her, singing "Y en mis manos si tuviera un puñal lo usaría / Y la vida yo te quitaría" [And if I had a dagger in my hands I'd use it / And I would take away your life]. The dagger, as well as the suffering that Ivy's ex-lover caused, evoke the story that La Lupe sings in "Amor Gitano." Importantly, however, Ivy Queen does not consider suicide, but rather fantasizes about using the dagger to kill her former lover. Through this call for violence and revenge, Ivy Queen reverses the typical bolero structure by actively rejecting the assumption that her role as the woman is to suffer, instead imagining that she would inflict particularly violent forms of suffering on her former male lover.

Songs on the album *Sentimiento* maintain this emphasis on suffering and revenge. The first single off the album, "Que Lloren," refutes the cultural standard that men should not cry, instead portraying men as vulnerable. But rather than sympathize with them, Ivy Queen calls for men to cry, singing in the chorus, "Que lloren, lo que yo quiero es / que lloren / que admitan de sus errores" (Cry, what I want is / for them to cry / to admit their errors). Here, Ivy denounces the assumption that men are somehow incapable of the same emotional vulnerability as women while simultaneously debunking the idea that women are willing to endure pain and inequality in their romances with men. At the same time, she enacts vengeance for women's suffering by demanding that men admit their wrongdoing, in many ways reversing what are otherwise considered the "typical" power relations between men and women.

In addition to lyrics, the body is also critical to bolero performance. Individuals' self-styling, fashion choices, glances, gestures, and movements amplify the sentiments in their lyrics.[91] This is evident in the descriptions of La Lupe's performances that consider her frenzied movements as part of the "excessive" and "uncontrollable" emotions in her songs. Although Ivy Queen is not known for her dramatic bodily movements, the gestures she makes with her fingernails similarly accentuate the feelings in her music. For example, in the music video for "Que Lloren," Ivy Queen's fingernails represent the tools with which she avenges women's suffering. Filmed in Miami by director Marlon Peña, the video begins when Ivy Queen enters a salon to have her nails done. There, Ivy encounters a woman whose male lover has been hitting on her. At the same time, a group of men are gathered at a conference called "The Power of Man," where a male speaker emphatically declares that they should never cry. Donning a white suit, Ivy Queen bursts into the room and starts rapping about men's vulnerability. Throughout, she points and gestures with her long nails at each man, sometimes even shoving him to the side, until the offender in question starts to weep. Ivy's fingernails serve as "weapons" attached to her body that she uses to make the men cry. Moreover, the fingernails comprise an important element of the video's narrative, for the salon serves as a site where women come together in a supportive community, and, ultimately, where Ivy Queen develops her strategy to reverse the power in their relationships, pointing out the vulnerability of men and avenging women's suffering.

Similar to the boleros that were her inspiration, Ivy Queen's songs on *Sentimiento* and elsewhere in her repertoire center romantic love and suffering at the hands of former lovers. However, Ivy Queen pushes the boundaries of traditional bolero performance. Rather than represent women as passive

FIGURE 4.2. Ivy Queen bursts into "The Power of Man" conference in her music video for "Que Lloren."

sufferers or evil *traicioneras*, Ivy Queen actively calls for vengeance and, as a result, troubles typical gender relations in both bolero and reggaetón. The demand for tenderness, understanding, and respect in her lyrics insists on the recognition of the humanity of the reggaetón woman who has been depicted as nonhuman within hegemonic discourses of racial democracy. Feeling, then, is more than a lament. Instead, it can be a political tool that allows for alternative imaginings of black womanhood in ways that both trouble dominant ideas of Puerto Ricanness and create opportunities for new alliances to emerge. In the process, Ivy Queen shatters the ties between whiteness, respectability, humanity, and Puerto Rican identity, and sets the stage for creating more inclusive ways of understanding Puerto Ricanness.

FRANCES APARICIO HAS argued that many critics discount *salsa romántica* often preferred by women audiences because they assume the music's focus on romance is not as political as salsa of the 1970s.[92] Similarly, Ivy Queen's music and persona may appear divorced from any political stance (except, perhaps, her active support of the gay community). However, Ivy

Queen's reggaetón presents love as a political project that advocates for a society where everyone is accepted for who they are, one that rejects the privileging of whiteness, patriarchy, and heteronormativity ingrained in Puerto Rico's racial democracy.

In this vein, Ivy Queen's shift in her look is not necessarily a desire to achieve whiteness, but rather makes evident its constructedness and, most important, the artificiality of the presumed connections between whiteness and respectability. Likewise, the suffering and intense longing for love that Ivy Queen describes in her lyrics are jarring not only because of the violence they relate, but also because their call for recognition discredits the assumption that working-class, nonwhite communities are not human, an assumption that is fundamental to hegemonic discourses of racial democracy. Her fingernails morph from a "gaudy" attempt to achieve normative standards of femininity to tools that both point out the artificiality of whiteness and help to defend the rights of those women left with no rights within Puerto Rico's so-called racial democracy. Beyond responding to romance gone awry, the suffering that Ivy describes in her lyrics addresses a system that does not recognize the humanity of everyone despite purporting to be a democracy. Feeling is central to the reimaginings of Puerto Ricanness that Ivy's work makes possible. Taking seriously the feelings of those whose emotions are often rendered nonexistent and irrelevant on the one hand, or excessive and extreme on the other, opens up possibilities for creating new alliances that reject the constrictive respectability politics of Puerto Rico's racial democracy in favor of more inclusive understandings of Puerto Ricanness.

To be sure, like other reggaetón artists, Ivy Queen is contradictory. These contradictions are not easy to explain and at times seem to reinforce some of the problematic constructions of race, gender, and sexuality that structure racial democracy discourses. It is important to remain critical of how broader structural inequalities may limit the effectiveness of Ivy's potential critiques, or how her performance may reify these same hierarchies. Still, reducing our analyses of Ivy Queen (and other reggaetón and pop music artists) to either the ways she fails to transform from one thing to another (as in the criticisms of her look) or the ways she merely navigates static constructions of race and gender (e.g., the analyses of her hyperfemininity overcompensating for her perceived masculinity) ignores the potential to explode these binaries that Ivy offers. While contradictory, Ivy Queen's music and persona break with many of the essentializing notions of whiteness and blackness, masculinity and femininity, and other binaries that inform dominant discourses of racial democracy, in the process pointing out their inherent contradictions. Consequently, these fingernails *con* feeling symbolize the creation of new, inclusive communities based on a love that recognizes and celebrates *all* Puerto Ricans.

CHAPTER FIVE
ENTER THE HURBANS

By 2005, the characteristic "boom-ch-boom-chick" of reggaetón had arrived in the United States. In 2004, Daddy Yankee released his smash hit "Gasolina," which climbed the *Billboard* charts and gained routine play on English-language radio and television. If Tego Calderón opened the doors to mainstream Puerto Rican audiences, Daddy Yankee spread the reggaetón sound beyond the Spanish-speaking community to the mainstream United States with one catchy hook. Produced by Luny Tunes, and written by Daddy Yankee and Eddie Dee, "Gasolina" represented a "quintessential example of contemporary, commercial reggaeton style."[1] The song was included in Daddy Yankee's *Barrio Fino* (2004) album, which debuted at number one on *Billboard's* Latin Albums chart, eventually reaching number twenty-six on *Billboard's* Top 200 list, and number sixteen on the rap charts. By 2006, *Barrio Fino* had sold two million copies.[2]

Born Raymond Ayala in 1977, Daddy Yankee grew up in the *caserío* Villa Kennedy. Like Ivy Queen, he began his career long before reggaetón reached commercial success. He performed as an underground artist with DJ Playero as a teenager, adopting the moniker "Daddy Yankee" when he was only thirteen years old. By twenty-one years old, Daddy Yankee was so popular that he began his own record label, El Cartel.[3] Many dominant narratives about the rise of reggaetón portray Daddy Yankee as the one who launched reggaetón into the mainstream United States, reaching English-speaking audiences despite his Spanish lyrics. As *Billboard* editor Leila

Cobo declared in an interview with *New York Times Magazine*, "If it weren't for 'Gasolina,' the mainstream wouldn't have heard about reggaetón."[4]

Wayne Marshall argues that "Gasolina" comprised "a musical text engaging with a long history of circulating sounds, people, and ideas about self and other, race and place."[5] And yet, the U.S.-based media ignored the complex musical and social histories that produced reggaetón, increasingly presenting the genre as Puerto Rican and, especially, Latino. Moreover, the success and popularity of reggaetón that preceded the release of "Gasolina"—including Daddy Yankee's own decade-long career—were virtually disregarded by the U.S. media, save for brief mentions of both Yankee's and reggaetón's long-standing connections to Puerto Rico's urban housing projects. The emphasis on reggaetón's "newness" follows a common trajectory in the U.S. Latin music industry in which "Latin American and U.S. Latino performers who perform primarily in Spanish are . . . repackaged as 'debut artists' and 'discoveries' of mainstream record companies."[6] Consequently, reggaetón became marketed as the next big thing, a musical "revolution" that would transform Latin music.

Still, there was something different about the coverage of reggaetón in the U.S. press, especially in relation to the so-called Latin Boom of the 1990s that immediately preceded it. In the late 1990s and early 2000s, Latin pop took center stage in the U.S. music industry. Artists who had firmly established themselves in Spanish-language markets such as Ricky Martin, Shakira, and Enrique Iglesias released English-language albums that climbed the pop music charts. Despite their histories as global pop stars with millions of record sales already under their belts, the music industry marketed these artists as novel discoveries. The coverage surrounding the Latin Boom in the mainstream U.S. press stressed many stereotypical tropes of Latinidad that presented these artists as hypersexual and "hot tamales." At the same time, however, the media also emphasized the artists' "*appearance* of whiteness."[7] Indeed, this representation of Latin Boom artists reflects broader processes of racialization of Latinos more generally who are seen as members of a racialized minority group even as they are viewed as harboring the potential for "whitening" and assimilation into the mainstream.[8] Latin Boom artists were thus inescapably Latino due to their Spanish-speaking origins, Latin-inflected pop, and embodiment of stereotypical images of Latinos as "tropicalized," hypersexual party people.[9] But at the same time, artists like Ricky Martin and Shakira were presented as whitened Latinos who could possibly become assimilated into the United States.

Despite characterizations of Daddy Yankee as a "cooler" version of Ricky Martin, reggaetón occupied a racial position distinct from its Latin Boom counterparts. If Ricky Martin was a "not quite white" artist who might be assimilated into U.S. mainstream culture, reggaetón artists were considered "not quite black." This racialization of reggaetón artists followed the historical racialization of Puerto Ricans as racial others who were thought to be similar, yet different from, African Americans. This is especially interesting given that Ricky Martin, arguably the most visible Latin Boom artist, is also Puerto Rican. And yet, while Ricky became the poster child for an assimilable, whitened Latinidad, Puerto Rican reggaetón artists came to embody stereotypes of urban Puerto Rican communities that had circulated throughout the twentieth century. These stereotypes racialized Puerto Ricans, and by extension reggaetón, as occupying an intermediary racial category between whites and African Americans; however, as mentioned in chapter 1, Puerto Ricans were located on the blacker end of the racial spectrum. Consequently, the racialization of reggaetón followed previous representations of Puerto Ricans as "not quite black" and therefore contrasted sharply with whitened, assimilable artists of the 1990s Latin Boom.

Regardless of the focus on reggaetón's similarities to blackness, reggaetón was still labeled a "Latino" phenomenon within the United States. As Wayne Marshall describes, this move changed reggaetón's framing from "*música negra* to 'Reggaeton Latino,' from a principally Afro–Puerto Rican or Puerto Rican audience to a pan-Latino and mainstream U.S. consumer base."[10] This shift included a pronounced move to market reggaetón to "Hurban"—or "Hispanic urban"—audiences that encompassed people of all Latin American national origins found throughout the United States.[11] It also involved a markedly more "tropicalized" sound that incorporated typical riffs from salsa, merengue, bachata and other Latin music genres as opposed to the more unembellished hip-hop and dancehall aesthetics of underground.[12]

Such moves are in line with dominant constructions of racial categories in the United States that separate blackness and Latinidad. Perceptions of blackness as property of African Americans in the United States often make Afro-Latinos' blackness suspect given their distinctive cultural backgrounds; at the same time, persistent antiblack racism within Latin America and many U.S. Latino communities presents obstacles for Afro-Latino inclusion within Latino communities.[13] Media and policy efforts reinforce these divisions by continuously representing blacks and Latinos as fundamentally distinct. The music industry also replicates these distinctions, with "black divisions" marketing and producing music intended for African American audiences.[14] On the other hand, the Latin music industry lumps together musical practices that share Spanish or Portuguese lyrics but come from a variety of musical genres and traditions, in pursuit of Latin American and U.S. Latino audiences.[15] Given this separation between blackness and Latinidad, did reggaetón offer the same possibilities for forging African diasporic connections once it was marketed as a Latino phenomenon in the United States? Wayne Marshall has argued that despite the commercial categorization of reggaetón as Latino, many audiences continue to recognize the music as affiliated with blackness due to its connections to hip-hop and its promotion of "longstanding myths about *negra* and *mulata* sexualities."[16] Likewise, while media coverage of reggaetón reinforces the music's characterization as "Latino," it also portrays reggaetón as "not quite black" in relation to other types of Latin music.

This complex process of racialization provides opportunities to consider the possibilities and limits of reggaetón as a space to elaborate African diasporic connections between Latinos and other black-identified groups within the United States, including the expression of distinctly Afro-Latino identities. In this chapter, I consider the racialization of reggaetón in the United States through a close examination of media coverage surrounding the music's move into the mainstream in the mid-2000s. More specifically, this process of racialization represented reggaetón and the communities associated with it as "not quite black" through the creation of a "Hurban" category that encompassed Hispanic urban audiences. This Hurban category linked Latinidad and blackness via stereotypes associated with poor, urban black and Latino communities while simultaneously maintaining the rigid separation between the two categories in the U.S. racial lexicon. Nevertheless, Hurban identity could also be resignified to create openings that erode the strict distinctions between blackness and Latinidad, particularly in relation to the connections between reggaetón and hip-hop routinely addressed in the media. After an analysis of the representations of reggaetón in the U.S. media, including profiles of artists Daddy Yankee and N.O.R.E., a brief discussion of the music of reggaetón/dancehall artist Notch reveals some of the possibilities reggaetón offers as a cultural practice of diaspora in the U.S. context. In the final analysis, considering the representation of reggaetón as a Latino phenomenon requires attention to the different ways Latinidad has been constructed, and how various national origin and racial groups become incorporated or not into hegemonic definitions of what it means to be Latino. Nevertheless, while U.S. media representations of a Latino reggaetón may appear to foreclose the possibility of the music's potential to articulate African diasporic connections, embedded within these representations of reggaetón exist opportunities to challenge the strict racial boundaries that continue to differentiate blackness and Latinidad by foregrounding Afro-Latino identities.

Hurban Discovery

The success of Daddy Yankee's "Gasolina" attracted the attention of record companies, music industry executives, and media outlets. Many large record companies signed reggaetón artists or obtained distribution rights for smaller labels owned by these artists. In 2005, both Daddy Yankee and Tego Calderón signed deals with major record labels (Interscope and Atlantic, respectively) that would sell the recordings from their own, smaller labels (Yankee's El Cartel and Calderón's Jiggiri Records).[17] In addition, many hip-hop labels added new sections exclusively devoted to reggaetón distribution, such as Bad Boy's Bad Boy Latino and Def Jam's Roc La Familia.[18]

Likewise, radio stations steadily incorporated reggaetón into their airplay as the music gained popularity. Clear Channel Radio decided to switch twenty-five stations in large, urban markets such as Houston, Miami, and Atlanta to predominantly reggaetón.[19] The switch even included stations that previously had not played Latin music, such as Houston's KLOL, which was formerly a classic rock station.[20] In New York, Univision's WCAA changed from a "Latino mix" to La Kalle, a station dedicated almost exclusively to reggaetón.[21] In addition to these reggaetón stations, some English-language radio, such as New York City's hip-hop station Hot 97 and Orlando's mainstream Power 95, as well as Spanish-language stations that had previously ignored reggaetón, began integrating it into their rotations.[22]

The rapid increase in corporate investment in reggaetón-oriented business ventures was motivated by the music's exposure of a supposedly new market—the Hurban. A combination of the phrase *Hispanic urban*, the term *Hurban* describes radio formats like La Kalle, which focused on reggaetón but also incorporated some English-language hits, primarily from genres such as hip-hop and R&B. Hurban audiences were assumed to be young Latinos who had grown up in the United States and were familiar with both English and Spanish music. As one reporter for USA *Today* described:

Right now, radio conglomerates and advertisers think they've hit on an untapped mother lode: second- and third-generation, young Hispanics. They're 18-to-34-year old-bilinguals who love urban music (i.e. hip-hop and R&B) but who yearn for their own twist on the sound . . . These stations offer a savvy mulch of reggaeton (the Puerto Rican rap-reggae export), Spanish hip-hop, and goosed-up remixes of mainstream R&B and hip-hop.[23]

Importantly, these stations were imagined as different from more traditional Spanish-language stations that prioritized specific genres such as Mexican regional music or salsa determined by whichever Latino subgroup dominated a specific local market. Consequently, not only did the Hurban moniker apply to younger generations of Latinos, but, as Clear Channel Radio senior vice president of Hispanic Radio, Alfredo Alonso, stated to *Billboard Magazine*, it was a "bilingual audience." He continued, "We've built a radio station to serve the young Latino whose needs, for years, weren't served. They do become acculturated, but they are still Latinos and they still have interests very different from the general market."[24]

This was not the first time that a musical phenomenon spurred U.S.-based companies to take notice of Latino markets. Several industries have focused on strategies to identify and market products to allegedly homogenous and culturally distinctive Latino consumers.[25] The rapid growth of the Latino population and recent discussions of the "browning of America" have also led to a recognition of the potentially massive profits for companies actively courting Latinos.[26] Considering these broader trends to pursue Latino markets, as well as the success of crossover artists like Ricky Martin just a few years before, it is hardly surprising that record labels and radio conglomerates would seek to capitalize on reggaetón's popularity. Indeed, the program director of Houston's Hurban station, Al Fuentes, observed, "When you see Daddy Yankee on MTV and Shakira doing a reggaeton remix of a song, you say, 'Wait a minute—something's happening here that's big.'"[27]

Still, reggaetón's long-standing popularity in Latin America, the fact that many Latinos in the United States already listened to reggaetón, and the prior existence of bilingual urban Latino communities elicits the question, what was so novel about Hurbans? It seems the most "new" thing about Hurban was the term itself. If the primary criterion for identifying Hurban audiences was that they were Latinos living in urban areas, then why weren't previous musical practices popular in these communities counted as Hurban? Mambo, boogaloo, salsa, and hip-hop all involved the critical participation of urban Latino communities. In fact, artists such as mambo and Latin jazz great Tito Puente and salsero Willie Colón could have been classified as "Hurban" given their backgrounds as Puerto Ricans who grew up in New York City. Moreover, while reggaetón speaks to the bicultural realities of many Latino youths in the United States, that aspect of the music is not new, either. Boogaloo, freestyle, and a whole host of other musical genres addressed the realities and desires of young, predominantly urban Latinos who related to both U.S. American and Latin American cultures, and who often worked together with African Americans and others to create new musical genres that reflected their bicultural sensibilities.[28] So what was it that made reggaetoneros and their audiences so Hurban compared to other types of Latin music?

The designation of these audiences as Hurban presents an interesting case for examining the assumptions about race that not only inform the music industry's marketing strategies, but also the racialization of Puerto Ricans more generally. To understand this process, it is critical to unpack the implications of both the Hispanic and urban components of the Hurban. The term *Hispanic* generally refers to all individuals of Latin American descent living in the United States. As such, it homogenizes the diverse experiences of Latino populations, collapsing differences of race, nationality, socioeconomic class, gender, religion, language, and other factors into one large group.[29] The category Hispanic thus promotes very specific characteristics such as Spanish language ability or a mixed race "look" to define Latinidad in the United States. Such rigid definitions of what it means to be Latino help to identify the population for companies seeking to market themselves to Latino consumers, including the Latin music industry. Beyond identifying potential markets, however, these characterizations of Latinidad also further the perceived distinctions between blackness and Latinidad, contributing to the marginalization of Afro-Latino identities and experiences in the United States. The *Hispanic* part of the *Hurban* term thus signals that reggaetón could attract a potentially massive, new, and distinct Latino audience—the "untapped mother lode" of millennial Latino consumers.

Still, Hurban signifies a different type of Hispanic identity. If the Hispanic part of the equation calls attention to the potential of a uniform and singular Latino audience, the urban element referenced the music's connections to Puerto Rican experiences and stereotypes about urban places. Juan Flores argues that the Puerto Rican experience in New York complicates the development of a "pan-Latino" identity in the city since "the Puerto Rican component too readily equates with the stigmatized, abject implications of the label."[30] The "stigma" of Puerto Rican identity comes from the on-going colonial relationship between the island and the United States that has linked Puerto Ricans and African Americans in the popular imagination. Flores's comments relate to the ways that the urban functions within the Hurban category. That is, even if the Hispanic element of Hurban strives to link the music to a homogenous Latino audience, reggaetón's intimate connections to the Puerto Rican experience signaled in the *urban* half of the term ultimately distinguishes the Hurban from other constructions of Latinidad.[31]

As I have already demonstrated, in Puerto Rico, reggaetón was tied to urban communities often marked as black and working class. Consequently, part of reggaetón's association with blackness in the Puerto Rican context relates to its classification as *música urbana* (urban music), in which the category urban serves as a euphemism for blackness.[32] In the United States, the term *urban* carries similar racial and class connotations. As scholars such as Robin D. G. Kelley and Murray Forman have shown, social science research, media representations, political debates, and other processes produce discourses that mark urban neighborhoods as predominantly black spaces.[33] More specifically, Murray Forman argues, "When mobilized in particular contexts, then, the term 'inner-city' implicitly refers to racialized images or racially inflected conditions of danger, violence, and depravity that can be contrasted with the ideals of calm, safety, and security attributed to nonurban or suburban spaces."[34] In other words, just as the perceived contrast between urban *caseríos* and the rest of Puerto Rico disclose underlying racial divisions and stereotypes, so too do the comparisons between urban and suburban places in the United States.

In addition, like Puerto Rican constructions of urban blackness, certain racialized subjects are understood to embody the stereotypes of the inner-city United States. Discursive representations of urban residents perpetuate several stereotypes attributed to African American and Latino communities, including figures such as the welfare queen, drug addict, or gang member.[35] These representations also assume "one discrete identifiable black urban culture," which not only neglects the diversity of black cultural practices but also reiterates suppositions about the so-called pathological behaviors of urban residents.[36] One of the segments of the urban population that has been most stigmatized is youth.[37] Forman argues that "the confluence of youth, race, and class that occurs within inner-city or urban environments has been discursively constructed, from the outside, as a visible and troubling blight on American society. It has accordingly been nominated across numerous discursive fields as a profound threat to American core values."[38] Importantly, these depictions are also gendered as masculine since many stereotypes of urban dysfunction are tied to tropes of black and Latino "thug" masculinity assumed to be hypersexual, inherently violent, and unrefined. Therefore, race, gender, class, and place converge in the U.S. imagination to produce images of urban neighborhoods as not only sites of danger, crime, and dysfunction, but also the counterpoint to the mainstream values represented by the supposedly homogenous, white, middle-class, and suburban United States.

Given the narrow parameters of U.S. racial classifications, the blackness emplaced within U.S. urban centers is often understood to be African American. In this context, Puerto Ricans (and, more specifically, Nuyoricans) play a critical role in situating Latinos within understandings of the urban in the United States. As described in chapter 1, Puerto Ricans in New York became racialized as similar to African Americans due to their characteristics as residents of urban neighborhoods; however, Puerto Ricans were also considered racially and, to a certain extent, culturally (e.g., regarding language or food) differentiated from African Americans. In New York, representations of Puerto Ricans as people who shared not only residences, but also certain dysfunctional behaviors with African Americans abounded in literature and media.[39] More recently, arguments about the "Puerto Rican exception" made famous by neoconservatives such as Linda Chavez claimed that Puerto Ricans' similarities to African Americans, both culturally and as U.S. citizens who qualified for social service programs, prevented them from fully assimilating into the U.S. mainstream.[40] As Ramón Grosfoguel and Chloé Georas point out, the status of African Americans and Puerto Ricans as "colonial/racial subjects" ultimately produced images of the two groups as suffering from "poverty and marginalization . . . due to a cultural problem within the ethnic community rather than a structural problem of discrimination by Euroamerican dominant groups."[41] These representations of Puerto Ricans and African Americans relied on the assumption that they were ensnared in a "culture of poverty"[42] or a "tangle of pathology"[43] that perpetuated their supposedly pathological behavior, ignoring the histories of segregation and colonialism that created the conditions in which many urban Puerto Rican and African American communities lived. As a result, Puerto Ricans and African Americans experience comparable forms of racialization marked by racial and class stereotypes that, in turn, position them as outside of the mainstream.

If the term *urban* refers to specific racialized and classed communities, it is also exemplified by cultural practices such as hip-hop, which has been racialized as black within both the music industry and society at large.[44] This occurs despite hip-hop's emergence from cultural exchanges between African Americans, West Indians, and Puerto Ricans, among others. Of course, as the work of Raquel Z. Rivera and Juan Flores shows, the diasporic connections that led to hip-hop's beginnings have not necessarily translated to the seamless integration of Puerto Ricans into the African Americanized "hip-hop zone."[45] Rather, several Puerto Ricans involved in early hip-hop reported occasional conflicts with African Americans. In fact, it is the presumption that hip-hop is exclusively African American that exacerbates these contentions and leads to suspicions of Puerto Ricans' contributions to the genre.

However, Raquel Z. Rivera argues that the 1990s saw a shift in perceptions of hip-hop from a black thing to a black and Latino one.[46] Part of this shift stems from a recognition of urban ghettos as the authentic sites of hip-hop production. Because of Latinos', and more specifically Puerto Ricans', participation in hip-hop as well as their shared experiences with African Americans in urban areas, a presumed ghettocentricity, in which urban ghetto life serves as a primary marker of belonging in hip-hop culture, links Latinos and blacks.[47] As Raquel Z. Rivera writes,

> The blackness formerly restricted by the bounds of an ethno-racialized African Americanness began expanding to accommodate *certain* Latino groups as a population of ethno-racial Others whose experience of class and ethno-racial marginalization is in many ways virtually indistinguishable from the ghettocentric African American experience. Such Latinos could even be perceived as closer to their class-based blackness than so-called bourgie (bourgeois) blacks, particularly in the case of Caribbean Latinos such as Puerto Ricans, given the growing acknowledgment that they were also part of the African diaspora in the Americas.[48]

In the end, these moves combined identities related to race, place, and culture such that hip-hop came to represent a fundamentally black and Latino urban experience in the popular imagination.

Despite the recognition of Caribbean Latinos as African diasporic, however, distinctions between black and Latino hip-hop audiences remained even after the shift toward a black and Latino hip-hop took place. That is, although Puerto Ricans participated in the development of hip-hop as a diasporic cultural practice, they eventually became a proxy for the inclusion of Latinos in the hip-hop community *not* as African diasporic populations, but rather as part of a decidedly *nonblack* Latino group.[49] As members of the Latino group, then, Puerto Ricans and other Caribbean Latinos became the conduit through which all Latinos (despite their differences) could make claims to hip-hop while keeping intact conventional racial categories in the United States that distinguish between blackness and Latinidad.

The creation of the *Hurban* term follows the same logic that situates Latinos within the "hip-hop zone" yet continues to obscure any links between blackness and Latinidad. The Hispanic component of the Hurban aimed to distance a genre that *sounded* more like "African American" hip-hop than "Latin" music from blackness by foregrounding its Latin roots and audience. As Hispanic urban communities, then, Hurbans were identifiably Latino, but a very specific type of Latino, which presumably shared with African Americans all of the alleged pathologies and dysfunction inherent to dominant constructions of the urban in the United States.

"A Caribbean Party with a Hip-Hop Beat"

Media coverage about reggaetón's connections to hip-hop furthered the assumptions about urban space that tie Puerto Ricans and African Americans together in the popular imagination. Even before the rapid growth of Hurban radio, some U.S. newspapers reported about reggaetón in articles such as "A Caribbean Party with a Hip-Hop Beat" (Jon Pareles, *New York Times*, August 2003), "Raperos Rule: As Rap Recedes on the U.S. Mainland, Reggaeton Rises on the Enchanted Island" (*Miami New Times*, May 2002), and "Spicy Mix of Salsa, Hip-Hop, and Reggae" (*New York Times*, August 2003). Newspaper coverage of reggaetón increased with the growth of Hurban radio and attention from major record corporations, and magazines such as *Vibe*, *The Source*, and *Latina* published profiles of major artists. *The Source* even launched a new version, *The Source Latino*, featuring interviews and stories on reggaetoneros and Latino hip-hop artists in 2005; chief editor Melanie Byron described it as an "invitation" into "everything that represents our Hip Hop [sic], urban Latin [sic] culture" in her introduction to the inaugural issue. Television stations such as MTV and BET produced specials meant to introduce reggaetón to English-speaking audiences. Overall, coverage included depictions of reggaetón's origins, its identifiable musical characteristics, and key artists. At the same time, portrayals of reggaetón frequently compared the music to hip-hop, presenting reggaetón artists and fans as similar to African Americans, but still unambiguously Latino (and, hence, nonblack) via common, tropicalized stereotypes of Latinos.

U.S. newspaper, magazine, and television accounts of reggaetón did not explore its shared African diasporic roots with hip-hop (although they often discussed the musics' comparable beginnings in poor urban areas), and they rarely mentioned hip-hop's critical influence on reggaetón (save for when reggaetoneros named specific hip-hop artists in interviews). Rather, the U.S. media depicted reggaetón as a Spanish-language version of U.S. American hip-hop that contained some influences from Jamaican dancehall, as well. Many articles touched on the combination of dancehall and hip-hop in reggaetón, but often privileged the hip-hop connection; one New York Times article described reggaetón as "the hip-hop sung in Spanish and some English that is laced with Caribbean rhythms."[50] Downplaying the dancehall influence on reggaetón helped naturalize the Spanish language music. That is, since dancehall is often recognized as "foreign" music from the Caribbean (usually Jamaica), the emphasis on hip-hop, understood to be autochthonous to the United States, allowed reggaetón to be considered a U.S. "urban Latino" phenomenon. This, in turn, made reggaetón more easily linked to the stereotypes of urban spaces given that, as Ejima Baker notes, "urban Latinos" are often thought to be distinct from immigrants even though many immigrants live in urban areas.[51] Consequently, despite brief mentions of Jamaican dancehall or other English-language influences, reggaetón ultimately was understood as a slightly modified form of hip-hop performed in Spanish.[52]

Despite the pan-ethnicity implied in labeling reggaetón as "Latin" hip-hop, accounts of the music in the U.S. press also stressed its ties to Puerto Rico, evident in the MTV special My Block as well as newspaper and magazine coverage. The series My Block featured local hip-hop scenes throughout the United States in places such as Atlanta, Chicago, and the Bay Area. In each episode, MTV VJ Sway, who often hosted hip-hop programming, followed producers and artists from these areas to their hometowns to learn about their upbringings and local hip-hop traditions. In 2006, MTV screened *My Block: Puerto Rico*, during which Sway traveled the island to learn about reggaetón. Dedicating an entire episode of the *My Block* series to Puerto Rico both acknowledged the unique, local characteristics of reggaetón and the island more generally (as it does with all of the "blocks" Sway visits), and situated reggaetón squarely within the hip-hop realm.

Many newspaper articles followed suit, often publishing an originary narrative that established dancehall and hip-hop as reggaetón's forebears but also distinguishing reggaetón from these two traditions because of its presumed Puerto Ricanness. Journalists described reggaetón as a "music born in Puerto Rican barrios,"[53] that "has fanned out from Puerto Rico"[54] with Puerto Rican "performers"[55] and "original fans."[56] The depiction of reggaetón's Puerto Ricanness reiterated its status as a "Latino" phenomenon given the aforementioned distinctions between Latinidad and blackness in the United States; at the same time, the representation of reggaetón as fundamentally Puerto Rican has larger implications for reggaetón's racialization and the specific type of Latinidad signified by the term *Hurban*.

Most often, many U.S. newspapers employed stereotypical tropes pertaining to "urban" culture, and, especially, poor African American and Puerto Rican inner city communities, to connect hip-hop and reggaetón. An article about the growing popularity of reggaetón published in the *Miami New Times* in 2002 began, "Growing up in Puerto Rico's projects, or *caseríos*, may be no different than in any other hood on the U.S. mainland. Bullets, drugs, and a rap sheet are part of everyday life."[57] Here, the comparison of a U.S. "hood" and Puerto Rican *caseríos* reiterates dominant associations between urban space and violence. Another description of reggaetón published in the *New York Times* stated, "Like gangsta rap before it, [reggaetón] rose out of tough neighborhoods with boasts about sex and violence."[58] Again, the links between "sex and violence" and "tough neighborhoods" connote stereotypes of urban areas in the United States. More specifically, this language conjures up images of urban black and Latino masculinity embodied by a "thug" figure, who is hypersexual, violent, delinquent, and always tied to the street. In these accounts, stereotypes of urban communities and thug masculinity serve as authenticating markers of reggaetón.

The media's emphasis on the presumed violence and hypersexuality of reggaetón furthers this trend. An article published in the *New York Times* described reggaetón as sharing certain characteristics with hip-hop and dancehall, stating that "like them, [reggaetón] was often raunchy and uninhibited, full of macho exploits involving guns, drugs, and women."[59] The *Los Angeles Times* printed another account of reggaetón that also emphasized sexuality, partying, and violence:

> The signature rhythm of reggaeton is based on the beat of Jamaican dancehall music, but with more muscle. It has the go-go energy of a cheerleading chant, the menacing undercurrent of gangsta rap and the chug-a-lug ethos of a fraternity party. It also has its own dance, a sexually suggestive bump-and-grind indelicately called el *perreo*— roughly translated, the doggie dance.[60]

Likewise, in a review of a 2003 Reggaeton Summerfest concert at Madison Square Garden in New York City, the *New York Times*'s critic described,

> Reggaeton's rappers are tough guys and party people. When they're not boasting like gangsta rappers about their fearlessness and weaponry, they're offering details of how they'll be dancing, drinking and putting the moves on women. Every few songs the rappers chanted, 'Hasta abajo' (roughly, 'Get down') and did a crouching, hip-thrusting update of limbo dancing.[61]

All of these descriptions openly compare reggaetón to rap, and, more specifically, gangsta rap; however, the basis of these comparisons reveals key aspects of the racialization of reggaetón as a "Hurban" phenomenon that is "not quite black."

Curiously, these descriptions do not address the musical qualities that reggaetón shares with hip-hop. Instead, the focus on lyrical themes related to "guns, drugs, and violence" becomes the linchpin on which similarities between reggaetón and gangsta rap rest. Similar to the anxieties surrounding reggaetón in Puerto Rico in the mid-1990s and early 2000s, many critics in the United States have demonized gangsta rap, arguing that it promotes violence (especially gang-related), drugs, hatred toward authority (particularly police officers), and misogyny.[62] These criticisms have moved beyond the realm of mere rhetoric; for example, concern about the impact of gangsta rap on the moral fabric of the United States prompted Congressional hearings in 1994. Moreover, the association between hip-hop and the inner city made hip-hop the symbol par excellence of urban life, resulting in the incorporation of stereotypes of urban communities as socially dysfunctional and culturally deficient into broader characterizations of hip-hop culture.[63] Like the censorship campaigns against underground and reggaetón in Puerto Rico, the hearings about gangsta rap as well as stereotypes about hip-hop culture more generally represent inner-city residents involved in hip-hop, be they producers, musicians, or fans, as inherently violent, sexist, criminal, and deviant.

Not only assumptions about the inner city but also blackness inform stereotypes about hip-hop. The anxieties around gangsta rap that motivated the Congressional hearings concerned the perceived threat of blackness, and young black men in particular, to mainstream society. The stereotype of rap music as primarily concerned with "guns, drugs, and women" forms part of a larger process of racialization that constructs blackness as deviant, and therefore as the inferior and primitive counterpoint to whiteness.[64] The descriptions of rap, and specifically gangsta rap, in much of the U.S media coverage of reggaetón thus reiterated these stereotypes with references to "fearlessness and weaponry," "macho exploits," and "menacing undercurrent[s]."

The stereotypical assumptions about blackness and Latinidad central to the comparisons between hip-hop and reggaetón ignore the socioeconomic realities and conditions of the inner city that impact the lives of hip-hop and reggaetón artists, fans, and urban residents. This is not surprising considering the historical representations of Puerto Ricans and African Americans as enmeshed in various cultural pathologies. In these discussions, reggaetón serves as a metonym for Hurbans, who are defined primarily through the Puerto Rican experience, and carries with it many of the same purportedly dysfunctional behaviors as rap. As a result, such depictions of reggaetón mark it—and, by extension, its Hurban fans and producers—as members of racialized urban communities motivated by alleged cultural deficiencies, ignoring larger social and structural inequalities that impact them.

At the same time, emphasizing that reggaetón is *like* gangsta rap means that it is *not* gangsta rap, thus signaling a difference between rap and reggaetón rooted in the perceived separation between blackness and Latinidad. Representations of reggaetón artists as tropicalized people emphasize these distinctions. Stereotypes of Latinos as "hot" and "spicy" hypersexual people who love to party and entertain have permeated U.S. popular culture for decades, embodied by artists who achieved crossover success such as Carmen Miranda, Desi Arnaz, Ricky Martin, and Shakira. Depictions of reggaetón in U.S. newspapers often employed similar tropes. Portrayals of reggaetoneros as party people who dance, drink, and "put the moves on women," or the comparisons of the music to a fraternity party, frame reggaetón artists within broader discourses that paint Latinos as hypersexual and fun-loving.[65] In addition, the emphasis on reggaetón artists' pursuit of women not only presents reggaetón as a masculine space (which it often is), but also connotes stereotypes of the Latin lover that depict Latino men as dangerous yet desirable sexual partners. The description of *perreo* as a "crouching, hip-thrusting update of limbo dancing" presents the clearest example of a tropicalized depiction of Latinidad that has been linked to reggaetón. The limbo is a Caribbean dance often included in Caribbean and tropical themed parties and resorts. Although the limbo involves movement of the hips, stylistically it shares little with *perreo*. The comparison of reggaetón with the limbo locates reggaetón within a tropicalized space in which Caribbean and Latin American culture is associated with sexual freedom and exotic "others." Most importantly in the U.S. context, representing reggaetón through tropicalized stereotypes of Latinidad problematically locates the music as an essentialized Latino phenomenon, ignoring, among other things, the diasporic routes that created it.

Taken together with the frequent discussion of reggaetón's similarities to gangsta rap, this representation of reggaetón as Latino ultimately reinforces dominant distinctions between blackness and Latinidad. On the one hand, the oft-cited commonalities between gangsta rap and reggaetón rehearse old stereotypes that connect violence to inner-city and minority communities. If gangsta rap—and hip-hop culture more generally—is usually imagined as an African American space, then reggaetón's framing within a tropicalized Latinidad forecloses its incorporation into blackness despite acknowledging their shared characteristics. In this vein, reggaetón and rap serve as racial code words that represent Latinidad (and, more specifically, a Latinidad marked by an urban Puerto Rican experience) and blackness, respectively. Similar depictions of reggaetón artists in the press also fortify these distinctions between blackness and Latinidad.

Daddy Yankee Is to Hurban as N.O.R.E. Is to Blackness

In addition to the media coverage regarding reggaetón, certain reggaetón artists received much media attention, particularly those artists credited with introducing English-language audiences to reggaetón. For example,

Daddy Yankee's success with "Gasolina" and potential crossover appeal sparked tremendous interest in his biography, and he was featured in publications from *Vibe Magazine* to *The New York Times Magazine*. In general, these profiles stressed his ties to the street and experiences with violence. Daddy Yankee frequently recalls his upbringing in the *caserío* Villa Kennedy in interviews, and articles often mention his beginnings in "San Juan projects,"[66] thus representing Daddy Yankee as an urban subject. It is not just any urban environment in which Yankee found himself, however, but also a particularly violent one, illustrated by the repeated story of Yankee being shot in the leg one night because of a mistaken identity.[67] It took one year to recover, and the bullet remains lodged in Daddy Yankee's thigh, causing him to walk with a permanent limp. Yankee describes the incident as a wakeup call that motivated him to pursue opportunities outside of the streets, stating in one interview, "I thank God because of that . . . if that didn't happen, I would be dead or in jail right now."[68] The frequent depiction of the shooting positions Daddy Yankee as a stereotypical thug located in an inner city understood to be a center of violence and danger, evident when one reporter described what happened after the incident as Yankee's "escape from thug life."[69] This move from a former thug to a reggaetonero—a story that Daddy Yankee also portrayed as the fictional character Edgar Dinero, a drug dealer turned reggaetón star, in his 2008 film *Talento del Barrio*—brings to mind images of young, so-called gang-banger men terrorizing urban areas that would be familiar to U.S. readers given the aforementioned stereotypes of inner cities pervasive in the United States. My point is not to discount the very real consequences of violence in urban Puerto Rico, particularly during the time that Yankee grew up. Rather, it is important to note that Daddy Yankee's experiences with violence became a critical aspect of his characterization as urban.

The frequent discussion of the violence Yankee experienced as opposed to the cursory mentions of other aspects of his life, such as his associate's degree in accounting, indicates the overdetermination of the urban in representations of both Daddy Yankee and reggaetón. Certainly, reggaetón artists often emphasize street life as proof of their authenticity in the genre.[70] Yankee contributes to this trend, positioning himself as a representative of *caserío* residents and describing reggaetón as, above all else, "a real urban movement that speaks for Latinos."[71] Reggaetoneros' representations of *caseríos* and other urban areas emphasize the "possibility of redemption" that acknowledges issues such as crime and poverty in their communities, but also expresses hope for change.[72] However, the U.S. media's focus on violence as an identifying marker of the urban blatantly ignores any discussion of the racist and classist policies that have produced violence in the Puerto Rican *caserío* or the U.S. inner city. Instead, these descriptions connect San Juan's *caseríos* to U.S. urban centers by foregrounding problematic stereotypes of urban spaces as sites of dysfunction, chaos, and danger.

At the same time, the accounts of Daddy Yankee's upbringing in San Juan contribute to the emphasis on his Latino identity. Although Daddy Yankee still lives in San Juan, stories of his travels to New York City and efforts to learn English to conduct business deals[73] connote common images of Latinos as immigrants (even if, as a Puerto Rican, Yankee is a U.S. citizen), perpetuating assumptions that *all* Latinos are new arrivals. In addition, Daddy Yankee embodies the whitened, racially mixed phenotype often associated with Latinidad. Daddy Yankee has been described as a "whiter" reggaetón artist, with the olive-toned skin color and wavy dark hair associated with stereotypical depictions of Latinidad; as Félix Jiménez notes, it is not surprising that "the internationalization of reggaeton was spearheaded by a white, lower-class, handsome Puerto Rican male—Daddy Yankee."[74] Even if Daddy Yankee acknowledges his own connections to blackness via his father, the U.S. press presents him as nonblack. Indeed, one might interpret Daddy Yankee's embrace of his blackness as a celebration of mestizaje, reiterating the representation of Puerto Ricans as racially mixed. Yankee's Puerto Ricanness and stereotypical Latin look allow him to be depicted as exclusively Latino within the U.S. racial context. Consequently, Daddy Yankee has become the ultimate Hurban—someone portrayed as distinctly Latino, yet also assumed to have shared an urban experience marked by stereotypical tropes of violence and thug life.

The other artist often credited with the breakout of reggaetón to the mainstream is Victor Santiago, better known as N.O.R.E., an English-language rapper who also released a reggaetón hit in 2004. Santiago grew up in Queens, New York, and began his professional rap career after meeting his partner, Kiam "Capone" Holloway, in prison. The duo released their first album in 1996. That N.O.R.E. began his career with someone he met in prison (and the attention he has received because of his subsequent run-ins with the law) is important because this narrative functions similarly to the stories of Yankee's experiences with violence, situating N.O.R.E.

FIGURE 5.1. Daddy Yankee in August 2005. *Credit:* AP Photo/Jim Cooper

FIGURE 5.2. N.O.R.E. performs at the Megaton 2004 concert in New York's Madison Square Garden in October 2004. *Credit:* AP Photo/Jennifer Szymaszek

within stereotypes of urban, thug masculinity. Following a successful rap career both with Capone and as a solo artist, N.O.R.E. released a bilingual reggaetón song, "Oye Mi Canto," in 2004, featuring reggaetón artists Daddy Yankee, Gem Star, and Big Mato as well as Latina English-language artists Nina Sky on the hook. "Oye Mi Canto" was a party song and pan-Latino anthem. The music video featured bikini-clad women representing different countries in Latin America while lounging on the shore, and later, at a beach party, as the artists extolled their pan-Latino identity. Importantly, the celebration of pan-Latinidad neglected connections between reggaetón (or Latinidad in general) and blackness, such as when N.O.R.E. raps, "no matter your race because you know you're Latino."[75] In an interview with MTV, N.O.R.E. asserted that one of his motivations for exploring reggaetón was his background, stating "Reggaeton is in my blood like hip-hop is in my blood because I am half Latino-American . . . so being both Latin and black, I wanted to rep my Latin side for once."[76] Here, N.O.R.E. distinguishes hip-hop and reggaetón along racial lines since it was presumably his experiences as a rapper that allowed him to experience blackness while reggaetón exclusively "reps [his] Latin side." This logic ignores both reggaetón's ties to blackness and Puerto Ricans' involvement in hip-hop.

The division between blackness and Latinidad continues in accounts of N.O.R.E.'s biography as a New Yorker born of a Puerto Rican father and a black mother. Ejima Baker describes the ways that blackness and Latinidad are presented as fundamentally distinct in the story of N.O.R.E.'s upbringing presented on BET's *Move Your Body: A Reggaeton Special*:

> The emcee N.O.R.E., whose real name is Victor Santiago, has an African American or Jamaican mother (there are conflicting narratives regarding his mother's ethnicity) and a Puerto Rican father, whose race is never discussed. It is simply assumed that his mother is Black and his Puerto Rican father is not; but how do we know that his Puerto Rican parent is not racially Black? And, to further problematize the issue, if his mother is indeed Jamaican, then why is she so often stripped of her ethnic identity and spoken of only as Black while his father's ethnicity is repeatedly emphasized?[77]

Baker's questions shed light on the ways that the complexity underlying N.O.R.E.'s racial and ethnic background becomes eclipsed through a narrative that definitively separates his blackness from his Latinidad. As Baker makes clear, this distinction links blackness in the U.S. exclusively to African Americans, obscuring the contributions and presence of other ethnic groups of African descent (Caribbean, African, Afro-Latino, and other populations).[78] Following this logic, whether or not N.O.R.E.'s mother is Jamaican does not matter since her presumed blackness supersedes any other identity. On the other hand, the race of N.O.R.E.'s father remains inconsequential because his Puerto Ricanness is subsumed under an overarching Latinidad that collapses racial and ethnic distinctions. In the end, the depiction of N.O.R.E.'s racial and ethnic background forecloses the possibility of describing him as an Afro-Latino by keeping intact the rigid distinctions between blackness and Latinidad found in the dominant systems of racial classification in the United States.

Unlike Hurbans who supposedly have a natural affinity for reggaetón, N.O.R.E. remains firmly positioned within the hip-hop sphere as a rapper who made a brief foray into reggaetón (emphasized in the frequent acknowledgments that N.O.R.E. encountered some difficulty releasing his hip-hop-reggaetón album, *N.O.R.E. Y La Familia ... Ya Tú Sabes* [2006], which did not sell as well as his previous rap albums). N.O.R.E.'s blackness, history as a rapper, and English-language music identify him as African American, even if his Puerto Rican ancestry legitimates his attempt at reggaetón. If Daddy Yankee is portrayed as a Hurban who has similarities with African Americans, then N.O.R.E. is considered black (if not exclusively African American) with similarities to urban Latinos who are imagined as racially distinct from him, despite the fact that N.O.R.E. could embrace an urban Latino identity given his upbringing in Queens and Puerto Rican background.

Media representations thus associate Daddy Yankee and N.O.R.E. with urban subjects, but situate them as either Latino or black (despite their shared ties to both identities) based on rigid assumptions about who makes and listens to hip-hop and reggaetón, respectively. What unites them as urban, however, is the popular association of urban places with black and Latino populations, particularly youth, as well as problematic stereotypes related to violence, sexuality, and a host of other issues. Although the depictions of these artists (and reggaetón more generally) appear to impede diasporic connections, other artists have taken advantage of reggaetón as a space to present a distinctly Afro-Latino identity in ways that break with these distinctions.

While media coverage of reggaetón replicates the dominant separation of blackness and Latinidad, some artists and fans express an alternative view of reggaetón as a space that emphasizes the links between blackness and Latinidad. Brief mentions in the newspaper coverage of reggaetón about African American fans of the music demonstrate these connections.[79] Likewise, musical collaborations between hip-hop artists and reggaetoneros, such as Wisin y Yandel with 50 Cent, Fabolous with Don Omar, and Luny Tunes' productions for several artists, flourished in the mid-2000s, showcasing not only reggaetón's crossover appeal, but also the types of connections that could be forged across hip-hop and reggaetón. One artist in particular, Notch, used reggaetón as a springboard to create a musical fusion that spoke to the shared experiences of African diasporic populations in the United States.

Born Norman Howell in Hartford, Connecticut, Notch describes himself as "a man without a country, but citizen of the world" whose father comes from a Jamaican family that initially immigrated to Cuba before arriving in the United States, and whose mother is both Puerto Rican and African American.[80] He began his career with the duo Born Jamericans in the early 1990s, infusing hip-hop and R&B influences with Jamaican dancehall. After the group disbanded, Notch achieved some success as a solo dancehall artist. In 2002, Notch moved to reggaetón, recording the hit "Hay Que Bueno" originally as a Spanish-language dancehall song remixed into a reggaetón version by Puerto Rico's DJ Blass. Afterward, Notch collaborated with several reggaetón artists, including Julio Voltio and Daddy Yankee, and eventually released his first solo album, *Raised by the People*, in 2007 on his own Cinco por Cinco label in conjunction with Machete Music. The album included previously released singles such as "Hay Que Bueno" and "Verme," a bilingual duet with reggaetón artist Baby Ranks included on Luny Tunes' *Más Flow 2* compilation, as well as the popular hit "Dale Pa' Tra (Back It Up)," which reached number eighteen on the *Billboard* Latin Rhythm Chart and was one of the most requested songs on New York radio in the spring of 2007.[81] Propelled by these singles, *Raised by the People* debuted at number twelve on *Billboard*'s Latin Rhythm Album Chart.

Raised by the People was not the typical reggaetón album. Including dancehall, reggaetón, merengue, roots reggae, and R&B fusions, the album was described as a "photo gallery of [Notch's] musical roots."[82] Likewise,

Notch described his goals for the album when he explained, "Musically, I am trying to connect the people of the African Diaspora who have been colonized by different languages."[83] For Notch, his Caribbean fusions speak not only to musical similarities between different groups, but also broader sociocultural connections between Latino and black populations. For example, when discussing his childhood in Hartford, Connecticut, home to large Puerto Rican and Jamaican populations, Notch emphasized the similarities between the two groups:

> I grew up in Hartford, Connecticut. There's not much of anything but Puerto Ricans and Black Americans. Everybody looking [sic] at themselves differently, but I've seen the similarities and have been able to use melodies to express the similarities and try to break down some of the barriers that people try to create for themselves when they limit themselves as just Puerto Rican, or Jamaican, or Black or whatever.[84]

Here, Notch makes clear that a critical aim of his music is to erase the strict boundaries between blackness and Latinidad that form part of the racial paradigm in the United States.

For Notch, the African diaspora serves as the unifying element that brings together Puerto Ricans, African Americans, and Jamaicans (among others). In another interview, Notch argued that musical similarities serve as evidence of these African diasporic connections:

> Growin' up I saw Puerto Ricans and blacks fighting... I refuse to stand around and watch that. Reggae, reggaeton, bachata—I've learned that there's always an African predecessor to it and they just givin' it different names. In San Juan [Puerto Rico], I went to a club where they had live drummers playing the bomba and plena over reggaeton, and I realized the reason why PR has taken to that particular dancehall sound from the [19]90's is because the frequency of the timbales is so similar to the pocomania drums Steely and Cleevie used.[85] I get it now. It's basically the same people; we're just separated by water.[86]

Importantly, a shared "African predecessor" marries Puerto Rican musical traditions with other practices from elsewhere in the African diaspora, in this case Jamaica. Moreover, Notch extends his observations to the people themselves, whom he identifies as the "same" despite living in different countries.

In addition to his musical fusions, Notch's use of Spatoinglish, a combination of Spanish, English, and Jamaican patois, also foregrounds African diasporic connections between Latinos, African Americans, and Caribbean people in the United States. Notch considers Spatoinglish to reflect the long histories of migration and collaboration between Caribbean communities:

> I think the best way to explain it is it's a dialect similar to speaking in Spanglish. First generation Spanish folks move here, they have kids, and carry the language with them over to America and they take on the native language. A lot of Jamaicans when they migrated to Cuba for work or Panama or Costa Rica, they took their patois with them but they spoke Spanish, and when they went back to speaking English, they spoke the broken dialect of like a patois. So it's nothing that I created, it's just something that's probably been on the low.[87]

In this vein, Spatoinglish constitutes a linguistic tradition that emerged from Jamaican migration to Latin America, and the cultural exchanges between Caribbean communities that produced new African diasporic traditions. The use of Spatoinglish in his own lyrics thus furthers Notch's project of dismantling hegemonic divisions between blackness and Latinidad.

It is critical to note that these fusions take place in the United States, especially because the distinctions that Notch aims to dissolve are based on U.S. racial categories. The album packaging of *Raised by the People* illuminates the importance of the United States, and New York City in particular, as the site where these African diasporic cultural fusions come together. The booklet accompanying the CD frequently pictures Notch in prototypical Caribbean spaces, near New York City landmarks, and sometimes in front of backgrounds that bring together both sites. In one photo, Notch sits at a *cafetería* sipping a *cafecito* and wearing a *guayabera*; although the photograph does not identify a specific geographic site, the cultural markers place him in a Caribbean place, and more specifically, a Spanish Caribbean site (evident in the advertisements for *batidos* and *jugos* painted on the *cafetería*). In another photograph, Notch leans against the wall of the Jamaica, Queens, subway stop on the New York City J and M lines. The tiling on the walls and the J and M markers in the characteristic circles of the New York City Metro make the location recognizable to anyone familiar with the city's subway system. That the stop where he waits is Jamaica is no accident, since not only

FIGURE 5.3. Album art from Notch's 2007 album, *Raised by the People*.
Note the way that the Caribbean landscape blends into the New York City skyline
and Brooklyn Bridge.

is Jamaica one of the countries whose music most influences Notch, but the
Jamaica neighborhood in Queens is home to a large West Indian population.

In addition to photos that situate Notch in either New York or the Caribbean, two pictures explicitly locate him in both sites simultaneously. In one,
Notch stands on a beach. Behind the water, one sees a distant tree line that
morphs into the New York City skyline with the Empire State Building tow-
ering prominently above. On the beach itself, a palm tree transforms into a
traffic sign directing drivers to New York. The second photograph features
Notch standing in front of two houses built in a traditional Caribbean style
surrounded by palm trees. Above the houses looms the Brooklyn Bridge
leading into downtown Manhattan. These photographs meld New York
City and the Caribbean together, a nod not only to Notch's background as
someone of Caribbean descent who grew up in the United States, but also
identifying New York City as the site where Caribbean communities come
together and where these African diasporic collaborations take place.

There are certain limitations to Notch's music. Like other reggaetón or dancehall artists, his music sometimes reinforces problematic gender representations. Notch's music and videos often portray women as hyper-sexual, and depict heterosexual men as the primary actors in the African diasporic community he builds.[88] Furthermore, for some fans, Spatoing-lish is unintelligible, and confusion over whether or not Notch is black or Latino expressed on Internet forums reveals the entrenched nature of the racial divisions Notch seeks to eliminate.[89]

Nevertheless, Notch's use of reggaetón as a platform for blurring the lines between blackness and Latinidad is significant. With the emphasis on the African diaspora as the link between Latino, West Indian, and African American communities in the United States, Notch demonstrates the pos-sibilities that reggaetón offers as an expression of an Afro-Latino identity that moves beyond the rigid distinctions between blackness and Latinidad. For Notch, blackness and Latinidad serve as important and malleable signi-fiers that expand and combine in different ways to be more inclusive of vari-ous experiences and subjectivities.[90] In this sense, the Afro-Latino identity that Notch endorses is more than just a combination of black and Latino. Instead, his definition of Afro-Latinidad foregrounds African diasporic connections that defy strict boundaries of here/there and us/them found in dominant and limiting definitions of blackness and Latinidad. Much the same way that Tego Calderón employs diaspora in his reconfiguration of Loíza (see chapter 3), the diasporic aspect of Notch's Afro-Latinidad calls attention to entrenched colonialism and racism that impact various groups of people, and situates reggaetón and its audiences within a larger African diaspora. Thus, Notch shows that while distinctions between Hurbans and African Americans in the U.S. media furthered divisions between black-ness and Latinidad, some reggaetón artists and fans also found opportuni-ties to disrupt these seemingly inflexible racial categories with expressions of a U.S. Afro-Latinidad rooted in U.S. experiences and African diasporic politics.

HIP-HOP HAS ALWAYS been a key ingredient of reggaetón. Not only do the two genres share important musical qualities, but they are also cultural practices of diaspora that developed out of cross-cultural exchanges be-tween different groups in the African diaspora in the Americas. And yet, despite their similar social moorings, once reggaetón became popular in the United States, the media presented it as distinct from hip-hop, save for the problematic stereotypes about inner-city communities that the two genres supposedly shared. Hip-hop and reggaetón served as racial code words that referenced blackness and Latinidad, respectively—two racial categories not only distinct from one another, but also from whiteness and the so-called mainstream.

Three critical points related to the social construction of U.S. Latinidad emerge in the story of reggaetón's racialization. First, like all socially constructed categories, Latinidad can be developed and interpreted in different ways depending on various factors, including country of origin, racial background, region of the United States where a given group lives, divergent histories of incorporation, and other issues. Consequently, the racialization of reggaetón as "not quite black" in the United States must be considered in relation to the larger processes of racializing Puerto Ricans (especially those in New York City) as similar to African Americans based on problematic stereotypes. Second, while constructions of Latinidad vary across time and place, the general tendency to consider all Latinidades as divorced from blackness remains. This holds even though many Latino groups are also part of the broader African diaspora. Finally, the dominant construction of Latinidad homogenizes the diversity of Latino experiences. Although the racialization of reggaetón in the United States must be understood in relation to the unique positionings of both Puerto Ricans and Afro-Latinos, its representation as a general Latino phenomenon followed larger moves to market reggaetón to an undifferentiated pan-Latino audience.

It is no mistake that the identification of a Hurban audience emerged with reggaetón. Despite previous music audiences that could have been defined as Hurban, reggaetón's relationship with hip-hop, a practice commonly identified with blackness, prompted the creation of a Hispanic urban category that was both fundamentally Latino and referenced an urban experience marked by specific stereotypes related to inner-city life. In the end, the creation of a Hurban category distanced reggaetón's connections to blackness while simultaneously providing record companies and other media industries access to "new" markets and potential profits.

Despite the insistence on dividing blackness and Latinidad, Afro-Latino communities in the United States have a rich history, documented in the myriad novels, songs, poems, essays, and other works describing their experiences straddling blackness and Latinidad. Reggaetón artists such as Notch continue this tradition, using reggaetón as a platform to promote a distinct Afro-Latino identity. Likewise, the frequent collaborations be-tween hip-hop artists and reggaetoneros not only serve as attempts to reach new markets (although they certainly do that) but also must be understood in relation to the larger history of reggaetón-hip-hop connections and the African diasporic exchanges that produced these musical genres in the first place.

In the end, although record companies, radio conglomerates, and the U.S. press promoted reggaetón as an exclusively Latino phenomenon, the music still functions as a space to articulate connections between black and La-tino identities in the United States. These links are not always guaranteed; indeed, it is important to remember that Puerto Ricans and African Ameri-cans have had conflicts, and reggaetón was not immediately embraced by everyone in the hip-hop community.[91] Still, it is critical to examine those in-stances when reggaetón operates as a space for the articulation of U.S. Afro-Latino identities. In this sense, the Hurban category created to identify the supposedly new markets associated with reggaetón might hold an alterna-tive meaning, one that sheds light on the experiences and histories of urban Latino communities in the United States. Intrinsic to these histories are not only the important collaborations between Latino and African American populations, but also the experiences of Afro-Latinos in the United States. As the steady beat that underlies all things Hurban, reggaetón is an impor-tant site for disrupting the boundaries between blackness and Latinidad that have become so entrenched in the United States. The consequences of this project are critical, for they address the realities of communities that are either stereotyped in ways that sustain white privilege in the United States, or neglected altogether. Though imperfect, reggaetón continues to serve as a cultural practice of diaspora in the United States, providing op-portunities to engage with Afro-Latino realities that break the hegemonic distinctions between blackness and Latinidad.

CONCLUSION
REGGAETÓN'S LIMITS, POSSIBILITIES, AND FUTURES

In August 2010, Don Omar released a music video of his new single, "Danza Kuduro," featuring France-based Portuguese artist, Lucenzo, on the Internet platform YouTube for U.S. and Latin America. The song immediately gained tremendous popularity, with 250,000 YouTube hits the first day (Lucenzo official website). "Danza Kuduro" became a hit of the summer, reaching number one on several *Billboard* music charts including Latin Pop Songs, Tropical Songs, and Latin Rhythm songs. Internationally, it charted in places like Argentina, Colombia, Venezuela, Israel, Spain, France, and Sweden. For their efforts, Don Omar and Lucenzo received nominations for several prestigious awards, including Latin Grammys and Latin Billboard awards, winning Billboard awards for Song of the Year and Digital Song of the Year. The music video continues to have millions of hits on YouTube and is widely recognized as one of the Latin music videos most viewed on the website.

"Danza Kuduro" is one of Don Omar's top reggaetón hits. Like colleagues Ivy Queen, Daddy Yankee, and Tego Calderón, Don Omar has had a long career that began with the release of his first studio album, *The Last Don* in 2003. Born William Omar Landrón Rivera, Don Omar grew up in the Villa Palmeras neighborhood in San Juan. As a teenager, he left home to join the Protestant church as a youth pastor for several years before dedicating himself to reggaetón. *The Last Don* sold more than one million copies and inspired the production of a live version, *Last Don Live*. Don Omar has since released several albums, achieved multiple number one hits, pursued acting in films such as *Fast and Furious*, started his own record label, the Orfanato Music Group, in 2007 (the label released the album *Don Omar Presents: Meet the Orphans* on which "Danza Kuduro" appeared), and has established himself as a notable Internet presence in the world of reggaetón.

While many of Don Omar's hits (including the first single from *Meet the Orphans*, "Hasta Abajo") sound like traditional reggaetón, "Danza Kuduro" does not. For example, there is no recognizable dembow beat. A reviewer from the *Washington Post* called the song a "sunny, up-tempo, utterly winning variation on Latin dance pop."[1] In many respects, this description of "Danza Kuduro" mirrors some of the larger trends in reggaetón. Many reggaetón artists have incorporated dance, house, and pop music into their songs, departing from what some fans consider more authentic reggaetón. Some critics accuse these performers of selling out and creating commercialized pop distinct from the allegedly more politicized nature of its underground forebear.

On one hand, the classification of reggaetón as Hurban in the United States exemplifies the assumption that the Latinization of reggaetón has disconnected it from potential African diasporic politics; on the other, artists such as Notch or Tego Calderón counter this presumption by foregrounding African diasporic connections in their music and performance. In many ways, "Danza Kuduro" represents both of these positions. The song's vast popularity reflects the globalization of popular music from the African diaspora, including some problematic aspects of this process. However, "Danza Kuduro" also illustrates the African diasporic affiliations within reggaetón. For all of its pop aesthetics (with "pop" often signifying mainstream whiteness), embedded within "Danza Kuduro" exists a story of diasporic connections based not only on transnational histories of migration, but also comparable experiences of displacement and racial discrimination across geographic sites.

Don Omar's "Danza Kuduro" was actually a remake of a Portuguese-language song recorded by his partner Lucenzo, "Vem Dançar Kuduro" [Come Dance Kuduro] in 2010. Born Luis Filipe Oliveira, Lucenzo, a Portuguese immigrant to France, had previously achieved success with the reggaetón hit, "Emigrante del Mundo" (Emigrant of the world) in 2008, a celebration of immigrants from Latin America (Brazil, Colombia, Venezuela, and Argentina) and Europe (Portugal, Spain, and Italy) sung predominantly in French. While reggaetón is one of Lucenzo's major influences, a second important musical ingredient in Lucenzo's repertoire is kuduro, an Angolan form of popular music.

Angolan kuduro does not sound like "Danza Kuduro." Instead, artists rap over sparse beats developed through intricate blends of cell phone ringtones.[2] The music speaks to communities of young Angolans displaced by wars and who currently face unemployment, limited access to education, and other issues that stem from urban poverty.[3] This displacement is evident in the "abrasive, grating, repetitive, and invasive metallizing beats," as well as the dance moves that incorporate a "specific celebration of the broken body" both figuratively and literally, because of the number of amputees who lost limbs in violence and who helped devise these dances.[4] The songs address struggles in poor, urban communities in Angola but also provide outlets for fun and to honor the resilience of these communities. As Marissa Moorman contends, Angolan popular music, such as kuduro, "is not immune to the difficult economic and social conditions, but by presenting them in new and different terms, music allows people to engage those conditions critically and mockingly and to celebrate their own survival."[5] Both kuduro and reggaetón thus speak to the larger racist and colonial practices that impact the lives of youth in Angola and Puerto Rico.

The influx of Angolan immigrants to Portugal brought with them their musical traditions, including kuduro, which has become popular in the suburbs and neighborhoods of Lisbon where many African immigrants live. According to Frank Nilton Marcon, kuduro grew popular among not only youth of Angolan descent, but also those of African descent more generally who encountered racial discrimination as black subjects in Portugal.[6] African people in Portugal are often viewed as perpetual foreigners within the country regardless of their citizenship status.[7] Moreover, these communities also face antiblack racism, in part due to Portugal's embrace of European modernity as a cornerstone of its national identity, especially since joining the European Union.[8] In this context, kuduro works as a space to bring together people who share similar experiences of racial discrimination and disenfranchisement; indeed, kuduro and other African diasporic musical practices in Portugal provide opportunities to develop an "African imaginary" that reflects both individuals' musical tastes and their comparable experiences as racialized subjects in Portugal, in the process establishing diasporic connections across different communities of African descent.[9] While the specific contexts surrounding kuduro and reggaetón are different, they function similarly as diasporic cultural practices that do not always explicitly address racism in their lyrics yet still provide spaces to bring together different people who face similar forms of racial exclusion.

Portuguese youth have also started producing their own styles of kuduro, and some mix kuduro with various genres of dance and electronic music. One of the groups that has received the most attention for "legitimating recognition" of kuduro is Buraka Som Sistema, a group of Lisbon-based musicians who combine kuduro with other types of music.[10] Buraka Som Sistema even performed at the indie music festival Coachella held in Indio, California, in 2009, and collaborated with internationally renowned U.K.-based artist M.I.A. As Jayna Brown notes, the types of kuduro produced in Lisbon by groups like Buraka Som Sistema differs significantly from the sounds of Angolan kuduro, in part due to the availability of new technologies and the various musical mash-ups that arise from access to other musical genres in Portugal.[11]

While Buraka Som Sistema's music may contain more flashy productions than many kuduro artists coming out of Angola, Lucenzo's "Vem Dançar Kuduro" departs even further from the intensely percussive and minimal sounds of Angolan kuduro. Certainly, the song features a rapid, percussive beat; however, it also foregrounds a synthesizer riff that mimics an accordion. Big Ali, a Paris-based hip-hop DJ originally from Queens, New York, acts as a "hype man," shouting phrases throughout the song in English and Spanish directing listeners to do certain dance moves and get "up" for Lucenzo. Importantly, Lucenzo sings rather than raps the song as one might do in more typical kuduro performance.

Lucenzo's kuduro can be interpreted as a whitened version of kuduro, similar to the ways in which contemporary reggaetón has also been thought of as whitened and removed from its original roots. This extends beyond the musical aesthetics of "Vem Dançar Kuduro" to his positionality as a white Portuguese man. Indeed, given Portugal's history as a colonizer of Angola (along with other sites of the African diaspora), Lucenzo's adaptation of kuduro might be seen as a problematic form of appropriation. As some scholars have argued regarding the world music scene, the appropriation of non-Western musical practices by Americans and Europeans not only tends to reinforce stereotypes of blackness as primitive and rhythmic but also reinscribes colonial relations in which European and American artists might use popular music from elsewhere without providing financial compensation to the original artists.[12] Moreover, Lucenzo's location in France offers him access to record companies and more advanced technologies to disseminate his music (and, thus, to accumulate more profits) that many Angolan artists may not have, further demonstrating the inequalities between the two places and their citizens. Therefore, the use of kuduro as a signifier for a song that sounds and looks very different from original Angolan kuduro may be understood as yet another example of the problematic appropriation of black popular culture.

Still, even in the case of "Vem Dançar Kuduro," the multiple circuits in which kuduro travels and the ways in which different communities in disparate locations have adapted the music to address their own experiences speaks to how it operates as a cultural practice of diaspora. Indeed, while he may borrow much of his style from popular African diasporic musical practices, Lucenzo himself is also framed within a larger Portuguese diaspora. Emigration from Portugal is a critical aspect of the country's history, which Lucenzo addressed with the title of his album *Emigrante del Mundo* (Emigrant of the World). In Western Europe, Portuguese emigrants have not always been wholly accepted within either their host communities or back in Portugal.[13] At the same time, studies of Portuguese immigrants in France, where Lucenzo's family settled, demonstrate that subsequent generations of Portuguese have fared better than immigrants from Africa, the Caribbean, or the Middle East, especially after Portugal joined the European Union.[14] In this context, one might surmise that Lucenzo did not face the same level of racism and exclusion as many African immigrants to France (and Portugal) do. Nevertheless, Lucenzo's own diasporic framing as an immigrant from Portugal is significant since many members of the Portuguese diaspora experience similar issues of displacement as other diasporic groups, even if it may not be affected by the same issues as the African diaspora. These larger questions of displacement provide fodder for the development of diasporic connections, even though "Vem Dançar Kuduro" also must be understood in relation to the long histories of colonization and unequal power relations between Angola and Portugal.

This rather long background of "Vem Dançar Kuduro" is important for understanding the diasporic aspects of Don Omar's "Danza Kuduro," demonstrating how the song draws from cultural practices that emerged out of similar circumstances of racial and class discrimination in the various geographic contexts where these musical practices developed. "Danza Kuduro" therefore represents another way in which reggaetón continues to participate in dialogues with other African diasporic traditions, incorporating musical aesthetics from genres that, like reggaetón, have also functioned as spaces of identification for communities facing racial exclusion. Although Don Omar's music may not always be overtly "political," he has crafted a persona that involves a critique of Puerto Rican racial and economic inequalities by situating himself in relation to poor, urban Puerto Rican communities as well as ideas about blackness (both in local contexts and the larger African diaspora), especially via his engagement with hip-hop.[15] This recalls similar moves by Ivy Queen who is perhaps not as openly "political" regarding issues of race and class as other artists, but who has also manipulated her performance and style in such a way that critiques broader discourses of racial democracy.

In the case of "Danza Kuduro," Don Omar's reference to a form of African popular music is even more significant in the context of dominant discourses of racial democracy that reproduce images of a fossilized and static Africa to promote a vision of contemporary Puerto Rico as a whitened, Hispanic society with limited connections to African culture. Instead, "Danza Kuduro" links Puerto Rico to modern Africa through actively engaging a cultural practice that addresses the experiences of Angolan youth whose local communities face challenges related to global processes of colonialism, displacement, and misrecognition that also impact the San Juan neighborhood where Don Omar grew up. In Don Omar's "Danza Kuduro," Angolan popular culture (though mediated by Lucenzo) becomes a critical resource that contributes to reggaetón's insertion of alternative conceptions of blackness into Puerto Rican culture, linking Puerto Rico to the broader African diaspora via an understanding of Africa that does not conform to the folkloric blackness consistent with hegemonic discourses of racial democracy.

Certainly, "Danza Kuduro" is by no means unproblematic. Jennifer Rudolph "cautions" reggaetón fans to "listen carefully to the lyrics and not simply allow the beats to seduce them," mentioning the ways that Don Omar sometimes reinforces a "chaos" that "occludes his call for Latino unity and black pride."[16] Among these more problematic aspects of Don Omar's performance is a hypermasculine stance that often promotes heterosexism, evident in the video for "Danza Kuduro." Filmed in Saint Martin, the video begins with Don Omar agreeing to pick Lucenzo up from his home, a large mansion with women lounging in bathing suits throughout the yard. The two men eventually arrive at a yacht that they sail to a small beach area. Don Omar and Lucenzo perform the first half of the song on the yacht while a

Figure c.1: Don Omar and Lucenzo perform on a yacht flanked by women in their music video for "Danza Kuduro."

group of women clad in black bikinis or revealing one-piece bathing suits stands around them. Sometimes the women flank the artists as they sing, and at other times they lie on the yacht as the camera pans over their bodies. The group of women is multiracial, but they all conform to whitened standards of beauty with European features and thin bodies. Likewise, the lyrics of the song focus on dancing and "shaking your hips." Lyrics identify the *morena* as the main dancer, referencing the hypersexualization of black and brown women common in Latin music; interestingly, although the *morena* is most frequently mentioned in the song, Lucenzo also calls on *loiras* [blonde women] to dance with *morenas*, too, perhaps a nod to ideals of racial democracy. In "Danza Kuduro," women literally embody the backdrop for Don Omar's and Lucenzo's performances, active only as hypersexualized *morenas* whose hips are made to shake to the beat of kuduro.

The heteronormative and patriarchal gender relations evident in "Danza Kuduro" are not surprising given that similar gender representations pervade many reggaetón music videos and lyrics. Indeed, the responses by male reggaetón artists, music industry executives, and music video producers to the Anti-Pornography Campaign in 2002 reinscribed problematic gender and racial representations of black women as hypersexual. This defense of reggaetón ultimately rehearsed deep-rooted assumptions about black female sexuality in order to situate the music in relation to hegemonic discourses of racial democracy. As scholars, fans, and listeners, we should be critical when reggaetón reproduces heterosexist hierarchies even if it may resist particular forms of racialization. At the same time, it is critical to recognize that the gender dynamics of reggaetón are also evident in other forms of popular music and in society more generally. To continuously blame reggaetón as the only arbiter of problematic gender relations limits the development of new strategies for disrupting heterosexist hierarchies by ignoring the larger social processes that perpetuate them. Moreover, we must also pay attention to the diversity within reggaetón, and the ways that some artists such as Ivy Queen utilize music and performance to challenge gender norms. Therefore, it is necessary to be critical of reggaetón's gender politics but also to place these critiques in relation to larger conversations about race and gender hierarchies in Puerto Rico and elsewhere.

In many ways, the mainstreaming of reggaetón may make these issues worse. The pressure to conform to music industry standards that eroticize and exoticize black and Latino performers may motivate some reggaetón artists to feel obligated to act out stereotypes in order to achieve broader success. As demonstrated in the racialization of reggaetón in U.S. newspapers, descriptions of the music as "hot," "spicy," and a nonstop "fiesta" reproduce old stereotypes of Latinidad that, while problematic, have also proven lucrative for many artists, including reggaetoneros, attempting to cross over into mainstream U.S. markets. Read in this way, a song like "Danza Kuduro" has less to do with diasporic connections and more to do with the so-called death of reggaetón as established artists such as Don Omar create more pop and dance tracks in order to appeal to wider audiences.

But this assumption that the mainstreaming of reggaetón has led to its demise must be treated with some skepticism. Indeed, one of the benefits of the so-called explosion of reggaetón in the mid-2000s is the diversity of styles and artists that have emerged. These include new artists in other countries such as Cuba, the Dominican Republic, or even non-Spanish speaking countries such as Belize or the Philippines. The establishment of reggaetón scenes in these places shows the on-going popularity of the supposedly monotonous and boring music. They also demonstrate the continued salience of reggaetón as a cultural practice of diaspora. Many new artists, in Puerto Rico and elsewhere, have access to new forms of distribution via the Internet, relying less on music industry channels to gain popularity and success. As Jayna Brown argues, these alternative distribution channels provide opportunities to create diasporic connections and express modern subjectivities in new and diverse ways.[17]

The establishment of new reggaetón scenes goes hand in hand with the creation of innovative mixes and fusions, such as the mixture of the South Asian music bhangra with reggaetón to produce "bhangraton." Traditionally, men in the Punjab region of India performed bhangra.[18] Bhangra then arrived in urban areas of the United Kingdom with the influx of Punjabi immigrants in the mid-twentieth century.[19] As time wore on, bhangra became a signifier of South Asian diasporic identities in cities throughout the Americas and the United Kingdom, and, like reggaetón, has become a more hybrid musical space that incorporates not only traditional bhangra aesthetics, but other diasporic musical practices such as rap and reggae.[20] At its most basic level, bhangraton could be considered a mixture of reggaetón and bhangra that emerged in urban centers such as London and New York City. Produced by groups such as the U.K.-based bhangra group Rishi Rich Project or the artist Deevani (incidentally, the sister of Luny, one half of the superstar reggaetón producers Luny Tunes), bhangraton exists, as Marisol Lebrón relates, "in the live remix, the YouTube video, and the bootlegged CD."[21] Lebrón argues that bhangraton shifts attention away from standard narratives of reggaetón's emergence in Puerto Rico to foreground what are often unrecognized connections between South Asian communities and the Caribbean, made all the more significant by the substantial histories of South Asian migration to the region.[22] Similar to "Danza Kuduro," through the combining of two musical practices that have already emerged from diasporic exchange, movement, and localized experiences of disenfranchisement and "otherness," bhangraton highlights diasporic connections in these popular music styles that expand beyond the exchange of sounds and styles to include the recognition of similar experiences of exclusion among different groups.

In addition to the globalization of reggaetón, the music continues to resonate with local communities in Puerto Rico. New Puerto Rican artists have emerged, and represent a diverse array of fusions and subgenres of reggaetón. Some are independent, like early underground artists, while others continue to produce songs that reference other Caribbean musical forms, from the *vallenato* of the Caribbean coast of Colombia to Jamaican dancehall and Dominican merengue. Still others fuse reggaetón with bachata or pop, creating *romantiqueo* love songs that appeal to teeny-boppers and adult pop lovers alike. For some Puerto Rican artists, reggaetón is a site for political commentary that continues to address issues of violence, police brutality, and disenfranchisement, while some extend their critiques to the island's ongoing colonial relationship with the United States. For others, reggaetón remains quintessential party music, a beat for dancing and having a good time. Finally, it is important to note that many more established artists, including several mentioned in this book such as Daddy Yankee, Tego Calderón, Ivy Queen, and Don Omar, are still tremendously popular, producing new albums, touring internationally, and collaborating with other reggaetoneros and artists from other genres.

Reggaetón is certainly no longer underground, but the conditions that created its emergence remain. Discourses of racial democracy endure as the defining ideology of Puerto Rican identity. Poverty, drug use, and violence continue to be key issues that impact Puerto Ricans, including youth living in urban areas. Racism also persists as the old stereotypes of blackness still circulate on the island, and black and nonwhite people face routine disenfranchisement and limited access to important resources. Certainly, reggaetón on its own is not the answer to these questions; still, it continues to be an important venue for contesting these structures of inequality, and offers an outlet for those communities who have been cast out of Puerto Rico's so-called racial democracy to express their own identities, opinions, and critiques.

The history of reggaetón is one of transformation. As a musical genre, reggaetón carries on despite attempts at censorship and constant disparagement from detractors. It has expanded to incorporate new sounds, new histories, and new identities. To be sure, reggaetón also maintains some of its more problematic elements, particularly around questions of gender and sexuality. As songs like "Danza Kuduro" make clear, although some aspects of the transformations in reggaetón may be problematic, they also point to the continued salience of reggaetón as a space to forge meaningful diasporic links across distinct geographic sites that introduce reggaetón artists and fans to musical influences and, more important, to diasporic resources that include different conceptions of blackness. While not the only space, reggaetón operates as a critical site for developing alternative configurations of Puerto Rican identities that foreground the island's African diasporic connections and refute racial democracy's attempts to limit blackness to either a primitive, premodern past, or to damaging stereotypes that position it outside the boundaries of respectable Puerto Ricanness. Reggaetón thus continues to insist on the creation of a more inclusive and equal Puerto Rican society.

NOTES

INTRODUCTION

1 Quoted in Sandra Barrera, "All Over the Musical Map at the Latin Grammys," *Daily News of Los Angeles*, November 3, 2005.

2 Kalefa Sennah, "Latin Grammys are Still Seeking an Identity," *New York Times*, November 3, 2005.

3 A second reggaetón performance featured Don Omar, who sang a medley of hits from his album *The Last Don*, which was nominated for Best Urban Album.

4 Unless otherwise stated, all Spanish translations are my own.

5 As I will discuss later, the origins of reggaetón are hotly debated. However, I focus my analysis on reggaetón in Puerto Rico because many of the most popular artists come from the island. Moreover, Puerto Rican artists and DJs played an essential role in developing reggaetón when they pieced together various musical practices from hip-hop, dancehall, and other traditions to create what we now recognize as the typical reggaetón sound. See chapter 1 for more information.

6 Colloquially, the phrase *la gran familia puertorriqueña* (the great Puerto Rican family) refers to Puerto Rico's racially mixed national identity (Alamo-Pastrana, "Disrupting Declarations of Freedom"; Jiménez-Román, "Un hombre (negro) del pueblo"; Rivero, *Tuning Out Blackness*; Torres, "La Gran Familia Puertorriqueña 'Ej Prieta de Beldá'" [The Great Puerto Rican Family Is Really Really Black]). Brazilian theorist Gilberto Freyre is credited with developing the concept of "racial democracy" to address similar racial dynamics in his country. Since then, several other scholars of Afro-Latin America have employed the term *racial democracy* to describe comparable systems of race relations in the region that celebrate race mixture and racial harmony while contradictorily embracing whiteness and maintaining racial hierarchies. Another common term in scholarship on

race in Latin America is *mestizaje*, which is used to describe the process of race mixture; however, *mestizaje* often connotes mixture between Spanish and indigenous groups (Godreau, *Scripts of Blackness*, 2). In this book, I use the term *racial democracy* to place Puerto Rican racial dynamics in larger conversations about race and identity in Latin America, particularly those countries that emphasize a racial triad of African, Indigenous, and European ancestry (indeed, I agree with Samuel Betances when he posits that scholars could "look toward Brazil as some kind of reasonable model" for understanding Puerto Rican race relations ["The Prejudice of Having No Prejudice in Puerto Rico Part I," 49]). At the same time, I also pay careful attention to the specificities of local understandings of racial identities in Puerto Rico throughout the text. Furthermore, I follow recent trends in scholarship about Puerto Rican race relations that use the term *racial democracy* (Arroyo, "Roots, or the Virtualities of Racial Imaginaries in Puerto Rico and the Diaspora"; Rodríguez-Silva, *Silencing Race*).

7   Some may consider my use of *national identity* a misnomer given Puerto Rico's lack of political sovereignty and the ongoing colonial relationship between Puerto Rico and the United States. However, several scholars such as Arlene Dávila (*Sponsored Identities*) and Jorge Duany (*The Puerto Rican Nation on the Move*) have argued that Puerto Ricans, including, in some cases, those living in the mainland United States, imagine themselves as members of a distinct cultural nation. This form of cultural nationalism recognizes a unique culture that unites Puerto Ricans despite the island's colonial status.

8   Marshall, R. Rivera, and Pacini Hernández, "Reggaeton's Socio-Sonic Circuitry," 9.

9   Negrón-Muntaner and R. Rivera, "Reggaeton Nation," 39.

10   I selected this time period because it encompasses reggaetón's crossover into the mainstream in Puerto Rico and, eventually, its entrance into Latin music markets in the United States.

11   See Fernandes, "Fear of a Black Nation"; Flores, *Diaspora Strikes Back*; Guilbault, *Governing Sound*; Pacini Hernández and Garofalo, "Hip Hop in Havana"; Thomas, *Modern Blackness*; Wade, *Music, Race, and Nation*; West-Durán, "Rap's Diasporic Dialogues."

12   Bomba is a folkloric music and dance that is generally considered emblematic of Afro–Puerto Rican culture on the island.

13   See Aparicio, *Listening to Salsa*; Arroyo, "Virtualities of Racial Imaginaries"; Berríos-Miranda and Dudley, "El Gran Combo, Cortijo, and the Musical Geography of Cangrejos/Santurce, Puerto Rico"; Flores, *Diaspora Strikes Back*; Rivera-Rideau, "Cocolos Modernos"; Santos-Febres, "Salsa as Translocation."

14   Juan Flores, "What's All the Noise About?" It is worth pointing out that other genres of popular music in Puerto Rico also developed from larger transnational processes of migration and cultural exchange. For more information, see Flores, *Diaspora Strikes Back*; Pacini Hernández, *Oye Como Va!*; Santos-Febres, "Salsa as Translocation."

15 Marshall, R. Rivera, and Pacini Hernández, "Reggaeton's Socio-Sonic Circuitry," 9.

16 I have used pseudonyms for all of the individuals I interviewed.

17 *Jincho* refers to someone very pale, usually with dark hair. At times, the term *jincho* can be considered derogatory.

18 My use of the term *discourses* is influenced by Shalini Puri's analysis of "discourses of hybridity" throughout the Caribbean (see *The Caribbean Postcolonial*). Puri focuses on discourses propagated by Caribbean states that mean to define a "distinct" national identity, "displac[e] discourses of equality, which has led to their importance in many instances for securing bourgeois nationalist hegemony," and "manag[e] racial politics—either by promoting cultural over racial hybridity or by producing racial mixtures acceptable to the elite" (*The Caribbean Postcolonial*, 46). Likewise, I employ the term *discourses* to refer to the rhetoric and imagery propagated by the state that define Puerto Rico as a racial democracy.

19 Hintzen, "Race and Creole Ethnicity"; Jiménez Román, "Looking at That Middle Ground"; Puri, *Caribbean Postcolonial*; Quijano, "Coloniality of Power, Eurocentrism, and Latin America."

20 In the late nineteenth and early twentieth centuries, many Latin American countries adopted immigration reforms in order to encourage Europeans to settle in their countries in the hope that this would encourage race mixture that would whiten their populations. However, this strategy did not work, and, by the 1920s and 1930s, many Latin American countries shifted their focus to a more cultural whitening that exalted European cultures and ideas as the most valuable to the development of Latin American identities. For more information, see Andrews, *Afro-Latin America*, 117–51.

21 For more information about how this works in various national contexts, see Andrews, *Afro-Latin America*; Gates, *Black in Latin America*; Graham, ed., *The Idea of Race in Latin America*; Hall, "Creolité and the Process of Creolization"; Hall, "Creolization, Diaspora, and Hybridity in the Context of Globalization"; Hanchard, *Orpheus and Power*; Hernández, *Racial Subordination in Latin America*; Hintzen, "Race and Creole Ethnicity"; Jiménez Román, "Looking at That Middle Ground"; Oboler and Dzidzienyo, eds., *Neither Enemies nor Friends*; Rahier, "Mestizaje, Mulataje, Mestiçagem in Latin American Ideologies of National Identities"; Torres and Whitten, Jr., eds., *Blackness in Latin America and the Caribbean*; Wade, *Race and Ethnicity in Latin America*.

22 Godreau, *Scripts of Blackness*.

23 Kinsbruner, *Not of Pure Blood*, 28–31.

24 Alamo-Pastrana, "Disrupting Declarations of Freedom," 21.

25 For example, historical accounts of life under Spanish rule by scholars such as Eileen Findlay (*Imposing Decency*), Jay Kinsbruner (*Not of Pure Blood*), and Ileana Rodríguez-Silva (*Silencing Race*) demonstrate that enslaved and free Afro–Puerto Ricans faced racial discrimination regularly on the island prior to the U.S. colonization.

26 For more about the concept of "silencing" and racial politics in Puerto Rico, see Rodríguez-Silva, *Silencing Race*.

27 Duany, *Puerto Rican Nation*; Flores, *Divided Borders*; López-Baralt, *Sobre Ínsulares Extrañas*.

28 Guerra, *Popular Expression and National Identity in Puerto Rico*, 37.

29 Pedreira, *Insularismo*, 12.

30 Blanco, *El Prejuicio Racial en Puerto Rico*.

31 Pedreira, *Insularismo*, 12.

32 Blanco, *El Prejuicio Racial*, 35.

33 For example, Pedreira wrote, "We are obliged to lovingly include all groups that are genuinely worthy, without feeling that horrible beast called social prejudice" (*Insularismo*, 15). Similarly, Blanco proclaimed that in Puerto Rico, "we still do not know what racial prejudice is" (*El Prejuicio Racial*, 9).

34 See Aparicio, *Listening to Salsa*; Duany, *Puerto Rican Nation*; Flores, *Divided Borders*; Jiménez Román, "Un hombre (negro) del pueblo"; Roy-Féquiere, *Women, Creole Identity, and Intellectual Life in Early Twentieth-Century Puerto Rico*.

35 Alamo-Pastrana, "Disrupting Declarations of Freedom," 178.

36 Zenón Cruz, *Narciso Descubre su Trasero*, 23.

37 González, *The Four Storeyed Country and Other Essays*, 11.

38 It is important to note that, although race mixture is not a problem in and of itself, these ideas have the potential to reinforce some of the more problematic aspects of discourses of racial democracy. In particular, they perpetuate static images of the racial triad that forms the basis for hegemonic depictions of Puerto Rican racial democracy. Nonetheless, Zenón Cruz and González provide important critiques of the racial biases inherent to racial democracy discourses, laying the groundwork for subsequent research and critiques of racial discrimination in Puerto Rico.

39 See Alamo-Pastrana, "Disrupting Declarations of Freedom"; Arroyo, "Virtualities of Racial Imaginaries"; Dinzey-Flores, *Locked In, Locked Out*; Flores, *Divided Borders*; Godreau, "Changing Space, Making Race"; Godreau, "Folkloric 'Others'"; Godreau, "Slippery Semantics"; Jiménez Román, "Un hombre (negro) del pueblo"; Quiñones Rivera, "From Trigueñita to Afro–Puerto Rican"; Rivera-Rideau, "Cocolos Modernos"; Rivera-Rideau, "From Carolina to Loíza"; Rivero, *Tuning Out Blackness*; Torres, "La familia puertorriqueña."

40 Godreau, "Slippery Semantics."

41 Rahier, "Blackness, the Racial/Spatial Order, Migrations, and Miss Ecuador"; Wade, *Blackness and Race Mixture*.

42 Godreau, "Missing the Mix"; Godreau, "Changing Space, Making Race"; Godreau, "Folkloric 'Others.'"

43 Godreau, "Changing Space, Making Race," 283–84.

44 Dinzey-Flores, *Locked In, Locked Out*.

45 It is important to note that other images of blackness also exist in Puerto Rico. For example, portrayals of Dominican immigrant communities or Nuyoricans (Puerto Ricans living in New York) as "black" reproduce understandings of

blackness as foreign to Puerto Rico, even though these communities comprise important sectors of the island's population. However, for the purposes of this discussion, I center my analysis on folkloric blackness and urban blackness.

46 Santos-Febres, "Geografía en decibeles."

47 Pacini Hernández, "The Name Game."

48 Pacini Hernández, "The Name Game."

49 Dávila, *Latino Spin*.

50 Pacini Hernández, *Oye Como Va!*, 13.

51 Pacini Hernández, *Oye Como Va!*, 6–7.

52 Perry, "Global Black Self-Fashionings."

53 Perry, "Global Black Self-Fashionings," 636.

54 Clifford, "Diasporas"; Butler, "Defining Diaspora, Refining Discourse."

55 A full exegesis of the term *diaspora* exceeds the limits of this introduction. For a detailed review of the debates regarding the various definitions of the African diaspora and their political implications, see Brent Hayes Edwards, "The Uses of Diaspora."

56 Livermon, "Diaspora Space/Kwaito Bodies"; Pierre, *The Predicament of Blackness*.

57 See Brah, *Cartographies of Diaspora*; Brown, "Black Liverpool, Black America, and the Gendering of Diasporic Space"; Butler, "Defining Diaspora"; Campt, "Diaspora Space, Ethnographic Space"; Edwards, *Practice of Diaspora*; Hall, "Cultural Identity and Diaspora"; Livermon, "Diaspora Space/Kwaito Bodies"; Patterson and Kelley, "Unfinished Migrations."

58 Gilroy, *The Black Atlantic*; Hintzen and Rahier, "Theorizing the African Diaspora"; Livermon, "Diaspora Space/Kwaito Bodies."

59 Gilroy, *The Black Atlantic*; Patterson and Kelley, "Unfinished Migrations."

60 Brown, *Dropping Anchor, Setting Sail*.

61 Hintzen and Rahier, "Theorizing the African Diaspora"; Livermon, "Diaspora Spaces/Kwaito Bodies."

62 Hintzen and Rahier, "Theorizing the African Diaspora," xvii.

63 Brown, "Black Liverpool, Black America"; Brown, *Dropping Anchor, Setting Sail*.

64 Madrid and Moore, *Danzón*, 17.

65 Flores, *Diaspora Strikes Back*, 4.

66 Flores, *Diaspora Strikes Back*, 48.

67 Flores, *Diaspora Strikes Back*, 46.

68 Hall, "Cultural Identity and Diaspora," 398.

69 I use the term *Afro-Latinidad* to mean an identity that integrates blackness and Latinidad—that is, one that does not assume blackness and Latinidad are discrete entities, but rather that they can be understood together. However, I also acknowledge that sometimes Afro-Latinidad and Puerto Ricanness are distinct. For example, for many people, *Latino* refers to individuals living in the United States, therefore excluding Puerto Ricans who live on the island. In these instances, Afro-Latinidad may refer solely to U.S.-based notions of identity. Similarly, Puerto Ricanness may refer to those individuals living on the island, or, at other times, to people both on the island and the mainland. Reggaetón offers a space

to articulate ideas that upend the alleged distinctions between blackness and Latinidad common in both the United States and Puerto Rico. While many of the chapters in this book focus on Puerto Rico, chapter 5, "Enter the Hurbans," provides a more detailed analysis of reggaetón as a space of Afro-Latinidad in the United States.

70 Lipsitz, *Dangerous Crossroads*.

71 Guilbault, *Governing Sound*; Lipsitz, *Footsteps in the Dark*.

72 It is important to note that reggaetón circulated in the United States prior to this time. For example, popular reggaetón producers Luny Tunes met in the suburbs of Boston, Massachusetts, where they had settled with their families from the Dominican Republic. They began producing their beats in the Boston area before attracting the attention of reggaetón producers in Puerto Rico.

CHAPTER ONE. Iron Fist against Rap

1 R. Rivera, "La música rap en Puerto Rico," 42.

2 Many individuals see a distinction between reggaetón and rap. Currently, these divisions are often based on questions of musical style, "political" lyrics, and commercialization. In addition, a note on terminology is important. Reggaetón is also sometimes referred to as "rap" or "reggae" in Puerto Rico. Artists are often called *raperos* [rappers] in addition to "reggaetoneros." Throughout the text, I have kept the terms *rap* and *rappers* in quotes by individuals who use them to refer to reggaetón. Otherwise, I use the terms *reggaetón* and *reggaetoneros* or *underground artists*.

3 Giovannetti, "Popular Music and Culture in Puerto Rico"; Marshall, "From Música Negra to Reggaeton Latino"; R. Rivera, "Policing Morality"; Santos-Febres, "Puerto Rican Underground."

4 For an in-depth analysis of the shift in reggaetón's sound, see Marshall, "From Música Negra to Reggaetón Latino," 48–58.

5 Marshall, "From Música Negra to Reggaeton Latino," 49.

6 Marshall, "From Música Negra to Reggaeton Latino," 50–53.

7 Marshall, "From Música Negra to Reggaeton Latino," 51.

8 According to Wayne Marshall, Raquel Z. Rivera, and Deborah Pacini Hernández ("Socio-Sonic Circuitry"), one principal difference between reggaetón and underground is their relationships to the market; that is, while reggaetón and underground share some basic musical characteristics (notwithstanding their different production qualities), contemporary reggaetón is "explicitly commercial" due to its circulation via larger record companies.

9 Some argue that Panamanian reggae en español was the primary precursor to reggaetón. Since I argue that reggaetón has been shaped by the urban Puerto Rican experience, I focus on underground here because many of the debates surrounding underground resurfaced once reggaetón became mainstream. I will also address the importance of Panamanian reggae en español and other musical influences later in this chapter.

10 In addition, it is important to point out that, as with hip-hop in the United States, the term *underground* also differentiates music considered more "street-oriented, vernacular, spontaneous, and uncensored . . . as opposed to the studio-oriented, glossy, sanitized aesthetic of the mainstream market" in contemporary Puerto Rico (R. Rivera, "Policing Morality," 113). For the purposes of this chapter, however, I refer to underground as the specific music that predates contemporary reggaetón.

11 See Santos-Febres, "Geografia en decibeles"; Santos-Febres, "Puerto Rican Underground"; Giovannetti, "Popular Music and Culture in Puerto Rico"; R. Rivera, "Rap in Puerto Rico: Reflections from the Margins"; R. Rivera, "Rapping Two Versions"; R. Rivera, "Cultura y poder en el rap puertorriqueño"; R. Rivera, "Policing Morality."

12 Brown, "Black Liverpool, Black America," 292; Brown, *Dropping Anchor, Setting Sail*, 5.

13 See Duany, *Puerto Rican Nation*; Flores, *Divided Borders*; Flores, *Diaspora Strikes Back*.

14 The term *Nuyorican* refers to Puerto Ricans from New York City; however, in some cases, Puerto Ricans on the island use the term to refer to all U.S. Puerto Ricans. For example, although I was raised in Ohio and Connecticut, many people called me a "Nuyorican."

15 Findlay, "Slipping and Sliding"; Flores, *Diaspora Strikes Back*; Jiménez Román, "Boricuas vs. Nuyoricans—Indeed!"

16 Findlay, "Slipping and Sliding"; Flores, *Diaspora Strikes Back*; Jiménez Román, "Boricuas vs. Nuyoricans."

17 Lebrón, "Con un flow natural"; Marshall, "From Música Negra to Reggaeton Latino."

18 Marshall, Rivera, and Pacini Hernández, "Socio-Sonic Circuitry," 8.

19 It is critical to note that other musical traditions such as salsa or Dominican bachata also inform reggaetón. For a discussion of the other musical influences on reggaetón, see Pacini Hernández, "Dominicans in the Mix"; Lebrón, "Con un flow natural"; and Rivera-Rideau, "Cocolos Modernos."

20 Santos-Febres, "Geografía en decibeles," 124.

21 Whalen, "Colonialism, Citizenship, and the Making of the Puerto Rican Diaspora," 32.

22 R. Rivera, *New York Ricans*, 23.

23 For a discussion about the shift from a "Puerto Rican" New York to a "Pan-Latino/Trans-Latino" New York, see Juan Flores, *From Bomba to Hip Hop*, 141–65.

24 Different entities such as the U.S. government or the Puerto Rican Office of Migration (which represented the Puerto Rican government) were invested in the racial classification of Nuyoricans. Puerto Ricans were sometimes classified as "white" or "black" depending on larger political motives, the particular individuals who filled out forms, or other issues (Haslip-Viera, "Changing Identities"; Thomas, *Puerto Rican Citizen*, 66–74). Therefore, while Puerto Ricans may be

understood to occupy an intermediary position within the black/white racial binary, the fact that they have been attributed different racial characteristics at different times reveals the ambiguity of race more generally.

25 R. Rivera, *New York Ricans*, 26.

26 See Flores, *From Bomba to Hip-Hop*; Grosfoguel and Georas, "Racialization of Latino Caribbean Migrants"; Grosfoguel and Georas, "'Coloniality of Power' and Racial Dynamics"; R. Rivera, *New York Ricans*; Rodríguez-Morazzani, "Beyond the Rainbow."

27 I discuss the construction of these stereotypes further in chapter 5.

28 R. Rivera, *New York Ricans*, 32–34; Thomas, *Puerto Rican Citizen*.

29 See Bonilla-Silva, "Reflections about Race by a *Negrito Acomplejao*"; Quiñones Rivera, "From Trigueñita to Afro-Puerto Rican"; Thomas, *Down These Mean Streets*.

30 Flores, *Diaspora Strikes Back*, 47.

31 Flores, *From Bomba to Hip-Hop*; Lipsitz, *Dangerous Crossroads*; Pacini Hernández, *Oye Como Va!*; R. Rivera, *New York Ricans*.

32 A full history of the development of hip-hop is beyond the scope of this chapter. There is an expansive bibliography that details the emergence and social significance of hip-hop in various urban contexts throughout the United States. For more information, see Jeff Chang, *Can't Stop, Won't Stop*; Murray Forman, *The 'Hood Comes First*; Murray Forman and Mark Anthony Neal, eds., *That's the Joint! The Hip Hop Studies Reader*; Raquel Rivera, *New York Ricans*; Tricia Rose, *Black Noise*, among others.

33 Flores, *From Bomba to Hip-Hop*; Flores, *Diaspora Strikes Back*; R. Rivera, *New York Ricans*.

34 Flores, *Diaspora Strikes Back*, 47.

35 R. Rivera, "Reflections from the Margins," 112.

36 Marshall, "From Música Negra to Reggaeton Latino," 47.

37 R. Rivera, "La música rap en Puerto Rico," 35.

38 Flores, *Diaspora Strikes Back*, 164.

39 Guilbault, "Audible Entanglements," 41.

40 Báez, "En mi imperio," 68.

41 Marshall, Rivera, and Pacini Hernández, "Socio-Sonic Circuitry," 11.

42 Thomas, *Modern Blackness*.

43 Thomas, *Modern Blackness*.

44 Gray, "Power and Identity among the Urban Poor of Jamaica."

45 Stolzoff, *Wake the Town*.

46 Peter Manuel and Wayne Marshall ("The Riddim Method," 449) date this "riddim-plus-voicing system" as beginning in the late 1970s.

47 Peter Manuel and Wayne Marshall ("The Riddim Method," 449) write that the use of prerecorded music rather than live band performance for dances was very popular in Jamaican dancehalls since the 1950s. Interestingly, one of the more popular musical practices to be played during these dances was U.S. R&B, further demonstrating the diasporic connections embedded in circum-Caribbean popular music.

48 Stolzoff, *Wake the Town*, 99, 108.

49 Stolzoff, *Wake the Town*, 2. See also Thomas, *Modern Blackness*.

50 Cooper, *Noises in the Blood*; Cooper, *Sound Clash*; Stolzoff, *Wake the Town*; Thomas, *Modern Blackness*.

51 Stolzoff, *Wake the Town*, 1–2. A full description of the debates surrounding dancehall and creole national identity in Jamaica is beyond the scope of this chapter; for more information see work by Carolyn Cooper (*Noises in the Blood*; *Sound Clash*) and Deborah Thomas (*Modern Blackness*).

52 Deborah A. Thomas, "Progress, 'America,' and the Politics of Popular Culture in Jamaica."

53 Putnam, "Eventually Alien."

54 Conniff, "Afro-West Indians"; Putnam, "Eventually Alien."

55 Conniff, "Afro-West Indians"; Putnam, "Eventually Alien."

56 Beginning in the 1920s, several Central American states passed laws restricting the immigration of black people to their countries. In Panama, a new law in 1928 stripped citizenship rights from Caribbean immigrants; in 1941, a new Panamanian constitution declared that children of West Indians born in Panama after 1928 were no longer Panamanian citizens (Putnam, "Eventually Alien," 290).

57 Priestley and Barrow, "The Black Movement in Panama," 51.

58 Priestley and Barrow, "The Black Movement in Panama," 51.

59 Priestley and Barrow, "The Black Movement in Panama," 51.

60 Priestley and Barrow, "The Black Movement in Panama," 51.

61 Conniff, "Afro-West Indians," 159; Modestín, "An Afro-Latina's Quest for Inclusion," 419; Priestley, "Post-Invasion Panama."

62 Twickel, "Muévelo," 88.

63 Marshall, "From Música Negra to Reggaeton Latino," 30.

64 Marshall, "Dem Bow, Dembow, Dembo," 133.

65 Nwankwo, "The Panamanian Origins of Reggae en Español," 92–93.

66 Marshall, "Dem Bow, Dembow, Dembo"; Marshall, "From Música Negra to Reggaeton Latino," 31.

67 Twickel, "Muévelo," 106.

68 Twickel, "Muévelo," 99–101; Nwankwo, "Panamanian Origins of Reggae en Español," 93.

69 Twickel, "Muévelo," 104.

70 Twickel, "Muévelo," 104–6.

71 Moore, *Music in the Hispanic Caribbean*, 8.

72 Marshall, "Dem Bow, Dembow, Dembo," 139.

73 Wayne Marshall, "Digital Rhythm: The Loopy Origins of Dembow and the Knotty Dancehall Roots of Reggaeton," *Wax Poetics*, January 28, 2014. www.waxpoetics.com/features/articles/digital-rhythm.

74 This new riddim circulated on the B-side of a dancehall recording of New York-based dancehall artists Bobo General and Sleepy Wonder as the *pounds* riddim; as a result, only Jamaican producer Dennis Thompson was credited on the record, while Pucho Bustamante was never recognized for his contributions. See Marshall, "Digital Rhythm."

75 Marshall, "Digital Rhythm."

76 Marshall, "From Música Negra to Reggaetón Latino," 40; see also Giovannetti, "Popular Music and Culture in Puerto Rico"; Santos-Febres, "Geografia en decibeles"; Santos-Febres, "Puerto Rican Underground."

77 See Dinzey-Flores, "De la Disco al Caserío"; Giovannetti, "Popular Culture and Music in Puerto Rico"; R. Rivera, "Reflections from the Margins"; Santos-Febres, "Geografia en decibeles"; Santos-Febres, "Puerto Rican Underground."

78 Fusté, "Colonial Laboratories."

79 Tyrrell, "Colonizing the New Deal," 74.

80 Dinzey-Flores, "Temporary Housing, Permanent Communities"; Dinzey-Flores, *Locked In, Locked Out*; Fusté, "Colonial Laboratories"; Tyrrell, "Colonizing the New Deal."

81 Tyrrell, "Colonizing the New Deal," 80.

82 Dinzey-Flores, "Temporary Housing, Permanent Communities"; Dinzey-Flores, "Caché vs. Cacheríos"; Dinzey-Flores, *Locked In, Locked Out*; Tyrrell, "Colonizing the New Deal."

83 Dinzey-Flores, *Locked In, Locked Out.*

84 Fusté, "Colonial Laboratories."

85 Rodríguez Beruff, "Guerra contra las drogas," 54.

86 Montalvo-Barbot, "Crime in Puerto Rico," 535; Rodríguez Beruff, "Guerra contra las drogas," 78–79.

87 Rodríguez Beruff, "Guerra contra las drogas," 55.

88 Montalvo-Barbot, "Crime in Puerto Rico," 536.

89 Montalvo-Barbot, "Crime in Puerto Rico," 535.

90 Santiago-Valles, "Policing the Crisis in the Whitest of All the Antilles."

91 Santiago-Valles, "Policing the Crisis in the Whitest of All the Antilles," 45, 47.

92 Santiago-Valles, "Policing the Crisis in the Whitest of All the Antilles," 45, 47.

93 Santiago-Valles, "Vigilando, administrando y patrullando a negros y trigueños," 33; Santiago-Valles, "Policing the Crisis in the Whitest of All the Antilles," 49.

94 Rivera-Bonilla, "Divided City"; Rodríguez Beruff, "Guerra contra las drogas," 56.

95 Santiago-Valles, "Vigilando, administrando y patrullando a negros y trigueños."

96 Simon, "Mano Dura."

97 Simon, "Mano Dura"; Simon, "Epilogue."

98 Simon, "Epilogue."

99 Simon, "Epilogue."

100 Rivera-Bonilla, "Divided City," 259.

101 Rivera-Bonilla, "Divided City," 252.

102 Rivera-Bonilla, "Divided City," 259.

103 Dinzey-Flores, *Locked In, Locked Out*, 30; Rivera-Bonilla, "Divided City," 255; Simon, "Epilogue."

104 Dinzey-Flores, *Locked In, Locked Out*, 30; Simon, "Epilogue."

105 Dinzey-Flores, *Locked In, Locked Out*, 30; Simon, "Epilogue."

106 Rivera-Bonilla, "Divided City"; Rodríguez Beruff, "Guerra contra las drogas"; Simon, "Epilogue."

107 Rivera-Bonilla, "Divided City," 252.

108 Montalvo-Barbot, "Crime in Puerto Rico," 543; Simon, "Epilogue."

109 Montalvo-Barbot, "Crime in Puerto Rico," 541.

110 Montalvo-Barbot, "Crime in Puerto Rico," 542; Rivera-Bonilla, "Divided City," 257; Simon, "Epilogue."

111 Rivera-Bonilla, "Divided City," 257.

112 Dinzey-Flores, *Locked In, Locked Out,* 32.

113 Gates formed part of the urban landscape in Puerto Rico since the 1980s, when the *Ley de Cierre* allowed neighborhoods to build gates in order to restrict access to certain areas; however, these gates enclosed middle- and upper-middle-class communities (*urbanizaciones*), serving as markers of upper-class identities. On the other hand, the gates surrounding *caseríos* were involuntary and constructed to control and restrict movement of *caserío* residents. As Zaire Dinzey-Flores argues, the gates surrounding housing projects ultimately contribute to racial and class segregation in Puerto Rico's urban areas by underscoring the perceived distinctions between *caseríos* and the rest of Puerto Rico. For more information, see Dinzey-Flores, "Caché vs. Cacheríos" and *Locked In, Locked Out.*

114 Dinzey-Flore, "Caché vs. Cacheríos," 216.

115 Dinzey-Flores, *Locked In, Locked Out.*

116 Marshall, "From Música Negra to Reggaeton Latino," 40.

117 Giovannetti, "Popular Culture and Music in Puerto Rico," 86; Marshall, "From Música Negra to Reggaeton Latino," 40.

118 Giovannetti, "Popular Culture and Music in Puerto Rico," 86; Marshall, "From Música Negra to Reggaeton Latino," 40.

119 R. Rivera, "Reflections from the Margins," 123; R. Rivera, "Rapping Two Versions," 254; Santos-Febres, "Puerto Rican Underground," 230.

120 Santos-Febres, "Puerto Rican Underground," 230.

121 Quoted in R. Rivera, "Rapping Two Versions," 251.

122 Juan Carlos Pérez, "Señor Oficial, esto es rap," *El Nuevo Día,* October 10, 1997.

123 Quoted in Pérez, "Señor Oficial, esto es rap."

124 Marshall, "From Música Negra to Reggaeton Latino," 38; R. Rivera, "Cultura y poder."

125 R. Rivera, "Policing Morality," 112, 116.

126 Emphasis added. Carmen Millán Pabón, "Vicios granel en las escuelas," *El Nuevo Día,* March 15, 1995.

127 Besides the actual raids, school policies also stigmatized underground music. For example, many schools enforced dress codes that banned the baggy blue jeans and T-shirts popular among underground fans. See Giovannetti, "Popular Culture and Music in Puerto Rico," 87.

128 Santos-Febres, "Geografía en decibeles," 122.

129 For more critique of the "cultural imperialism" arguments, see R. Rivera, "Reflections from the Margins"; R. Rivera, "Cultura y Poder"; R. Rivera, "Policing Morality."

130 Fernando Clemente, "Entrando por la Salida," *Claridad,* February 18–24, 1994.

131 R. Rivera, "Policing Morality," 124; R. Rivera, "Cultura y poder," 130.

132 Edwin Reyes, "Rapeo sobre el rap en Ciales," *Claridad,* December 29–January 4, 1995–96; for more commentary on this editorial, see R. Rivera, "Cultura y poder"; R. Rivera, "Policing Morality."

133 Jiménez Román, "Boricuas vs. Nuyoricans"; Flores, *Diaspora Strikes Back*; Findlay, "Slipping and Sliding."

134 Giusti Cordero, "AfroPuerto Rican Cultural Studies," 59; Alan West-Durán, "The Pleasures and Traumas of Race," 56.

135 Yolanda Rosaly, "¡Alto a la música underground!" *El Nuevo Día,* February 7, 1995.

136 Mateo Mateo, "El escándolo y la aplicación de la ley," *El Nuevo Día,* February 25, 1995.

137 Rosaly, "¡Alto a la música underground!"

138 Emphasis added. Mateo, "El escándolo."

139 Santos-Febres, "Puerto Rican Underground," 226.

140 R. Rivera, "Policing Morality," 126.

141 Jorge Luis Medina, "Rappers rap bum rap and hypocrisy," *San Juan Star,* February 19, 1995.

142 R. Rivera, "Policing Morality," 118, 119.

143 R. Rivera, "Policing Morality," 118–20.

144 R. Rivera, "La música rap en Puerto Rico"; R. Rivera, "Cultura y poder."

145 Rafael Bernabe, "Rap: Soy Boricua pa' que tú lo sepas," *Claridad,* January 19–25, 1996.

146 Huaralí Reyes Avíles, "Playero DJ revela la historia del Underground," *El Vocero,* August 5, 1999.

147 Huaralí Reyes Avíles, "Playero DJ . . . el genio detrás del rap," *El Vocero,* August 6, 1999.

CHAPTER TWO. The Perils of Perreo

1 Quoted in María Vera, "Firme Velda contra la pornografía," *El Vocero,* May 30, 2002.

2 Quoted in Francisco Rodríguez-Burns, "Educar a los hijos al son del perreo," *Primera Hora,* May 19, 2003.

3 This preference for models with fair complexions and European features is similar to other music video genres, including those performed by and marketed to nonwhite communities. For example, many hip-hop videos in the United States reveal a preference for lighter women, including Puerto Ricans and other Latinas as well as African Americans. For more information, see R. Rivera, *New York Ricans*, 128, 134, 135.

4 Báez, "En mi imperio," 65.

5 See Aparicio, *Listening to Salsa,* for an analysis of the gendered representations in Puerto Rican salsa.

6 Similar tropes related to respectability and hypersexuality can be found in a variety of national contexts. For example, see Hammonds, "Genealogy of Black

Female Sexuality," for discussions related to race and sexuality in the United States; Rahier, *Blackness in the Andes*, 147–73, for analysis of Ecuador; and Findlay, *Imposing Decency*, and Quiñones Rivera, "From Trigueñita to Afro-Puerto Rican," for examinations of these tropes in Puerto Rico.

7   The Anti-Pornography Campaign has similarities with the U.S. trial of rap group 2 Live Crew, who were charged with obscenity in the 1990s due to their misogynistic rap lyrics. Kimberlè Williams Crenshaw argues that while 2 Live Crew did include problematic lyrical and visual representations of black women in their music and videos, the obscenity charges "selectively" focused on 2 Live Crew as opposed to other musicians partly because of racial stereotypes that marked black sexuality as "deviant" in the United States. Moreover, although the court case against 2 Live Crew attempted to address concerns about their music videos' impact on violence against women, Crenshaw claims that the issue of women's safety centered on white women even though black women dominated most of the representations in these music videos. See "Beyond Racism and Misogyny," 120–27.

8   Alexander, *Pedagogies of Crossing*.

9   Alexander, *Pedagogies of Crossing*, 23.

10   Carby, "Policing the Black Woman's Body in an Urban Context," 740.

11   Higginbotham, *Righteous Discontent*, 187. Evelyn Brooks Higginbotham argues that this politics of respectability among early twentieth-century African American women in the United States centered on reforming individuals' behavior as part of a broader political project for full incorporation of African Americans into the United States. While I draw from Higginbotham's work, it is also important to emphasize that the Anti-Pornography Campaign employed a politics of respectability in order to *reinforce*, not disrupt, the hegemony of racial democracy discourses.

12   Leonor Mulero, "Cinco medidas contra la difusión del perreo," *El Nuevo Día*, May 15, 2002; Nadesha Karina González, "Aprueban proyectos contra la obscenidad," *El Vocero*, June 15, 2002.

13   Carolina is a municipality located between San Juan and Loíza, and often associated with the development of reggaetón (see Rivera-Rideau, "From Carolina to Loíza," 626–27).

14   Quiñones Rivera, "From Trigueñita to Afro–Puerto Rican," 167–68.

15   Quiñones Rivera, "From Trigueñita to Afro-Puerto Rican," 168. See also Jorge, "The Black Puerto Rican Woman in Contemporary American Society"; Cruz-Janzen, "Latinegras."

16   Alegría, *Discovery, Conquest, and Colonization of Puerto Rico*, 157.

17   Díaz Soler uses *mestización* to mean *mestizaje*.

18   Díaz Soler, *Historia de la esclavitud negra en Puerto Rico*, 225.

19   McClintock, *Imperial Leather*; Stoler, *Carnal Knowledge and Imperial Power*.

20   Hintzen, "Race and Creole Ethnicity."

21   Edmonson, "Public Spectacles"; Hintzen, "Race and Creole Ethnicity"; Rahier, "Racial/Spatial Order."

22   Findlay, *Imposing Decency*, 25.

23 Findlay, *Imposing Decency*, 23.

24 Findlay, *Imposing Decency*, 24.

25 Findlay, *Imposing Decency*.

26 Findlay, *Imposing Decency*, 91, 178–79.

27 Findlay, *Imposing Decency*, 86.

28 Findlay, *Imposing Decency*, 205.

29 Findlay, *Imposing Decency*, 108.

30 Alexis Rolón, "La valentía de Velda González," *El Nuevo Día*, June 17, 2002.

31 Hilda Iriarte, "Respaldo a Velda González," *El Nuevo Día*, May 18, 2002.

32 Quoted in María Vera, "Pentacostales endorsan medidas de Velda," *El Vocero*, May 21, 2002.

33 Quoted in Ivonne Y. Rosario and Gladyra I. Archilla, "Urge se estudien proyectos de Velda," *El Vocero*, May 16, 2002.

34 Irene Garzón Fernández, "A vistas la pornografía," *Primera Hora*, May 22, 2002; María Vera, "Apoya controles Procuradora de la Mujer," *El Vocero*, May 30, 2002; María Vera, "Hay poder para regular vídeos del 'perreo,'" *El Vocero*, June 6, 2002.

35 Miried González Rodríguez, "Niña en custodia de DF: Huye y sale en un vídeo," *Primera Hora*, May 17, 2002; Carmen Millán, "A atacar las agencias el 'perreo,'" *El Nuevo Día*, June 11, 2002.

36 Miried González Rodríguez, "Niña en custodia de DF."

37 Millán, "A atacar"; María Vera, "Operativos contra producciones 'perreo,'" *El Vocero*, June 11, 2002.

38 Irene Garzón Fernández, "Ofensiva legislativa contra el 'perreo,'" *Primera Hora*, May 15, 2002; María Vera, "Ofensiva legislativa contra pornografía," *El Vocero*, May 15, 2002.

39 Sandra Morales Blanes, "Frente apoya una ley contra el 'perreo.'" *El Nuevo Día*, June 12, 2002.

40 Quoted in Leonor Mulero, "Clave la comunicación contra la pornografía," *El Nuevo Día*, May 16, 2002.

41 Adria Cruz, "Darse a respetar," *Primera Hora*, May 17, 2002; Nanny Torres, "Acá Entre Nos," *El Nuevo Día*, May 19, 2002.

42 Quoted in Gladys Nieves Ramírez, "Caravana pro perreo bloquea a tránsito," *El Nuevo Día*, May 28, 2002.

43 Quoted in Gladys Nieves Ramírez, "Caravana pro perreo bloquea a tránsito."

44 Nieve Vásquez, "La bomba fue el rap de hoy," *Primera Hora*, May 16, 2002.

45 Nieve Vásquez, "La bomba fue el rap de hoy," *Primera Hora*, May 16, 2002.

46 Cruz, "Darse a respetar."

47 Cruz, "Darse a respetar."

48 See Chasteen, *National Rhythms, African Roots*.

49 Ana Lydia Vega, "El jaleo del perreo," *El Nuevo Día*, May 23, 2002.

50 Ana Lydia Vega, "El jaleo del perreo," *El Nuevo Día*, May 23, 2002.

51 Aparicio, *Listening to Salsa*, 145.

52 Negrón-Muntaner, *Boricua Pop*, 251.

53 Negrón-Muntaner, *Boricua Pop*, 251.

54 Negrón-Muntaner, *Boricua Pop*, 256.

55 Jaime Garay, "Antes de legislar hay que definir," *El Nuevo Día*, May 22, 2002.

56 Rubén Arrieta Vilá, "De todo un poco," *El Nuevo Día*, May 27, 2002; Candida Cotto, "Violan derechos los proyectos sobre obscenidad," *Claridad*, July 19–25, 2002.

57 Cruz, "Darse a respetar"; Esther Vicente, "La Controversia sobre las 'Leyes del Perreo' . . . Libertad de Expresión, ¿Para Quién?" *Diálogo*, November 2002.

58 Ángel Casiano, "Opinión diferente sobre el 'perreo,'" *El Nuevo Día*, June 7, 2002.

59 Alberto Meléndez Juarbe, "Las personas que disfrutan la música 'underground' merecen respeto," *El Nuevo Día*, May 19, 2002.

60 Quoted in Leonor Mulero, "Productor critica la postura antirrap," *El Vocero*, May 16, 2002.

61 Quoted in Miried González Rodríguez, "Baile divide a los raperos," *Primera Hora*, May 17, 2002.

62 Quoted in González Rodríguez, "Baile divide a los raperos."

63 Quoted in González Rodríguez, "Baile divide a los raperos."

64 Quoted in Rosalina Marrero-Rodríguez, "El rap de los marginados," *Primera Hora*, February 2, 2002.

65 Liz Arelis Cruz Maisonave, "Raperos Wisin y Yandel respaldan que se limite contenido videos," *El Vocero*, May 18, 2002; Mulero, "Productor critica la postura antirrap."

66 Sandra Molares Blanes, "Discriminatoria la medida contra la pornografía," *El Nuevo Día*, June 13, 2002.

67 Quoted in Mulero, "Productor critica la postura antirrap."

68 Cruz Maisonave, "Wisin y Yandel"; González Rodríguez, "Baile divide a los raperos."

69 Quoted in Miried González Rodríguez, "Con esposa e hijos en vídeo: Familia unida en el perreo," *Primera Hora*, May 16, 2002.

70 Dinzey-Flores, *Locked In, Locked Out*, 87, 95, 137.

71 Miried González Rodríguez, "Niña en custodia del DF."

72 Miried González Rodríguez, "Niña en custodia del DF."

73 Miried González Rodríguez, "Niña en custodia del DF."

74 Miried González Rodríguez, "Bailarina ve su perreo como arte," *Primera Hora*, May 22, 2002.

75 Lewis, *La Vida*.

76 Dinzey-Flores, *Locked In, Locked Out*, 131.

77 Dinzey-Flores, *Locked In, Locked Out*, 132.

78 González Rodríguez, "Con esposa e hijos en video."

79 Miried González Rodríguez, "Bailarina ve su perreo."

80 Miried González Rodríguez, "Bailarina ve su perreo."

81 Quoted in González Rodríguez, "Bailarina ve su perreo."

82 Quoted in González Rodríguez, "Bailarina ve su perreo."

83 Quoted in González Rodríguez, "Bailarina ve su perreo."

84   Rosalina Marrero-Rodríguez, "Lo que bailan hoy los jóvenes: Erotismo en el 'perreo,'" *Primera Hora*, February 17, 2002; González Rodríguez, "Bailarina ve su perreo."

85   Quoted in González Rodríguez, "Bailarina ve su perreo."

86   Quoted in González Rodríguez, "Baile divide a los raperos."

87   Quoted in Tatiana Pérez Rivera, "Opinan 'las chicas del perreo,'" *El Nuevo Día*, May 28, 2002.

88   Quoted in Pérez Rivera, "Opinan las chicas."

89   Quoted in Pérez Rivera, "Opinan las chicas."

90   Francisco Rodríguez-Burns, "Niños en discoteca en Caguas: Escuela del perreo," *Primera Hora*, May 8, 2003.

91   Antonio R. Gómez, "Preocupados por los menores: Truenan Velda y líderes del Gobierno," *Primera Hora*, May 9, 2003.

92   Frances Tirado, "Padres raperos preocupados por lo que oyen los suyos," *Primera Hora*, May 19, 2003.

93   Nieve Vásquez, "Baile con alto contenido erótico," *Primera Hora*, September 1, 2003.

94   Esterlitz Dávila, "Perreo: puro 'show' sexual de los jóvenes," *Primera Hora*, November 18, 2003

95   Magdalys Rodríguez, "Diálogo sobre sexo y violencia en los medios," *El Nuevo Día*, November 12, 2002; María Vera, "A discusión violencia en medios," *El Vocero*, November 12, 2002.

96   Sara M. Justicia Doll, "Discusión de alumnos: Analiza el perreo en los videos," *Primera Hora*, December 17, 2003.

97   Mabel M. Figueroa, " 'Rankea'o' el reggaetón," *Primera Hora*, November 17, 2003.

98   Mabel M. Figueroa, " 'Rankea'o' el reggaetón," *Primera Hora*, November 17, 2003.

99   Francisco Rodríguez-Burns, "Educar a los hijos al son del perreo."

CHAPTER THREE. Loíza

1   Puerto Rican television has featured several popular blackface performers such as Ramón Rivero in the 1940s and Chianita in the 1970s. For more information about these and other representations of blackness on Puerto Rican television, see Rivero, *Tuning Out Blackness*.

2   Ritesh Gupta, *My Block: Puerto Rico*. MTV News and Docs. Aired April 16, 2006.

3   Jiménez, *Las prácticas de la carne*, 144.

4   It is worth mentioning that Don Omar's segment, which focused on a local cockfight, included a brief discussion about Puerto Rican culture in Piñones, although he did not discuss race. Located within the *municipio* of Loíza, many people recognize Piñones as another site associated with Afro–Puerto Rican life and culture. Jennifer Rudolph argues that Don Omar's segment of *My Block: Puerto Rico* represented Piñones as a site of poverty and blight, linking it to urban communities with which Don Omar often affiliates himself. Rudolph contends

that Don Omar's discussion in Piñones thus situates him in relation to blackness (see Rudolph, *Embodying Latino Masculinities*, 128–29). However, this blackness is more akin to urban blackness than the folkloric blackness associated with Loíza and Tego Calderón.

5   Tego Calderón first established himself as a local rapper before participating in reggaetón. In fact, he does not consider himself a reggaetón artist ("Guest DJ: Puerto Rican Rap Legend Tego Calderón," *Alt.Latino: Latin Alternative Music and Rock en Español*, August 9, 2012). However, since people generally consider Calderón to be a reggaetón artist, I incorporate his work into my discussion of reggaetón's racial politics.

6   Negrón-Muntaner and Rivera, "Reggaeton Nation," 37.

7   Negrón-Muntaner and Rivera, "Reggaeton Nation," 36.

8   José R. Pagán Sánchez, "Ritmos al compás de Tego," *El Nuevo Día*, February 7, 2003; José R. Pagán Sánchez, "Tego con todos los hierros," *El Nuevo Día*, February 28, 2003; José R. Pagán Sánchez, "Tego se prepara para su concierto," *El Nuevo Día*, March 6, 2003.

9   Laura Rivera Meléndez, "Brilla el 'negro Calde,' " *El Nuevo Día*, March 16, 2003.

10   Laura Rivera Meléndez, "Brilla el 'negro Calde,' " *El Nuevo Día*, March 16, 2003.

11   Negrón-Muntaner and Rivera, "Reggaeton Nation," 37.

12   Negrón-Muntaner and Rivera, "Reggaeton Nation," 37.

13   Rose, *Black Noise*.

14   Godreau, "Changing Space, Making Race."

15   Puri, *Caribbean Postcolonial*.

16   Many scholars document that, historically, large black populations lived in the coastal regions of Puerto Rico, where the sugar industry was most dominant during the nineteenth century (see Álvarez Nazario, *El Elemento Afronegroide en el Español de Puerto Rico*; Figueroa, *Sugar, Slavery, and Freedom*; Mintz, *Caribbean*; Scarano, *Sugar and Slavery in Puerto Rico*). As a result, places such as the neighborhood of San Antón in Ponce and the southern town of Guayama are likewise popularly recognized as sites with majority black populations (Figueroa, *Sugar, Slavery, and Freedom*; Godreau, "Missing the Mix"). Loíza also has a history of plantation life when several Spaniards established large sugar plantations there in the sixteenth century; sugar cultivation continued well into the twentieth century, especially when U.S. companies purchased sugar plantations at the end of the nineteenth century (see Pérez, "The Place of Abandonment," 26). Although the southern coast may have a more substantial history of plantation life, Loíza is often recognized as the primary "black place" in Puerto Rico, including in many of the other places also marked by folkloric blackness (Godreau, "Folkloric 'Others,' " 181).

17   Pérez, "The Place of Abandonment," 16, 73.

18   Hernández Hiraldo, *Black Puerto Rican Identity*; Pérez, "The Place of Abandonment." Despite Loíza's reputation, it is not the case that the town has always been isolated from the rest of the island. Juan Giusti Cordero documents that Loíza was a center for food production and trade at various points in Puerto Rico's history.

Thus, the perception of Loíza's isolation contradicts its history of economic and social connections with other places in Puerto Rico. See Giusti Cordero, "Labor, Ecology, and History in a Caribbean Sugar Plantation Region," 407.

19 Rivera-Rideau, "From Carolina to Loíza."

20 Alegría, *La Fiesta de Santiago Apóstol en Loíza Aldea*, 5.

21 Alegría, *La Fiesta de Santiago Apóstol en Loíza Aldea*, xxii.

22 Godreau, "Folkloric 'Others.'"

23 Barton, "The Drum Dance Challenge," 111; Barton, "The Challenges of Puerto Rican Bomba," 188; Barton, "A Challenge for Puerto Rican Music," 81.

24 Dávila, *Sponsored Identities*, 92–93.

25 Amanda Rivera, "Felicitación para Tego Calderón," *El Nuevo Día*, March 22, 2003.

26 R. Rivera, "Entrevista a Tego Calderón," 274.

27 Marshall, "From Música Negra to Reggaeton Latino," 64n3.

28 Quoted in R. Rivera, "Entrevista a Tego Calderón," 274. Some may argue that being from Río Grande gives Tego Calderón license to claim belonging to Loíza since the towns neighbor one another. Still, Loíza remains the place with the most institutional investment from both government-affiliated agencies and the tourism industry to support and develop cultural practices there that are perceived to be "black." Because Loíza is one of the officially recognized sites of folkloric blackness, then, I argue that many people imagine the town as unique within Puerto Rico's geography. Thus, the specific associations between Calderón and Loíza are critical for understanding his portrayal in Puerto Rico.

29 Another artist who visually and musically incorporates bomba into her performance is La Sista from Loíza. I attended a concert by La Sista in New York City's Central Park on July 14, 2007. In addition to a DJ (typical of most reggaetón artists), La Sista also included two bomba drummers, four back-up vocalists, and several dancers dressed in folkloric costumes. Besides Tego Calderón, La Sista is one of the very few artists who includes such overt bomba signifiers in her performance (see also Marshall, "From Música Negra to Reggaeton Latino," 64n3).

30 R. Rivera, "Entrevista a Tego Calderón," 277.

31 Here, Calderón refers to the process of spirit possession typical of many African-based religions in the Americas such as Santería. Saints are said to "mount" individuals during religious ceremonies. Loíza is popularly considered one of the major centers for African-based religions in Puerto Rico. Consequently, religion is another element that positions Loíza as the epicenter of black life and culture. See Hernández Hiraldo, *Black Puerto Rican Identity*.

32 Quoted in R. Rivera, "Entrevista a Tego Calderón," 274.

33 Rivera-Rideau, "Cocolos Modernos."

34 Aparicio, *Listening to Salsa*, 35; Rivero, *Tuning Out Blackness*. It is interesting to note that while Cortijo y su Combo is often credited with breaking these racial barriers, a fierce debate regarding whether or not to name the Centro de Bellas Artes after Rafael Cortijo brought issues about blackness in the island into stark relief. Many opponents of naming Bellas Artes after Cortijo claimed that such "popular" and working-class art forms could not be associated with such a presti-

gious venue. Juan Flores has argued that Cortijo y su Combo's musical sounds and lyrical themes that celebrated working-class, black, urban life were perceived as threatening to Puerto Rican elites, who sought to maintain a whitened construction of Puerto Rican national identity; see Juan Flores, *Divided Borders*, 92–97.

35 See Aurora Flores, "¡Ecua Jei! Ismael Rivera, El Sonero Mayor (A Personal Reflection)"; Rafael Figueroa Hernández, *Ismael Rivera*.

36 Rivera-Rideau, "Cocolos Modernos," 10–11.

37 Here it is important to note that Calderón does not racially distinguish himself from artists like Don Omar. In fact, Calderón not only has collaborated with Don Omar on several recordings (e.g., "Los Bandoleros" and "Chillin'"), he has also praised Don Omar's embracing of a black identity (see Calderón, "Black Pride," 325).

38 Daniel Rivera Vargas, "Bajo arresto el rapero Don Omar," *El Nuevo Día*, July 21, 2003; Frances Tirado, "Nada ilegal con guagua a nombre de Don Omar, dice su abogado," *Primera Hora*, August 10, 2006; Alex Figueroa Cancel, "Arrestan al reggaetonero Don Omar por caso de violencia del género," *El Nuevo Día*, September 17, 2014.

39 Rudolph, "'Pidieron Cacao.'"

40 Rudolph, *Embodying Latino Masculinities*, 129.

41 Indeed, many youth who perform bomba in Puerto Rico use the music to address concerns about racism, colonialism, sexism, and a host of other social issues. Bomba performance thus serves as an important site for the critique of many of the issues that underpin dominant discourses of racial democracy throughout the island and in the Puerto Rican diaspora. See Alamo-Pastrana, "Con el Eco de los Barriles."

42 Calderón's pride in his *bemba* also brings to mind Cortijo y su Combo's hit "El negro bembón." This song tells the story of a young policeman with a *bemba* who hides it when confronting a murderer who killed a young man for also having large lips. Although some have criticized "El negro bembón" for replicating stereotypes that equate blackness with ugliness, the song can also be read as an account of both the physical and emotional violence faced by black communities on the island. From Calderón's perspective, "El negro bembón" is an example of how artists like Rafael Cortijo tried to use humor to address racial politics on the island (see Jasmine Garsd, "Black, Puerto Rican, and Proud: Guest DJ Tego Calderón," *Alt.Latino: Latin Alternative Music and Rock en Español*, May 23, 2013).

43 See Melanie Byron, "The Top Dog," *Source Latino*, fall 2005; Calderón, "Black Pride."

44 Rahier, "Racial/Spatial Order."

45 *LatinHop*, "Orgulloso de su raza," 2006; Marcos Pérez Ramírez, "Tego batea una línea dura," *El Nuevo Día*, October 16, 2006.

46 Quoted in Pérez Ramírez, "Tego batea una línea dura."

47 Quoted in María Ivette Vega Calles, "Consciente de su Misión," *El Nuevo Día*, July 11, 2010.

48 Wade, *Blackness and Race Mixture*.

49 Calderón, "Black Pride."
50 Quoted in Byron, "Top Dog."
51 The editorial was reprinted in *Reggaeton*, edited by Raquel Z. Rivera, Wayne Marshall, and Deborah Pacini Hernández.
52 Calderón, "Black Pride," 325.
53 Jiménez Román and Flores, eds., *The Afro-Latin@ Reader.*
54 Calderón, "Black Pride," 324.
55 Quoted in Byron, "Top Dog," 62.
56 Garsd, "Black, Puerto Rican, and Proud."
57 Garsd, "Black, Puerto Rican, and Proud"; Byron, "Top Dog."
58 Calderón, "Black Pride," 326.
59 Calderón, "Black Pride," 325.
60 Calderón, "Black Pride," 325.
61 In this context, I believe the interviewer uses the term *negroide* to refer to an artistic movement in Puerto Rico that celebrates blackness. Some scholars have criticized the *negroide* cultural movement in Puerto Rico for replicating stereotypical tropes of blackness, particularly associations between blackness and nature; see Giusti Cordero, "AfroPuerto Rican Cultural Studies."
62 Muñequitos de Matanzas is a rumba group from Cuba. Rumba and bomba are different musical genres, although they have several similarities in their structure and performance. Furthermore, like bomba does in Puerto Rico, rumba has come to represent Afro-Cuban heritage in dominant depictions of Cuban national identity (see Daniel, *Rumba*). Although Muñequitos de Matanzas is not Puerto Rican, this quote recognizes the musical and cultural similarities between bomba and rumba as well as Calderón's recognition of the African diasporic connections between Puerto Rico and Cuba. Indeed, Berta Jottar has documented how Cuban rumba became an expression of pan-Latino solidarity in New York City, where many Nuyorican musicians adopted rumba performance as an expression of their own Afro-Latinidad (see Jottar, "Central Park Rumba").
63 Quoted in Byron, "Top Dog," 64.
64 Rivera-Rideau, "Cocolos Modernos," 12.
65 Quoted in Garsd, "Black, Puerto Rican, and Proud."
66 Jiménez, *Las prácticas de la carne*, 144.
67 Reyes-Santos, "Race, Empire, and Development in the Caribbean."
68 Reyes-Santos, "Race, Empire, and Development in the Caribbean."
69 Reyes-Santos, "Race, Empire, and Development in the Caribbean."
70 Hall, "What Is This 'Black' in Black Popular Culture?" 471.
71 Hall, "What Is This 'Black' in Black Popular Culture?" 470.

CHAPTER FOUR. Fingernails con Feeling

1 Báez, "En mi imperio," 68.
2 Quoted in *Primera Hora*, "Ivy Queen apoya la unión entre parejas del mismo sexo," June 12, 2002.

3 José R. Pagán Sánchez, "Se desborda con alegría Ivy Queen," *El Nuevo Día*, June 9, 2004; Christian del Moral, "Ivy Queen sigue adelante," *El Diario La Prensa*, November 29, 2002.

4 José R. Pagán, "Se da a respetar," *El Nuevo Día*, December 2, 2007; del Moral, "Ivy Queen sigue adelante."

5 Quoted in del Moral, "Ivy Queen sigue adelante."

6 Marcos Billy Guzmán, "Sin miedo a ser problemática," *El Nuevo Día*, April 9, 2010.

7 Aponte-Parés et al., "Puerto Rican Sexualities"; Negrón-Muntaner, "When I Was a Puerto Rican Lesbian"; Rodríguez, "Getting F****d in Puerto Rico."

8 Quoted in Rita Portela López, "Mintió, el Nuevo de Ivy Queen," *El Nuevo Día*, September 6, 2001.

9 Quoted in Tatiana Pérez Rivera, "Los inicios del perreo en el isla," *El Nuevo Día*, May 27, 2002.

10 Báez, "En mi imperio," 69.

11 Báez, "En mi imperio," 73.

12 Vazquez, "Salon Philosophers."

13 Vazquez, "Salon Philosophers," 301.

14 Ayala Ben-Yehuda, "Queen Mother," *Billboard—The International Newsweekly of Music Video and Home Entertainment*, July 31, 2010.

15 At the time of this writing, Ivy Queen appears to have cut her nails. In one interview, she stated that she would only cut her nails if she had a baby (see Patricia Vargas, "Se cortaría las garras . . . sólo por un hijo," *El Nuevo Día*, August 12, 2008), and her first child was born in late 2013—perhaps this is what prompted the new style. Nevertheless, Ivy Queen has maintained her long acrylics for most of her career to date, and they remain important attributes of her persona.

16 Butler, *Bodies That Matter*, 126; Hobson, *Body as Evidence*, 48.

17 Cruz-Janzen, "Latinegras." See also Jorge, "The Black Puerto Rican Woman," and Quiñones Rivera, "From Trigueñita to Afro–Puerto Rican."

18 Jiménez Román, "Looking at That Middle Ground," 64.

19 Báez, "En mi imperio," 69.

20 Báez, "En mi imperio," 67.

21 See Bonilla-Silva, "*Negrito Acomplejao*," 451; Rivera-Rideau, "From Carolina to Loíza," 12.

22 Arroyo, "Virtualities of Racial Imaginaries," 199n2.

23 Rebollo-Gil, "Entre Cafres y Blanquitos," 102.

24 Rebollo-Gil, "Entre Cafres y Blanquitos," 101–2.

25 "Sin freno La Caballota," *El Nuevo Día*, November 18, 2007.

26 Doty, "There's Something about Mary," 4.

27 Báez, "En mi imperio," 73–74.

28 Báez, "En mi imperio," 74.

29 Jiménez, "(W)rapped in Foil," 240.

30 Caballota translates to "female horse."

31 Jiménez, "(W)rapped in Foil," 230.

32 Cepeda, *Musical ImagiNation*, 75; Valdivia, "Is Penélope to J.Lo as Culture Is to Nature?," 138.

33 Richard Araujo, "Cautiva la visión de Ivy Queen," *El Nuevo Día*, November 16, 2003; Báez, "En mi imperio," 72; "Ivy Queen: 'Pienso como hombre, rapeo como tal, pero no soy lesbiana,'" *Hoy Online*, November 19, 2008.

34 "Ivy Queen: 'Pienso como hombre, rapeo como tal, pero no soy lesbiana,'" *Hoy Online*, November 19, 2008.

35 *Move Your Body: A Reggaeton Special*, BET, aired January 25, 2005.

36 Eliezer Rivera, "Ivy Queen, diva y reina," *El Nuevo Herald*, August 13, 2003.

37 Miriam Fernández-Soberon, "Ivy Queen, madrina de los boricuas," *El Nuevo Día*, May 29, 2004; Nuria Net, "Ivy Queen," *Latina Magazine*, March 2006.

38 Negrón-Muntaner, "Celia's Shoes," 108.

39 Negrón-Muntaner, "Celia's Shoes," 108.

40 Jiménez, "(W)rapped in Foil," 242.

41 Muñoz, *Disidentifications*, 31.

42 Nicole Fleetwood and Jennifer Dawn Whitney make similar observations of U.S.-based black women rappers Lil' Kim and Nicki Minaj, respectively. See Fleetwood, *Troubling Vision*; Whitney, "Some Assembly Required."

43 Fleetwood, *Troubling Vision*, 109, 144.

44 Moore, "Tina Theory," 72.

45 Patricia Vargas, "Se cortaría las garras."

46 Patricia Vargas, "Ya tiene su propia muñeca," *El Nuevo Día*, June 24, 2009.

47 Nelly Apaza Retamoso, "Ivy Queen, un pilar del reggaetón," *La Opinión*, April 12, 2007.

48 Quoted in Yoselín Acevedo, "Ivy Queen: I've Had My Heart Broken Many Times," *People en Español* online, March 26, 2008.

49 For more information, see Ahmed-Ghosh, "Writing the Nation on the Beauty Queen's Body"; Banet-Weiser, *The Most Beautiful Girl in the World*; Edmonson, "Public Spectacles."

50 P. Rivera, "*Orgulloso de mi Caserío y de Quien Soy*," 87–88.

51 Jiménez, "(W)rapped in Foil," 239.

52 Quoted in Retamoso, "Un pilar del reggaetón."

53 Retamoso, "Un pilar del reggaetón."

54 Eduardo Alegría, "Ivy Queen: Giro de 360 Grados." *El Diario la Prensa*, April 12, 2007; Retamoso, "Un pilar del reggaetón."

55 Ayala Ben-Yehuda, "The Ladies of Latin Hip Hop," *Billboard—The International Newsweekly of Music, Video and Home Entertainment*, March 31, 2007. Sometimes called *reggaetón romántico, romantiqueo* is a subset of reggaetón that is usually performed by male duos who infuse reggaetón with contemporary R&B.

56 Jon Pareles, "Two Romeos Romance the World to an Adrenalized Reggaetón Beat," *New York Times*, June 9, 2008.

57 Brooks, "'All That You Can't Leave Behind,'" 201.

58 Brooks, "'All That You Can't Leave Behind,'" 186.

59 Muñoz, "Feeling Brown," 70.

60 Muñoz, "Feeling Brown," 70.

61 Aparicio, *Listening to Salsa*, 128.

62 Aparicio, *Listening to Salsa*, 135.

63 Aparicio, *Listening to Salsa*, 136.

64 García Yero, "Is It Just about Love?"; Washburne, "Play It 'Con Filin!'"

65 Knights, "Tears and Screams," 87.

66 Aparicio, *Listening to Salsa*, 175. Deborah Vargas makes a similar observation in her analysis of the bolero performances of Chelo Silva. She contends that Silva's boleros disrupt the hypermasculine ethos of much of Chicano popular music. See Vargas, *Dissonant Divas in Chicana Music*, 54–107.

67 Alegría, "Giro de 360 Grados."

68 Quoted in José R. Pagán Sánchez, "'Flashback' de once años," *El Nuevo Día*, October 22, 2005.

69 Quoted in Retamoso, "Un pilar del reggaetón."

70 Quoted in Acevedo, "I've Had My Heart Broken."

71 Jorge J. Muñiz Ortiz, "Ivy Queen se desahoga con 'Drama Queen,'" *El Diario La Prensa*, April 13, 2010.

72 Quoted in María I. Vega, "Con sus sentimientos a flor de piel," *El Nuevo Día*, April 10, 2007.

73 Quoted in Ayala Ben-Yehuda, "Reggaetón Royalty," *Billboard—The International Newsweekly of Music, Video and Home Entertainment*, March 31, 2007.

74 Aparicio, *Listening to Salsa*, 179; Aparicio and Valentín-Escobar, "Memorializing La Lupe and Lavoe," 81; Salazar, *Mambo Kingdom*, 173.

75 Aparicio, *Listening to Salsa*, 179–83.

76 Aparicio, *Listening to Salsa*, 178; Aparicio and Valentín-Escobar, "Memorializing La Lupe and Lavoe," 185; Muñoz, *Disidentifications*, 192; Poey, "¡La Lupe!," 79.

77 Knights, "Tears and Screams," 89.

78 Poey, "¡La Lupe!," 79. Poey considers La Lupe's performance in relation to representations of the racially mixed *mulata* figure in Cuba. Though different from blackness, many of the tropes and stereotypes associated with the *mulata*, particularly concerning hypersexuality, are similar to those of black women more generally. This comparison is especially salient given Cuba's constructions of national identity, which, like Puerto Rican racial democracy discourses, have celebrated race mixture while simultaneously disregarding blackness. For more information, see de la Fuente, *A Nation for All*; Helg, "Race in Argentina and Cuba, 1880–1930"; Sawyer, *Racial Politics in Post-Revolutionary Cuba*.

79 Aparicio, *Listening to Salsa*, 177.

80 Aparicio, *Listening to Salsa*, 177.

81 Aparicio and Valentín-Escobar, "Memorializing La Lupe and Lavoe."

82 Aparicio, *Listening to Salsa*, 179.

83 Poey, "¡La Lupe!"

84 Aparicio, *Listening to Salsa*, 179–82.

85 See F. Mexía, "La 'diva' del reguetón revelará todo," *El Diario La Prensa*, August 20, 2008.

86 Quoted in Aparicio, *Listening to Salsa*, 181.

87 Quoted in Aparicio, *Listening to Salsa*, 181–82.

88 The concert took place in the Coliseo de Puerto Rico José Miguel Agrelot in San Juan, Puerto Rico, on November 30, 2007. A recording of the concert is available on the DVD *Ivy Queen—Live! From the Coliseum of Puerto Rico* (Drama Records, Inc./Machete Music/Universal Music, 2008).

89 Pacini Hernández, *Bachata*, 5–6.

90 Rudolph, " 'Roncamos Porque Podemos,' " 37.

91 Vargas, *Dissonant Divas*, 92.

92 Aparicio, "La Lupe, La India, and Celia," 140.

CHAPTER FIVE. Enter the Hurbans

1 Marshall, "From Música Negra to Reggaeton Latino," 19.

2 Carolina A. Miranda, "Daddy Yankee: Reigning Champ of Reggaeton," *Time Magazine*, May 8, 2006.

3 Sarah Corbett, "The King of Reggaeton: How a Poor, Pudgy Kid from the San Juan Projects Reinvented Latin Music for the Hip-Hop Generation and Became an International Star," *New York Times*, February 5, 2006.

4 Quoted in Corbett, "The King of Reggaeton."

5 Marshall, "From Música Negra to Reggaeton Latino," 19.

6 Cepeda, *Musical ImagiNation*, 52.

7 Cepeda, *Musical ImagiNation*, 58.

8 Dávila, *Latino Spin*.

9 Aparicio and Chávez-Silverman, eds., *Tropicalizations*.

10 Marshall, "From Música Negra to Reggaeton Latino," 57.

11 Marshall, "From Música Negra to Reggaeton Latino," 60; Pacini Hernández, *Oye Como Va!*, 75, 160.

12 Marshall, "From Música Negra to Reggaeton Latino," 57.

13 Jiménez Román and Flores, *The Afro-Latin@ Reader*.

14 Negus, "The Music Business and Rap."

15 Pacini Hernández, "The Name Game," 50.

16 Marshall, "From Música Negra to Reggaeton Latino," 58.

17 Angie Romero, "Latin Kings," *Vibe Magazine*, November 2005.

18 Steve Jones, "Spanish-spiced Hip Hop," *USA Today*, August 5, 2005; Romero, "Latin Kings."

19 Leila Cobo and Tony Sanders, "Radio Hooked on Latin," *Billboard Magazine*, April 6, 2005.

20 Jim Farber, "A New Spin on Spanish: With Its 'Hurban' Mix, Radio Is Getting Hip to Hispanic Youth," *New York Daily News*, May 30, 2005.

21 Kalefa Sanneh, "Reggaeton's Rise on Radio Show Isn't Bad," *New York Times*, June 30, 2005.

22 Cobo and Sanders, "Radio Hooked on Latin"; Sanneh, "Reggaeton's Rise on Radio."

23 Farber, "A New Spin on Spanish."

24 Quoted in Cobo and Sanders, "Radio Hooked on Latin."

25 Dávila, *Latinos, Inc.*

26 Dávila, *Latino Spin*, 71–94.

27 Quoted in Farber, "A New Spin on Spanish."

28 Pacini Hernández, *Oye Como Va!*

29 Oboler, *Ethnic Labels, Latino Lives.*

30 Flores, *From Bomba to Hip Hop*, 164.

31 This includes the distinct racialization of other Latino groups such as Cubans or Mexicans, who do not necessarily share the same stereotypes as Nuyoricans or other urban Puerto Rican communities.

32 It is important to acknowledge that the racialization of *Hurban* is distinct from the adjective *urbana* in the phrase *música urbana* that is often associated with reggaetón in Latin American and Latino communities. In the case of *música urbana*, the *urban* label connotes ties to blackness and black popular culture. Indeed, this is not surprising given reggaetón's connections to blackness in Puerto Rico and elsewhere. For the purposes of this chapter, however, I am interested in theorizing how the urban operates within the broader construction of the Hurban category, which, I argue, is a uniquely U.S. development that attempts to diminish the links to blackness that reggaetón already contained as *música urbana*.

33 Forman, *The 'Hood Comes First*; Kelley, "Looking for the 'Real' Nigga."

34 Forman, *The 'Hood Comes First*, 43.

35 Forman, *The 'Hood Comes First*, 43.

36 Kelley, "Looking for the 'Real' Nigga," 120.

37 Forman, *The 'Hood Comes First*, 49–50.

38 Forman, *The 'Hood Comes First*, 51.

39 Many scholars have analyzed and critiqued these images of Puerto Ricans in New York. For example, see Grosfoguel and Georas, " 'Coloniality of Power' and Racial Dynamics"; R. Rivera, *New York Ricans.*

40 Chavez, *Out of the Barrio*. For a critique of Chavez, see R. Rivera, *New York Ricans*, 28–29.

41 Grosfoguel and Georas, " 'Coloniality of Power' and Racial Dynamics," 105.

42 Lewis, *La Vida.*

43 Moynihan, "The Negro Family."

44 Forman, *The 'Hood Comes First*; Kelley, "Looking for the 'Real' Nigga"; Negus, "The Music Business and Rap"; R. Rivera, *New York Ricans.*

45 Flores, *From Bomba to Hip-Hop*; R. Rivera, *New York Ricans.*

46 R. Rivera, *New York Ricans*, 99.

47 R. Rivera, *New York Ricans*, 98–99.

48 R. Rivera, *New York Ricans*, 99.

49 R. Rivera, *New York Ricans*, 107.

50 Mireya Navarro, "Mad Hot Reggaeton," *New York Times*, July 17, 2005.

51 Baker, "Can BET Make You Black?," 359.

52 It is important to note that many artists are classified or identify themselves as Latin hip-hop artists, who are distinct from reggaetón, despite U.S. media's tendency to lump them together.

53 Agustin Gurza, "A Rowdy Sound Leaves Salsa Behind on the Dance Floor," *Los Angeles Times*, April 30, 2005.

54 Navarro, "Mad Hot Reggaeton."

55 Jon Pareles, "Reggaeton's Big Star Hits the Big Time," *New York Times*, August 25, 2005.

56 Navarro, "Mad Hot Reggaeton."

57 Juan Carlos Perez-Duthrie, "Raperos Rule: As Rap Recedes on the U.S. Mainland, Reggaeton Rises on the Enchanted Island," *Miami New Times*, May 9, 2002.

58 Pareles, "Reggaeton's Big Star."

59 Jon Pareles, "A Caribbean Party with a Hip Hop Beat," *New York Times*, August 12, 2003.

60 Gurza, "A Rowdy Sound."

61 Pareles, "Caribbean Party."

62 For a detailed analysis of the debates surrounding gangsta rap, see Lipsitz, *Footsteps in the Dark*, 154–83.

63 Rose, *The Hip Hop Wars*, 9, 62.

64 I do not mean to suggest that cultural practices such as hip-hop or reggaetón do not have any problematic content. Certainly, many individuals involved in both rap and reggaetón reinforce the very same stereotypes that affiliate blackness and/or Latinidad with hypersexuality, violence, and a host of other behaviors. However, here I am interested in unpacking the broader constructions of these stereotypes and their imposition on racial groups.

65 In some instances, dancing to popular music and having fun might be considered liberatory because it can serve as a respite from harsh living conditions and build community among people disenfranchised by colonialism, social inequality, or other forms of injustice (for example, see Berríos-Miranda, "Salsa Music as Expressive Liberation"; Guilbault, "Music, Politics, and Pleasure"). However, the representation of reggaetón in the U.S. media ignores the inequalities against which reggaetón might serve as a space for liberation. Instead, these representations situate reggaetón within problematic frames that reinforce stereotypes of the fun-loving and fiesta Latino.

66 See Corbett, "The King of Reggaeton"; Pareles, "Reggaeton's Big Star"; Romero, "Latin Kings."

67 Corbett, "The King of Reggaeton"; Pareles, "Reggaeton's Big Star"; Romero, "Latin Kings."

68 Quoted in Pareles, "Reggaeton's Big Star."

69 Romero, "Latin Kings."

70 Dinzey-Flores, "De la Disco al Caserío," 45.

71 Quoted in Pareles, "Reggaeton's Big Star." See also Dinzey-Flores, "De la Disco al Caserío," 41–42.

72 Dinzey-Flores, "De la Disco al Caserío," 43–44.

73 See Corbett, "The King of Reggaeton."

74 Jiménez, "W(rapped) in Foil," 236; see also Dinzey-Flores, "De la Disco al Caserío," 53.

75 Marshall, "From Música Negra to Reggaeton Latino," 59; Vazquez, "Salon Philosophers," 301–2.

76 Quoted in Rashaun Hall, "N.O.R.E. Reps His Latin Side with Reggaeton, 'Oye Mi Canto,'" MTV News Online, November 3, 2004.

77 Baker, "Can BET Make You Black?" 360.

78 Indeed, this assumption is so common that several scholars have documented the ways in which many other black-identified people attempt to assert their ethnic backgrounds in order to distance themselves from African Americans, either to avoid the discrimination faced by African Americans or because they also harbor stereotypes of African Americans and do not wish to be confused with them. For more information, see Candelario, "Displaying Identity"; Hintzen, West Indians in the West; Waters, Black Identities.

79 See Navarro, "Mad Hot Reggaeton"; Pareles, "Reggaeton's Big Star."

80 Quoted in In the House Magazine, "Notch: Citizen of the World," no. 34, 2007.

81 "Notch Lanza su Primer Album Como Solista Titulado, 'Raised by the People,'" Terra.com, May 24, 2007.

82 Ayala Ben-Yehuda, "Notch," Billboard.com, June 29, 2007.

83 Quoted in New York Beacon, "Notch Hopes His Musical Styles Will Tear Down Cultural Barriers," October 11, 2007.

84 Quoted in Kathy Iandoli, "Notch Cross Colors," All HipHop, June 6, 2007.

85 Steely and Cleevie are popular Jamaican dancehall producers. Pocomania is a Jamaican religion.

86 Quoted in Edwin Houghton, "Stats: Cuban Links: Notch Lays It Down Over Troubled Water," Fader, no. 40 (2006).

87 Quoted in Iandoli, "Notch Cross Colors."

88 P. Rivera, "Tropical Mix," 228–30.

89 P. Rivera, "Tropical Mix," 231.

90 Notch's project is similar to the Latinities described by Claudia Milian (Latining America). Milian proposes Latinities as a concept that acknowledges the ways that Latino identity might serve as a moving signifier, departing from narrow definitions of Latinidad and instead acknowledging the diverse experiences within groups of Latin American descent in the United States.

91 Marshall, Rivera, and Pacini Hernández, "Socio-Sonic Circuitry," 1. While there is undeniable cross-fertilization between hip-hop and reggaetón, these connections have been contested. Wayne Marshall, Raquel Z. Rivera, and Deborah Pacini Hernández note that several critics admonished reggaetón once it emerged in the United States, presenting the music as the "enemy" of hip-hop in ways that align with the perceived conflict between African Americans and Latinos. Moreover, they point out that reggaetón's emergence at the same time as intense debates about immigration fueled this tension. Reggaetón and hip-hop are often perceived in opposition to each other in other contexts as well; for

example, see Baker, "The Politics of Dancing"; Romero Joseph, "From Hip-Hop to Reggaeton."

CONCLUSION

1   Allison Stewart, "Album Review: Don Omar, Meet the Orphans," *Washington Post Blog*, November 16, 2010.
2   Brown, "Buzz and Rumble," 140.
3   Rodrigues, "Youth in Angola," 8; Moorman, *Intonations*, 193.
4   Brown, "Buzz and Rumble," 141.
5   Moorman, *Intonations*, 193.
6   Marcon, "Identidade e estilo em Lisboa."
7   Reiter, "National Pride and Imperial Neurosis," 88–89; Reiter, "The Perils of Empire."
8   Reiter, "National Pride and Imperial Neurosis"; Reiter, "The Perils of Empire."
9   Marcon, "Identidade e estilo em Lisboa," 6–7.
10 Brown, "Buzz and Rumble," 140.
11 Brown, "Buzz and Rumble," 140–41.
12 Taylor, *Global Pop*, 50.
13 For example, see Klimt, "European Spaces."
14 Silberman, Alba, and Fournier, "Segmented Assimilation in France?"
15 Rudolph, "Pidieron Cacao."
16 Rudolph, "Pidieron Cacao," 48.
17 Brown, "Buzz and Rumble," 132.
18 Gopinath, "Bombay, U.K., Yuba City," 307.
19 Gopinath, "Bombay, U.K., Yuba City," 307.
20 Gopinath, "Bombay, U.K., Yuba City"; Lebrón, "Con un flow natural," 220.
21 Lebrón, "Con un flow natural," 223.
22 Lebrón, "Con un flow natural," 223.

BIBLIOGRAPHY

Ahmed-Ghosh, Huma. "Writing the Nation on the Beauty Queen's Body: Implications for a 'Hindu' Nation." *Meridians: Feminism, Race, Transnationalism* 4, no. 1 (2003): 205–27.

Alamo-Pastrana, Carlos. "Con el Eco de los Barriles: Race, Gender, and the Bomba Imaginary in Puerto Rico." *Identities* 16, no. 5 (2009): 573–600.

Alamo-Pastrana, Carlos. "Disrupting Declarations of Freedom: The Enlistment of Race within and against Racial Regimes in Puerto Rico." PhD diss., University of California, Santa Barbara, 2009.

Alegría, Ricardo E. *La Fiesta de Santiago Apóstol en Loíza Aldea.* Madrid: Artes Gráficas, 1954.

Alegría, Ricardo E. *Discovery, Conquest, and Colonization of Puerto Rico, 1493–1599.* San Juan: Centro de Estudios Puertorriqueños, 1971.

Alexander, M. Jacqui. *Pedagogies of Crossing: Meditations on Feminism, Sexual Politics, Memory, and the Sacred.* Durham, NC: Duke University Press, 2005.

Álvarez Nazario, Manuel. *El elemento afronegroide en el español de Puerto Rico.* San Juan: Instituto de Cultura Puertorriqueña, 1974.

Andrews, George Reid. *Afro-Latin America, 1800–2000.* New York: Oxford University Press, 2004.

Aparicio, Frances R. *Listening to Salsa: Latin Popular Music and Puerto Rican Culture.* Hanover, NH: University Press of New England, 1998.

Aparicio, Frances R. "La Lupe, La India, and Celia: Toward a Feminist Genealogy of Salsa Music." In *Situating Salsa: Global Markets and Local Meanings in Latin Popular Music,* edited by Lise Waxer, 135–60. New York: Routledge, 2002.

Aparicio, Frances R., and Susana Chávez-Silverman, eds. *Tropicalizations: Transcultural Representations of Latinidad.* Hanover, NH: University Press of New England, 1997.

Aparicio, Frances R., and Wilson A. Valentín-Escobar. "Memorializing La Lupe and Lavoe: Singing Vulgarity, Transnationalism, and Gender." CENTRO: Journal of the Center for Puerto Rican Studies 16, no. 2 (2004): 78–101.

Aponte-Parés, Luis, Jossianna Arroyo, Elizabeth Crespo-Kebler, Lawrence La Fountain-Stokes, and Frances Negrón-Muntaner. "Puerto Rican Sexualities: Introduction." CENTRO: Journal of the Center for Puerto Rican Studies 19, no. 1 (2007): 4–24.

Arroyo, Jossianna. "'Roots,' or the Virtualities of Racial Imaginaries in Puerto Rico and the Diaspora." Latino Studies 8, no. 2 (2010): 195–219.

Báez, Jillian M. "'En mi imperio': Competing Discourses of Agency in Ivy Queen's Reggaetón." CENTRO: Journal of the Center for Puerto Rican Studies 18, no. 1 (2006): 63–80.

Baker, Ejima. "Can BET Make You Black? Remixing and Reshaping Latin@s on Black Entertainment Television." In The Afro-Latin@ Reader: History and Culture in the United States, edited by Miriam Jiménez Román and Juan Flores, 358–63. Durham, NC: Duke University Press, 2010.

Baker, Geoff. "The Politics of Dancing: Reggaetón and Rap in Havana, Cuba." In Reggaeton, edited by Raquel Z. Rivera, Wayne Marshall, and Deborah Pacini Hernández, 165–99. Durham, NC: Duke University Press, 2009.

Banet-Weiser, Sarah. The Most Beautiful Girl in the World: Beauty Pageants and National Identity. Berkeley: University of California Press, 1999.

Barton, Halbert E. "The Drum Dance Challenge: An Anthropological Study of Gender, Race, and Class Marginalization of Bomba in Puerto Rico." PhD diss., Cornell University, 1995.

Barton, Halbert E. "The Challenges of Puerto Rican Bomba." In Caribbean Dance from Abakuá to Zouk: How Movement Shapes Identity, edited by Susanna Sloat, 183–96. Gainesville: University Press of Florida, 2002.

Barton, Halbert E. "A Challenge for Puerto Rican Music: How to Build a Soberao for Bomba." CENTRO: Journal of the Center for Puerto Rican Studies 16, no. 2 (2004): 69–89.

Berríos-Miranda, Marisol. "Salsa Music as Expressive Liberation." CENTRO: Journal of the Center for Puerto Rican Studies 16, no. 2 (2004): 159–73.

Betances, Samuel. "The Prejudice of Having No Prejudice in Puerto Rico: Part I." Rican: Revista de Pensamiento Contemporáneo Puertorriqueño 2 (1972): 41–54.

Blanco, Tomás. El prejuicio racial en Puerto Rico. 2nd ed. San Juan: Editorial Biblioteca de Autores Puertorriqueños, 1948.

Bonilla-Silva, Eduardo. "Reflections about Race by a Negrito Acomplejao." In The Afro-Latin@ Reader: History and Culture in the United States, edited by Miriam Jiménez Román and Juan Flores, 445–52. Durham, NC: Duke University Press, 2010.

Brah, Avtar. Cartographies of Diaspora: Contesting Identities. London: Routledge, 1996.

Brooks, Daphne A. "'All That You Can't Leave Behind': Black Female Soul Singing and the Politics of Surrogation in the Age of Catastrophe." Meridians: Feminism, Race, Transnationalism 8, no. 1 (2006): 180–204.

Brown, Jacqueline Nassy. "Black Liverpool, Black America, and the Gendering of Diasporic Space." *Cultural Anthropology* 13, no. 3 (1998): 291–325.

Brown, Jacqueline Nassy. *Dropping Anchor, Setting Sail: Geographies of Race in Black Liverpool.* Princeton, NJ: Princeton University Press, 2005.

Brown, Jayna. "Buzz and Rumble: Global Pop Music and Utopian Impulse." *Social Text* 28, no. 1 102 (2010): 125–46.

Butler, Judith. *Bodies That Matter: On the Discursive Limits of "Sex."* New York: Routledge, 1993.

Butler, Kim. "Defining Diaspora, Refining a Discourse." *Diaspora* 10, no. 2 (2001): 189–219.

Calderón, Tego. "Black Pride." In *Reggaeton*, edited by Raquel Z. Rivera, Wayne Marshall, and Deborah Pacini Hernández, 324–26. Durham, NC: Duke University Press, 2009.

Campt, Tina M. "Diaspora Space, Ethnographic Space: Writing History Between the Lines." In *Globalization and Race: Transformations in the Cultural Production of Blackness*, edited by Kamari Maxine Clarke and Deborah A. Thomas, 93–111. Durham, NC: Duke University Press, 2006.

Candelario, Ginetta E. B. "Displaying Identity: Dominicans in the Black Mosaic of Washington, D.C." In *The Afro-Latin@ Reader: History and Culture in the United States*, edited by Miriam Jiménez Román and Juan Flores, 326–42. Durham, NC: Duke University Press, 2010.

Carby, Hazel V. "Policing the Black Woman's Body in an Urban Context." *Critical Inquiry* 8, no. 4 (1992): 738–55.

Cepeda, María Elena. *Musical ImagiNation: U.S.-Colombian Identity and the Latin Music Boom.* New York: New York University Press, 2010.

Chang, Jeff. *Can't Stop, Won't Stop: A History of the Hip-Hop Generation.* New York: Picador, 2005.

Chasteen, John Charles. *National Rhythms, African Roots: A Deep History of Latin American Popular Dance.* Albuquerque: University of New Mexico Press, 2004.

Chavez, Linda. *Out of the Barrio: Toward a New Politics of Hispanic Assimilation.* New York: Beacon Books, 1991.

Clarke, Kamari Maxine, and Deborah A. Thomas, eds. *Globalization and Race: Transformations in the Cultural Politics of Blackness.* Durham, NC: Duke University Press, 2006.

Clifford, James. "Diasporas." *Cultural Anthropology* 9, no. 3 (1994): 302–38.

Colón, Jesús. "A Puerto Rican in New York and Other Sketches." In *The Afro-Latin@ Reader: History and Culture in the United States*, edited by Miriam Jiménez Román and Juan Flores, 113–19. Durham, NC: Duke University Press, 2010.

Conniff, Michael. "Afro-West Indians on the Central American Isthmus: The Case of Panama." In *Slavery and Beyond: The African Impact on Latin America and the Caribbean*, edited by Darién J. Davis, 147–72. Wilmington, DE: Scholarly Resources.

Cooper, Carolyn. *Noises in the Blood: Orality, Gender, and the "Vulgar" Body of Jamaican Popular Culture.* London: Macmillan Caribbean, 1993.

Cooper, Carolyn. *Sound Clash: Jamaican Dancehall Culture at Large.* New York: Palgrave Macmillan, 2004.

Crenshaw, Kimberlè Williams. "Beyond Racism and Misogyny: Black Feminism and 2 Live Crew." In *Words that Wound: Critical Race Theory, Assaultive Speech, and the First Amendment*, edited by Mari J. Matsuda, Charles R. Lawrence, Richard Delgado, and Kimberlè Williams Crenshaw, 111–32. Boulder, CO: Westview Press, 1993.

Cruz-Janzen, Marta I. "Latinegras: Desired Women—Undesirable Mothers, Daughters, Sisters, and Wives." In *The Afro-Latin@ Reader: History and Culture in the United States*, edited by Miriam Jiménez Román and Juan Flores, 282–95. Durham, NC: Duke University Press, 2010.

Daniel, Yvonne. *Rumba: Dance and Social Change in Contemporary Cuba.* Bloomington: Indiana University Press, 1995.

Dávila, Arlene M. *Sponsored Identities: Cultural Politics in Puerto Rico.* Philadelphia: Temple University Press, 1997.

Dávila, Arlene M. *Latinos, Inc.: The Marketing and Making of a People.* Berkeley: University of California Press, 2001.

Dávila, Arlene M. *Latino Spin: Public Image and the Whitewashing of Race.* New York: New York University Press, 2008.

De la Fuente, Alejandro. *A Nation for All: Race, Inequality, and Politics in Twentieth-Century Cuba.* Chapel Hill: University of North Carolina Press, 2001.

Díaz Soler, Luis M. *Historia de la esclavitud negra en Puerto Rico.* San Juan: Editorial de la Universidad de Puerto Rico, 1953.

Dinzey-Flores, Zaire Z. "Temporary Housing, Permanent Communities: Public Housing Policy and Design in Puerto Rico." *Journal of Urban History* 33, no. 3 (2007): 467–92.

Dinzey-Flores, Zaire Z. "Caché vs. Caseríos: Urban Development, Distinction, and Segregation in Puerto Rican Neighborhoods." In *The Caribbean City*, edited by Rivke Jaffe, 209–26. Kingston, Jamaica: Ian Randle Publishers, 2008.

Dinzey-Flores, Zaire Z. "De la Disco al Caserío: Urban Spatial Aesthetics and Policy to the Beat of Reggaetón." CENTRO: *Journal of the Center for Puerto Rican Studies* 20, no. 2 (2008): 34–69.

Dinzey-Flores, Zaire Z. *Locked In, Locked Out: Gated Communities in a Puerto Rican City.* Philadelphia: University of Pennsylvania Press, 2013.

Doty, Alexander. "Introduction: There's Something about Mary." *Camera Obscura* 22, no. 2 (2007): 1–8.

Duany, Jorge. "Popular Music in Puerto Rico: Toward an Anthropology of Salsa." *Latin American Music Review/Revista de Música Latinoamericana* 5, no. 2 (1984): 186–216.

Duany, Jorge. *The Puerto Rican Nation on the Move: Identities on the Island and in the United States.* Chapel Hill: University of North Carolina Press, 2002.

Edmonson, Belinda. "Public Spectacles: Caribbean Women and the Politics of Public Performance." *Small Axe* 13 (2003): 1–16.

Edwards, Brent Hayes. "The Uses of Diaspora." *Social Text* 19, no. 1 (2001): 45–73.

Edwards, Brent Hayes. *The Practice of Diaspora: Literature, Translation, and the Rise of Black Internationalism.* Cambridge, MA: Harvard University Press, 2003.

Fernandes, Sujatha. "Fear of a Black Nation: Local Rappers, Transnational Cross-ings, and State Power in Contemporary Cuba." *Anthropological Quarterly* 76, no. 4 (2003): 575–608.

Figueroa, Luis A. *Sugar, Slavery, and Freedom in Nineteenth-Century Puerto Rico.* Chapel Hill: University of North Carolina Press, 2005.

Figueroa Hernández, Rafael. *Ismael Rivera: El Sonero Mayor.* 2nd ed. San Juan: Instituto de Cultura Puertorriqueña, 2002.

Findlay, Eileen J. Suárez. *Imposing Decency: The Politics of Sexuality and Race in Puerto Rico, 1870–1920.* Durham, NC: Duke University Press, 1999.

Findlay, Eileen J. "Slipping and Sliding: The Many Meanings of Race in Life Histories of New York Puerto Rican Return Migrants in San Juan." *CENTRO: Journal of the Center for Puerto Rican Studies* 24, no. 1 (2012): 20–43.

Fleetwood, Nicole R. *Troubling Vision: Performance, Visuality, Blackness.* Chicago: University of Chicago Press, 2011.

Flores, Aurora. "¡Ecua Jei! Ismael Rivera, El Sonero Mayor (A Personal Reflection)." *CENTRO: Journal of the Center for Puerto Rican Studies* 16, no. 2 (2004): 63–77.

Flores, Juan. *Divided Borders: Essays on Puerto Rican Identity.* Houston: Arte Público Press, 1993.

Flores, Juan. *From Bomba to Hip-Hop: Puerto Rican Culture and Latino Identity.* New York: Columbia University Press, 2000.

Flores, Juan. "Foreword: What's All the Noise About?" In *Reggaeton*, edited by Wayne Marshall, Raquel Z. Rivera, and Deborah Pacini Hernández, ix–xii. Durham, NC: Duke University Press, 2009.

Flores, Juan. *The Diaspora Strikes Back: Caribeño Tales of Learning and Turning.* New York: Routledge, 2009.

Forman, Murray. *The 'Hood Comes First: Race, Space, and Place in Rap and Hip-Hop.* Middletown, CT: Wesleyan University Press, 2002.

Forman, Murray, and Mark Anthony Neal, eds. *That's the Joint!: The Hip-Hop Studies Reader.* New York: Routledge, 2004.

Fusté, José I. "Colonial Laboratories, Irreparable Subjects: The Experiment of (B)ordering San Juan's Public Housing Residents." *Social Identities* 16, no. 1 (2010): 41–59.

García Yero, Cary Aileen. "Is It Just about Love? Filin and Politics in Postrevolutionary Cuba." *Studies in Latin American Popular Culture* 30 (2012): 138–61.

Gates, Henry Louis, Jr. *Black in Latin America.* New York: New York University Press, 2011.

Gilroy, Paul. *The Black Atlantic: Modernity and Double Consciousness.* Cambridge, MA: Harvard University Press, 1993.

Giovannetti, Jorge L. "Popular Music and Culture in Puerto Rico: Jamaican Reggae and Rap Music as Cross-Cultural Symbols." In *Musical Migrations: Transnationalism and Cultural Hybridity in Latin/o America*, edited by Frances R. Aparicio, Cándida F. Jáquez, and María Elena Cepeda, 81–98. New York: Palgrave Macmillan, 2003.

Giusti Cordero, Juan A. "Labor, Ecology, and History in a Caribbean Sugar Plantation Region: Piñones (Loíza), Puerto Rico, 1770–1950." PhD diss., State University of New York, Binghamton, 1994.

Giusti Cordero, Juan A. "AfroPuerto Rican Cultural Studies: Beyond cultura negroide and antillanismo." CENTRO: Journal of the Center for Puerto Rican Studies 8, nos. 1–2 (1996): 56–77.

Godreau, Isar P. "Missing the Mix: San Antón and the Racial Dynamics of 'Nationalism' in Puerto Rico." PhD diss., University of California, Santa Cruz, 1999.

Godreau, Isar P. "Changing Space, Making Race: Distance, Nostalgia, and the Folklorization of Blackness in Puerto Rico." Identities: Global Studies in Culture and Power 9, no. 2 (2002): 281–304.

Godreau, Isar P. "Folkloric 'Others': Blanqueamiento and the Celebration of Blackness as an Exception in Puerto Rico." In Globalization and Race: Transformations in the Cultural Production of Blackness, edited by Kamari Maxine Clarke and Deborah A. Thomas, 171–87. Durham, NC: Duke University Press, 2006.

Godreau, Isar P. "Slippery Semantics: Race Talk and Everyday Uses of Racial Terminology in Puerto Rico." CENTRO: Journal of the Center for Puerto Rican Studies 20, no. 2 (2008): 5–33.

Godreau, Isar P. Scripts of Blackness and the Dynamics of Nationalism in Puerto Rico. Cuadernos de Investigación, vol. 6. Cayey, Puerto Rico: Universidad de Puerto Rico en Cayey Instituto de Investigaciones Interdisciplinarias, 2009.

González, José Luis. Puerto Rico: The Four Storeyed Country and Other Essays. Translated by Gerald Guiness. Princeton, NJ: Markus Wiener Publishing, 1993.

Gopinath, Gayatri. "Bombay, U.K., Yuba City: Bhangra Music and the Engendering of Diaspora." Diaspora: A Journal of Transnational Studies 4, no. 3 (1995): 303–21.

Graham, Richard, ed. The Idea of Race in Latin America, 1870–1940. Austin: University of Texas Press, 1990.

Gray, Obika. "Power and Identity among the Urban Poor of Jamaica." In Globalization and Survival in the Black Diaspora, ed. Charles Green, 199–226. Albany: State University of New York Press, 1997.

Grosfoguel, Ramón, and Chloé Georas. "The Racialization of Latino Caribbean Migrants in the New York Metropolitan Area." CENTRO: Journal of the Center for Puerto Rican Studies 8, nos. 1–2 (1996): 190–201.

Grosfoguel, Ramón, and Chloé Georas. " 'Coloniality of Power' and Racial Dynamics: Notes toward a Reinterpretation of Latino Caribbeans in New York City." Identities 7, no. 1 (2000): 85–125.

Guerra, Lillian. Popular Expression and National Identity in Puerto Rico: The Struggle for Self, Community, and Nation. Gainesville: University Press of Florida, 1998.

Guilbault, Jocelyne. "Audible Entanglements: Nation and Diaspora in Trinidad's Calypso Music Scene." Small Axe 9, no. 1 (2005): 40–63.

Guilbault, Jocelyne. Governing Sound: The Cultural Politics of Trinidad's Carnival Music. Chicago: University of Chicago Press, 2007.

Guilbault, Jocelyne. "Music, Politics, and Pleasure: Live Soca in Trinidad." Small Axe 14, no. 1 (2010): 16–29.

Gupta, Ritesh. My Block: Puerto Rico. Directed by Ritesh Gupta and Sean Lee. MTV News and Docs. Aired April 16, 2006.

Hall, Stuart. "Cultural Identity and Diaspora." In *Colonial Discourse and Postcolonial Theory: A Reader*, edited by Patrick Williams and Laura Chrisman, 392–403. New York: Columbia University Press, 1994.

Hall, Stuart. "What Is This 'Black' in Black Popular Culture?" In *Stuart Hall: Critical Dialogues in Cultural Studies*, edited by David Morley and Kuan-Hsing Chen, 465–75. London: Routledge, 1996.

Hall, Stuart. "Creolité and the Process of Creolization." In *Creólité and Creolization: Documenta 11_Platform 3*, edited by Okwui Emwezor et al., 27–41. Ostfildern-Ruit, Germany: Hatje Cantz, 2003.

Hall, Stuart. "Creolization, Diaspora, and Hybridity in the Context of Globalization." In *Creólité and Creolization: Documenta 11_Platform 3*, edited by Okwui Enwezor et al., 185–98. Ostfildern-Ruit, Germany: Hatje Cantz, 2003.

Hammonds, Evelynn M. "Towards a Genealogy of Black Female Sexuality: The Problematic of Silence." In *Feminist Genealogies, Colonial Legacies, Democratic Futures*, edited by M. Jacqui Alexander and Chandra Talpade Mohanty, 170–82. New York: Routledge, 1997.

Hanchard, Michael. *Orpheus and Power: The Movimento Negro of Rio de Janeiro and São Paulo, Brazil, 1945–1988*. Princeton, NJ: Princeton University Press, 1994.

Haslip-Viera, Gabriel. "Changing Identities: An Afro-Latin@ Family Portrait." In *The Afro-Latin@ Reader: History and Culture in the United States*, edited by Miriam Jiménez Román and Juan Flores, 142–49. Durham, NC: Duke University Press, 2010.

Helg, Aline. "Race in Argentina and Cuba, 1880–1930." In *The Idea of Race in Latin America*, edited by Richard Graham, 37–69. Austin: University of Texas Press, 1990.

Hernández, Tanya Katerí. *Racial Subordination in Latin America: The Role of the State, Customary Law, and the New Civil Rights Response*. New York: Cambridge University Press, 2012.

Hernández Hiraldo, Samiri. *Black Puerto Rican Identity and Religious Experience*. Gainesville: University Press of Florida, 2006.

Higginbotham, Evelyn Brooks. *Righteous Discontent: The Women's Movement in the Black Baptist Church, 1880–1920*. Cambridge, MA: Harvard University Press, 1993.

Hintzen, Percy C. *West Indians in the West: Self-Representations in an Immigrant Community*. New York: New York University Press, 2001.

Hintzen, Percy C. "Race and Creole Ethnicity." In *Companion to Racial and Ethnic Studies*, edited by David Theo Goldberg and John Solomos, 475–94. Malden, MA: Blackwell Publishers, 2002.

Hintzen, Percy C., and Jean Muteba Rahier. "Introduction: Theorizing the African Diaspora: Metaphor, Miscognition, and Misrecognition." In *Global Circuits of Blackness: Interrogating the African Diaspora*, edited by Jean Muteba Rahier, Percy C. Hintzen, and Felipe Smith, ix–xxv. Champaign: University of Illinois Press, 2010.

Hobson, Janell. *Body as Evidence: Mediating Race, Globalizing Gender*. Albany: State University of New York Press, 2012.

Jiménez, Félix. *Las prácticas de la carne: Construcción y representación de las masculinidades puertorriqueñas*. San Juan: Ediciones Vértigo, 2004.

Jiménez, Félix. "(W)rapped in Foil: Glory at Twelve Words a Minute." In *Reggaeton*, edited by Raquel Z. Rivera, Wayne Marshall, and Deborah Pacini Hernández, 229–51. Durham, NC: Duke University Press, 2009.

Jiménez Román, Miriam. "Un hombre (negro) del pueblo: José Celso Barbosa and the Puerto Rican 'Race' Toward Whiteness." CENTRO: *Journal of the Center for Puerto Rican Studies* 8, nos. 1–2 (1996): 8–29.

Jiménez Román, Miriam. "Looking at That Middle Ground: Racial Mixing as a Panacea?" *Wadabagei: Journal of the Caribbean and Its Diaspora* 8, no. 1 (2005): 65–79.

Jiménez Román, Miriam. "Boricuas vs. Nuyoricans—Indeed!" *ReVista: Harvard Review of Latin America* 7, no. 3 (2008): 8–11.

Jiménez Román, Miriam, and Juan Flores, eds. *The Afro-Latin@ Reader: History and Culture in the United States*. Durham, NC: Duke University Press, 2010.

Jorge, Angela. "The Black Puerto Rican Woman in Contemporary American Society." In *The Puerto Rican Woman: Perspectives on Culture, History, and Society*, edited by Edna Acosta-Belén, 180–87. New York: Praeger Publishers, 1986.

Jottar, Berta. "Central Park Rumba: Nuyorican Identity and the Return to African Roots." CENTRO: *Journal of the Center for Puerto Rican Studies* 13, no. 1 (2011): 5–29.

Kelley, Robin D. G. "Looking for the 'Real' Nigga: Social Scientists Construct the Ghetto." In *That's the Joint!: The Hip-Hop Studies Reader*, edited by Murray Forman and Mark Anthony Neal, 119–36. New York: Routledge, 2004.

Kinsbruner, Jay. *Not of Pure Blood: The Free People of Color in Nineteenth-Century Puerto Rico*. Durham, NC: Duke University Press, 1996.

Klimt, Andrea. "European Spaces: Portuguese Migrants' Notions of Home and Belonging." *Diaspora: A Journal of Transnational Studies* 9, no. 2 (2000): 259–85.

Knights, Vanessa. "Tears and Screams: Pleasure and Pain in the Bolero." In *Queering the Popular Pitch*, edited by Sheila Whiteley and Jennifer Rycenga, 83–100. New York: Routledge, 2006.

Lebrón, Marisol. " 'Con un flow natural': Sonic Affinities and Reggaeton Nationalism." *Women and Performance: A Journal of Feminist Theory* 21, no. 2 (2011): 219–33.

Lewis, Oscar. *La Vida: A Puerto Rican Family in the Culture of Poverty—San Juan and New York*. New York: Random House, 1966.

Lipsitz, George. *Dangerous Crossroads: Popular Music, Postmodernism, and the Poetics of Place*. London: Verso, 1994.

Lipsitz, George. *Footsteps in the Dark: The Hidden Histories of Popular Music*. Minneapolis: University of Minnesota Press, 2007.

Livermon, Xavier. "Diaspora Space/Kwaito Bodies: The Politics of Popular Music in Post-Apartheid South Africa." PhD diss., University of California, Berkeley, 2006.

López-Baralt, Mercedes. *Sobre Ínsulares Extrañas: El clásico de Pedreira anotado por Tomás Blanco*. San Juan: Editorial de la Universidad de Puerto Rico, 2001.

Madrid, Alejandro L., and Robin D. Moore. *Danzón: Circum-Caribbean Dialogues in Music and Dance*. New York: Oxford University Press, 2013.

Manuel, Peter. "Salsa and the Music Industry: Corporate Control or Grassroots Expression?" In *Essays on Cuban Music: North American and Cuban Perspectives*, edited by Peter Manuel, 159–80. Lanham, MD: University Press of America, 1991.

Manuel, Peter, and Wayne Marshall. "The Riddim Method: Aesthetics, Practice, and Ownership in Jamaican Dancehall." *Popular Music* 25, no. 3 (2006): 447–70.

Marcon, Frank Nilton. "Identidade e estilo em Lisboa: Kuduro juventude e imigração africana." *Cadernos de Estudos Africanos* 24 (2012): 95–116. doi:10.4000/cea.706.

Marshall, Wayne. "Dem Bow, Dembow, Dembo: Translation and Transnation in Reggaeton." *Lied und populäre Kultur/Song and Popular Culture* 53 (2008): 131–51.

Marshall, Wayne. "From Música Negra to Reggaeton Latino: The Cultural Politics of Nation, Migration, and Commercialization." In *Reggaeton*, edited by Raquel Z. Rivera, Wayne Marshall, and Deborah Pacini Hernández, 19–76. Durham, NC: Duke University Press, 2010.

Marshall, Wayne, Raquel Z. Rivera, and Deborah Pacini Hernández. "Introduction: Reggaeton's Socio-Sonic Circuitry." In *Reggaeton*, edited by Raquel Z. Rivera, Wayne Marshall, and Deborah Pacini Hernández, 1–16. Durham, NC: Duke University Press, 2010.

McClintock, Anne. *Imperial Leather: Race, Gender, and Sexuality in the Colonial Contest*. New York: Routledge, 1995.

Milian, Claudia. *Latining America: Black-Brown Passages and the Coloring of Latina/o Studies*. Athens: University of Georgia Press, 2013.

Mintz, Sidney W. *Caribbean Transformations*. Chicago: Aldine Publishing Company, 1974.

Modestín, Yvette. "An Afro-Latina's Quest for Inclusion." In *The Afro-Latin@ Reader: History and Culture in the United States*, edited by Miriam Jiménez Román and Juan Flores, 417–21. Durham, NC: Duke University Press, 2010.

Montalvo-Barbot, Alfredo. "Crime in Puerto Rico: Drug Trafficking, Money Laundering, and the Poor." *Crime and Delinquency* 43, no. 4 (1997): 533–47.

Moore, Madison. "Tina Theory: Notes on Fierceness." *Journal of Popular Music Studies* 24, no. 1 (2012): 71–86.

Moore, Robin D. *Nationalizing Blackness: Afrocubanismo and Artistic Revolution in Havana, 1920–1940*. Pittsburgh: University of Pittsburgh Press, 2001.

Moore, Robin D. *Music in the Hispanic Caribbean: Experiencing Music, Expressing Culture*. New York: Oxford University Press, 2010.

Moorman, Marissa J. *Intonations: A Social History of Music and Nation in Luanda, Angola, from 1945 to Recent Times*. Athens: Ohio University Press, 2008.

Moynihan, Daniel Patrick. "The Negro Family: The Case for National Action." 1965. In *Call and Response: Key Debates in African American Studies*, edited by Henry Louis Gates Jr. and Jennifer Burton, 638–51. New York: W. W. Norton, 2011.

Muñoz, José Esteban. *Disidentifications: Queers of Color and the Performance of Politics*. Minneapolis: University of Minnesota Press, 1999.

Muñoz, José Esteban. "Feeling Brown: Ethnicity and Affect in Ricardo Bracho's *The Sweetest Hangover (and other STDs)*." *Theatre Journal* 52, no. 1 (2000): 67–79.

Negrón-Muntaner, Frances. "When I Was a Puerto Rican Lesbian." *GLQ: A Journal of Lesbian and Gay Studies* 5, no. 4 (1999): 511–26.

Negrón-Muntaner, Frances. *Boricua Pop: Puerto Ricans and the Latinization of American Culture*. New York: New York University Press, 2004.

Negrón-Muntaner, Frances. "Celia's Shoes." In *From Bananas to Buttocks: The Latina Body in Popular Film and Culture*, edited by Myra Mendible, 95–116. Austin: University of Texas Press, 2007.

Negrón-Muntaner, Frances, and Raquel Z. Rivera. "Reggaeton Nation." NACLA *Report on the Americas*, November/December 2007, 35–39.

Negus, Keith. "The Music Business and Rap: Between the Street and the Executive Suite." *Cultural Studies* 13, no. 3 (1999): 488–508.

Nwankwo, Ifeoma C. K. "The Panamanian Origins of Reggae en Español: Seeing History through 'Los Ojos Café' of Renato." In *Reggaeton*, edited by Raquel Z. Rivera, Wayne Marshall, and Deborah Pacini Hernández, 89–98. Durham, NC: Duke University Press, 2009.

Oboler, Suzanne. *Ethnic Labels, Latino Lives: Identity and the Politics of (Re)Presentation in the United States*. Minneapolis: University of Minnesota Press, 1995.

Oboler, Suzanne, and Anani Dzidzienyo, eds. *Neither Enemies nor Friends: Latinos, Blacks, Afro-Latinos*. New York: Palgrave Macmillan, 2005.

Pacini Hernández, Deborah. *Bachata: A Social History of Dominican Popular Music*. Philadelphia: Temple University Press, 1995.

Pacini Hernández, Deborah. "The Name Game: Locating Latina/os, Latins, and Latin Americans in the US Popular Music Landscape." In *A Companion to Latina/o Studies*, edited by Juan Flores and Renato Rosaldo, 49–59. Malden, MA: Blackwell Publishing, 2007.

Pacini Hernández, Deborah. "Dominicans in the Mix: Reflections on Dominican Identity, Race, and Reggaeton." In *Reggaeton*, edited by Raquel Z. Rivera, Wayne Marshall, and Deborah Pacini Hernández, 136–64. Durham, NC: Duke University Press, 2009.

Pacini Hernández, Deborah. *Oye Como Va! Hybridity and Identity in Latino Popular Music*. Philadelphia: Temple University Press, 2010.

Pacini Hernández, Deborah, and Reebee Garofalo. "Hip Hop in Havana: Rap, Race, and National Identity in Contemporary Cuba." *Journal of Popular Music Studies* 11/12 (1999/2000): 18–47.

Patterson, Tiffany Ruby, and Robin D. G. Kelley. "Unfinished Migrations: Reflections on the African Diaspora and the Making of the Modern World." *African Studies Review* 43, no. 1 (2000): 11–45.

Pedreira, Antonio S. *Insularismo: An Insight into the Puerto Rican Character*. 1934. Translated by Aoife Rivera Serrano. New York City: Ausubo Press, 2005.

Pérez, Moira Alexandra. "The Place of Abandonment: Geography, Race, and Nature in Puerto Rico." PhD diss., University of California, Berkeley, 2002.

Perry, Marc D. "Global Black Self-Fashionings: Hip Hop as Diasporic Space." *Identities: Global Studies in Culture and Power* 15 (2008): 635–44.

Pierre, Jemima. *The Predicament of Blackness: Postcolonial Ghana and the Politics of Race*. Chicago: University of Chicago Press, 2012.

Poey, Delia. "¡La Lupe! Performing Race, Gender, Nation, and Excess." *Women and Performance: A Journal of Feminist Theory* 15, no. 2 (2005): 79–98.

Priestley, George. "Post-Invasion Panama: Urban Crisis and Social Protests." In *Globalization and Survival in the Black Diaspora*, edited by Charles Green, 85–104. Albany: State University of New York Press, 1997.

Priestley, George, and Angela Barrow. "The Black Movement in Panama: A Historical and Political Interpretation, 1994–2004." In *New Social Movements in the African Diaspora: Challenging Global Apartheid*, edited by Leith Mullings, 49–78. New York: Palgrave Macmillan, 2009.

Puri, Shalini. *The Caribbean Postcolonial: Social Equality, Post-Nationalism, and Cultural Hybridity*. New York: Palgrave Macmillan, 2004.

Putnam, Lara. "Eventually Alien: The Multigenerational Saga of the British West Indians in Central America, 1870–1940." In *Blacks and Blackness in Central America: Between Race and Place*, edited by Lowell Gudmundson and Justin Wolfe, 278–306. Durham, NC: Duke University Press, 2010.

Quijano, Anibal. "Coloniality of Power, Eurocentrism, and Latin America." *Neplanta: Views from the South* 1, no. 3 (2000): 533–80.

Quiñones Rivera, Maritza. "From Trigueñita to Afro–Puerto Rican: Intersections of the Racialized, Gendered, and Sexualized Body in Puerto Rico and the U.S. Mainland." *Meridians: Feminism, Race, Transnationalism* 7, no. 1 (2006): 162–82.

Rahier, Jean Muteba. "Blackness, the Racial/Spatial Order, Migrations, and Miss Ecuador, 1995–96." *American Anthropologist* 100, no. 2 (1998): 421–30.

Rahier, Jean Muteba. "Mestizaje, Mulataje, Mestiçagem in Latin American Ideologies of National Identities." *Journal of Latin American Anthropology* 8, no. 1 (2003): 40–51.

Rahier, Jean Muteba. *Blackness in the Andes: Ethnographic Vignettes of Cultural Politics in the Time of Multiculturalism*. New York: Palgrave Macmillan, 2014.

Rebollo-Gil, Guillermo. "Entre Cafres y Blanquitos: Perceptions of Race and Racism in Puerto Rico." PhD diss., University of Florida, 2005.

Reiter, Bernd. "Portugal: National Pride and Imperial Neurosis." *Race and Class* 47, no. 1 (2005): 79–91.

Reiter, Bernd. "The Perils of Empire: Nationhood and Citizenship in Portugal." *Citizenship Studies* 12, no. 4 (2008): 397–412.

Reyes-Santos, Irmary. "Race, Empire, and Development in the Caribbean." Paper presented at the Annual Meeting of the American Studies Association, San Juan, Puerto Rico, November 2012.

Reynolds, Tom. *Straight Outta Puerto Rico: Reggaeton's Rough Road to Glory*. Directed by Leigh Savidge and James Chankin. Santa Monica, CA: Xenon Pictures, 2008.

Rivera, Petra R. "'*Orgulloso de mi Caserío y de Quien Soy*': Race, Place, and Space in Puerto Rican Reggaetón." PhD diss., University of California, Berkeley, 2010.

Rivera, Petra R. "Tropical Mix: Afro-Latino Space in Notch's Reggaetón." *Popular Music and Society* 34, no. 2 (2011): 221–35.

Rivera, Raquel Z. "La música rap en Puerto Rico: Consumo, revisión y resistencia." *CENTRO: Journal of the Center for Puerto Rican Studies* 5, no. 2 (1992/1993): 30–51.

Rivera, Raquel Z. "Rap in Puerto Rico: Reflections from the Margins." In *Globalization and Survival in the Black Diaspora: The New Urban Challenge*, edited by Charles Green, 109–27. Albany: State University of New York Press, 1997.

Rivera, Raquel Z. "Rapping Two Versions of the Same Requiem." In *Puerto Rican Jam: Rethinking Colonialism and Nationalism*, edited by Ramón Grosfoguel and Frances Negrón-Muntaner, 243–56. Minneapolis: University of Minnesota Press, 1997.

Rivera, Raquel Z. "Cultura y poder en el rap puertorriqueño." *Revista de Ciencias Sociales* 4 (1998): 124–45.

Rivera, Raquel Z. *New York Ricans from the Hip Hop Zone.* New York: Palgrave Macmillan, 2003.

Rivera, Raquel Z. "Entrevista a Tego Calderón." CENTRO: *Journal of the Center for Puerto Rican Studies* 16, no. 2 (2004): 272–81.

Rivera, Raquel Z. "Will the 'Real' Puerto Rican Culture Please Stand Up? Thoughts on Cultural Nationalism." In *None of the Above: Puerto Ricans in the Global Era*, edited by Frances Negrón-Muntaner, 217–31. New York: Palgrave Macmillan, 2007.

Rivera, Raquel Z. "Policing Morality, *Mano Dura Stylee*: The Case of Underground Rap and Reggae in Puerto Rico in the Mid-1990s." In *Reggaeton*, edited by Raquel Z. Rivera, Wayne Marshall, and Deborah Pacini Hernández, 111–34. Durham, NC: Duke University Press, 2009.

Rivera, Raquel Z., Wayne Marshall, and Deborah Pacini Hernández, eds. *Reggaeton*. Durham, NC: Duke University Press, 2009.

Rivera-Bonilla, Ivelisse. "Divided City: The Proliferation of Gated Communities in San Juan." PhD diss., University of California, Santa Cruz, 2003.

Rivera-Rideau, Petra R. "Cocolos Modernos: Salsa, Reggaetón, and Puerto Rico's Cultural Politics of Blackness." *Latin American and Caribbean Ethnic Studies* 8, no. 1 (2013): 1–19.

Rivera-Rideau, Petra R. "From Carolina to Loíza: Race, Place, and Puerto Rican Racial Democracy." *Identities: Global Studies in Culture and Power* 20, no. 5 (2013): 616–32.

Rivero, Yeidy M. *Tuning Out Blackness: Race and Nation in the History of Puerto Rican Television.* Durham, NC: Duke University Press, 2005.

Rodrigues, Cristina Udelsmann. "Youth in Angola: Keeping the Pace Towards Modernity." *Cadernos de Estudos Africanos* 18/19 (2010): 165–79. doi 10.4000/cea.116.

Rodríguez, Juana María. "Getting F****d in Puerto Rico: Metaphoric Provocations and Queer Activist Interventions." In *None of the Above: Puerto Ricans in the Global Era*, edited by Frances Negrón-Muntaner, 129–46. New York: Palgrave Macmillan, 2007.

Rodríguez Beruff, Jorge. "Guerra contra las drogas, militarización y democracia: Políticas y fuerzas de seguridad en Puerto Rico." In *Fronteras en conflicto: Guerra contra las drogas, militarización y democracia en el Caribe, Puerto Rico, y Vieques*, edited by Humberto García Muñiz and Jorge Rodríguez Beruff, 51–115. San Juan: Red Caribeña de Geopolítica, Seguridad Regional y Relaciones Internacionales afiliada al Proyecto ATLANTEA, 1999.

Rodríguez-Morazzani, Roberto P. "Beyond the Rainbow: Mapping the Discourse on Puerto Ricans and 'Race.'" CENTRO: *Journal of the Center for Puerto Rican Studies* 8, nos. 1–2 (1996): 141–69.

Rodríguez-Silva, Ileana M. *Silencing Race: Disentangling Blackness, Colonialism, and National Identities in Puerto Rico.* New York: Palgrave Macmillan, 2012.

Romero Joseph, Welmo E. "From Hip-Hop to Reggaeton: Is There Only a Step?" In *Reggaeton,* edited by Raquel Z. Rivera, Wayne Marshall, and Deborah Pacini Hernández, 312–23. Durham, NC: Duke University Press, 2009.

Rose, Tricia. *Black Noise: Rap Music and Black Culture in Contemporary America.* Middletown, CT: Wesleyan University Press, 1994.

Rose, Tricia. *The Hip Hop Wars: What We Talk About When We Talk About Hip Hop—And Why It Matters.* New York: Basic Books, 2008.

Roy-Féquiere, Magali. *Women, Creole Identity, and Intellectual Life in Early Twentieth-Century Puerto Rico.* Philadelphia: Temple University Press, 2004.

Rudolph, Jennifer Domino. "'Roncamos Porque Podemos': Racialization, Redemption, and Mascu-latinidad." PhD diss., University of Illinois at Chicago, 2008.

Rudolph, Jennifer Domino. "'Pidieron Cacao': Latinidad and Black Identity in the Reggaetón of Don Omar." CENTRO: *Journal of the Center for Puerto Rican Studies* 23, no. 1 (2011): 30–53.

Rudolph, Jennifer Domino. *Embodying Latino Masculinities: Producing Masculatinidad.* New York: Palgrave Macmillan, 2012.

Salazar, Max. *Mambo Kingdom: Latin Music in New York.* New York: Schirmer Trade Books, 2002.

Santiago-Valles, Kelvin A. "Vigilando, administrando y patrullando a negros y trigueños: Del cuerpo del delito al delito de los cuerpos en la crisis del Puerto Rico urbano contemporáneo." *Bordes* 2 (1995): 28–42.

Santiago-Valles, Kelvin A. "Policing the Crisis in the Whitest of All the Antilles." CENTRO: *Journal of the Center for Puerto Rican Studies* 8, nos. 1–2 (1996): 42–57.

Santos-Febres, Mayra. "Puerto Rican Underground." CENTRO: *Journal of the Center for Puerto Rican Studies* 8, nos. 1–2 (1996): 219–31.

Santos-Febres, Mayra. "Geografía en decibeles: Utopías pancaribeñas y el territorio del rap." In *Primer Simposio del Caribe 2000: re-Definiciones: Espacios global/nacional/cultural/personal-caribeño,* edited by Lowell Fiet and Janette Becerra, 121–37. Río Piedras: Facultad de Humanidades, Universidad de Puerto Rico, 1996.

Santos-Febres, Mayra. "Salsa as Translocation." In *Everynight Life: Culture and Dance in Latina/o America,* edited by José E. Muñoz, 175–88. Durham, NC: Duke University Press, 1997.

Sawyer, Mark Q. *Racial Politics in Post-Revolutionary Cuba.* New York: Cambridge University Press, 2005.

Scarano, Francisco A. *Sugar and Slavery in Puerto Rico: The Plantation Economy of Ponce, 1800–1850.* Madison: University of Wisconsin Press, 1984.

Silberman, Roxanne, Richard Alba, and Irene Fournier. "Segmented Assimilation in France? Discrimination in the Labour Market against the Second Generation." *Ethnic and Racial Studies* 30, no. 1 (2007): 1–27.

Simon, Harvey. "Mano Dura: Mobilizing the National Guard to Battle Crime in Puerto Rico." *Kennedy School of Government Case Program Number C109-97-1390.0.* Cambridge, MA: Harvard University, 1997.

Simon, Harvey. "Mano Dura: Mobilizing the National Guard to Battle Crime in Puerto Rico (Epilogue)." *Kennedy School of Government Case Program Number C109–97–1390.1.* Cambridge, MA: Harvard University, 1997.

Stoler, Ann Laura. *Carnal Knowledge and Imperial Power: Race and the Intimate in Colonial Rule.* Berkeley: University of California Press, 2002.

Stolzoff, Norman C. *Wake the Town and Tell the People: Dancehall Culture in Jamaica.* Durham, NC: Duke University Press, 2000.

Taylor, Timothy D. *Global Pop: World Music, World Markets.* New York: Routledge, 1997.

Thomas, Deborah A. *Modern Blackness: Nationalism, Globalization, and the Politics of Culture in Jamaica.* Durham, NC: Duke University Press, 2004.

Thomas, Deborah A. "Modern Blackness: Progress, 'America,' and the Politics of Popular Culture in Jamaica." In *Globalization and Race: Transformations in the Cultural Production of Blackness,* edited by Kamari Maxine Clarke and Deborah A. Thomas, 335–54. Durham, NC: Duke University Press, 2006.

Thomas, Lorrin. *Puerto Rican Citizen: History and Political Identity in Twentieth-Century New York City.* Chicago: University of Chicago Press, 2010.

Thomas, Piri. *Down These Mean Streets.* Thirtieth Anniversary Edition. New York: Vintage Books, 1997.

Torres, Arlene. "La Gran Familia Puertorriqueña 'Ej Prieta de Beldá' (The Great Puerto Rican Family Is Really Really Black)." In *Blackness in Latin America and the Caribbean Volume Two,* edited by Arlene Torres and Norman Whitten, 285–306. Bloomington: Indiana University Press, 1998.

Torres, Arlene, and Norman Whitten Jr., eds. *Blackness in Latin America and the Caribbean.* Bloomington: Indiana University Press, 1998.

Twickel, Christoph. "Muévelo (Move It!): From Panama to New York and Back Again, the Story of El General." In *Reggaeton,* edited by Raquel Z. Rivera, Wayne Marshall, and Deborah Pacini Hernández, 99–108. Durham, NC: Duke University Press, 2009.

Tyrrell, Marygrace. "Colonizing the New Deal: Federal Housing in San Juan, Puerto Rico." In *The Caribbean City,* edited by Rivke Jaffe, 69–93. Kingston, Jamaica: Ian Randle Publishers, 2008.

Valdivia, Angharad. "Is Penélope to J.Lo as Culture Is to Nature?" In *From Bananas to Buttocks: The Latina Body in Popular Film and Culture,* edited by Myra Mendible, 129–48. Austin: University of Texas Press, 2007.

Vargas, Deborah R. *Dissonant Divas in Chicana Music: The Limits of La Onda.* Minneapolis: University of Minnesota Press, 2012.

Vazquez, Alexandra T. "Salon Philosophers: Ivy Queen and Surprise Guests Take Reggaetón Aside." In *Reggaeton,* edited by Raquel Z. Rivera, Wayne Marshall, and Deborah Pacini Hernández, 300–311. Durham, NC: Duke University Press, 2009.

Wade, Peter. *Blackness and Race Mixture: The Dynamics of Racial Identity in Colombia.* Baltimore: Johns Hopkins University Press, 1993.

Wade, Peter. *Race and Ethnicity in Latin America.* London: Pluto Press, 1997.

Wade, Peter. *Music, Race, and Nation: Música Tropical in Colombia.* Chicago: University of Chicago Press, 2000.

Washburne, Christopher. "Play It 'Con Filin!': The Swing and Expression of Salsa." *Latin American Music Review/Revista de Música Latinoamericana* 19, no. 2 (1998): 160–85.

Waters, Mary C. *Black Identities: West Indian Dreams and American Realities.* Cambridge, MA: Harvard University Press, 2001.

West-Durán, Alan. "Rap's Diasporic Dialogues: Cuba's Redefinition of Blackness." *Journal of Popular Music Studies* 16, no. 1 (2004): 4–39.

West-Durán, Alan. "Puerto Rico: The Pleasures and Traumas of Race." CENTRO: *Journal of the Center for Puerto Rican Studies* 17, no. 1 (2005): 47–69.

Whalen, Carmen Teresa. "Colonialism, Citizenship, and the Making of the Puerto Rican Diaspora: An Introduction." In *The Puerto Rican Diaspora: Historical Perspectives*, edited by Carmen Teresa Whalen and Victor Vásquez-Hernández, 1–42. Philadelphia: Temple University Press, 2005.

Whitney, Jennifer Dawn. "Some Assembly Required: Black Barbie and the Fabrication of Nicki Minaj." *Girlhood Studies* 5, no. 1 (2012): 141–59.

Zenón Cruz, Isabelo. *Narciso descubre su trasero: El negro en la cultura puertorriqueña.* Humacao, Puerto Rico: Editorial Furidi, 1974.

Discography

Calderón, Tego. *El Abayarde.* White Lion/BMG U.S. Latin 82876 53021-2, 2003, compact disc.

Calderón, Tego. *The Underdog/El Subestimado.* Jiggiri Records/Atlantic Records, 94121-2, 2006, compact disc.

Daddy Yankee. *Barrio Fino.* V.I. Music/Universal Music, 545-450-639-2-IN02, 2004, compact disc.

Don Omar. *Don Omar Presenta: Meet the Orphans.* Orfanato Music Group/Machete Music, 001495800, compact disc.

Ivy Queen. *Sentimiento.* Drama Records, Inc./Univision Music, 0883 11140 2, 2007, compact disc.

Los Bandoleros. V.I. Music/All Star Records, 874286, 2007, compact disc.

Lucenzo. *Emigrante del Mundo.* Yanis/B1M1, 2782130, 2011, compact disc.

Luny Tunes. *Más Flow 2.* Universal International, 2300001, 2005, compact disc.

N.O.R.E. *N.O.R.E. Y La Familia . . . Ya Tú Sabe.* Roc La Familia/Def Jam Records, 000626602, 2006, compact disc.

Notch. *Raised by the People.* Machete Music/Cinco por Cinco Records, B0008970-02, 2007, compact disc.

Vico C. *Greatest Hits.* Prime/RCA Records, 74321-24329-2, 1994, compact disc.

INDEX

Page numbers followed by *f* refer to illustrations.

diasporic resources: bhangraton and, 167; blackness and, 15; defined, 15; racial democracy and, 16–17; Tego Calderón and, 86–87, 93–101, 103

Díaz Soler, Luis, 57

Dinzey-Flores, Zaire, 10–11, 34, 37, 181n113

discrimination: Eddie Dee's "Señor Oficial" on police harassment and, 39–41; against rappers and reggaetón fans, 50–51, 69–70

DJ Blass, 152

DJ Charlie Chase, 28

DJ Negro, 21, 104

DJ Nelson, 22

DJ Playero, 38, 50, 130

Don Omar (William Omar Landrón Rivera): background and career of, 159–60; collaboration and, 152; "Danza Kuduro," 159–60, 163–68, 165f; Ivy Queen and, 117; *The Last Don* and *Last Don Live*, 159; Latin Grammys performance, 171n3; on *My Block: Puerto Rico* (MTV), 186n4; Tego Calderón and, 81, 83, 91, 92–93, 188n37

Doty, Alexander, 109

dress codes in schools, 181n127

drug use: crime rates and, 35; Eddie Dee on, 40; *Mano Dura* campaign and, 36–37; school raids, 42–43; songs about, 39, 40

Duany, Jorge, 25, 172n7

Eddie Dee, 2, 3f, 39–42, 41f, 84, 130

El General (Edgardo Franco), 32

"Entrando por la Salida" (Clemente), 44–45, 45f

erotic autonomy, 55, 62, 74, 76–77

Fabolous, 152

Fania All-Stars, 2

fashion and "look": cultural imperialism critique, 44; dress codes in schools, 181n127; Ivy Queen's shift from "tomboy" to "diva" look, 106, 110–14; underground and, 38

female sexuality. *See* Anti-Pornography Campaign; sexuality and hypersexuality

femininity. *See* gender and gender politics

Fernández, Ruth, 123

Las Fiestas de Santiago Apóstol, 88

50 Cent, 152

Figueroa, Héctor "El Flaco," 69–70, 71–72, 73

filin, 120–21, 123–25

Findlay, Eileen, 59

Fleetwood, Nicole, 114, 192n42

Flores, Juan, 15–16, 25, 27, 137, 139, 188n34

Flores Osuna, Héctor, 125

folkloric blackness. *See* blackness, folkloric

Forman, Murray, 137

Franco, Edgardo (El General), 32

Freyre, Gilberto, 171n6

Fuentes, Al, 135

Fusté, José, 34

gangsta rap, 143–44

"Gasolina" (Daddy Yankee), 1, 130–31, 134, 146

gates, 37, 181n113

gay community and Ivy Queen, 104–5

Gelpí Mehreb, Enrique, 78

Gem Star, 150

gender and gender politics: Anti-Pornography Campaign and racialized female hypersexuality vs. respectability, 54–55, 56–59, 70, 73–77; bolero and, 193n66; *caserío* resident stereotypes, female, 72; Don Omar's "Danza Kuduro" and, 164–65; Ivy Queen and, 108, 111–12, 114–17, 120; La Lupe and, 123; Latin lover stereotype, 66–67, 145; Notch and, 156; reggaetón as problematic on gender hierarchies, 17; Tego Calderón and, 102; thug masculinity, 138, 142–44, 146, 150. *See also* sexuality and hypersexuality

Generación de los 1930s, 7–8, 46

Generación de los 1970s, 8–9

Georas, Chloé, 138

ghettocentricity, 139

Giusti Cordero, Juan, 187n18

globalization, 147, 167

Godreau, Isar P., 9, 10, 88

González, José Luis, 8–9, 174n38

González, Velda, 52–54, 56, 59–61, 68, 69, 77, 78, 84. *See also* Anti-Pornography Campaign

race and racialization (*continued*)
Tego Calderón and problematic of,
102–3; United States as locus of racism,
6–7, 97; U.S. classification of, 27. *See also*
blackness; *blanqueamiento* (whitening)
and whiteness
race mixture: black women, Puerto Rican
identity, and, 57; Daddy Yankee and, 147;
la gran familia puertorriqueña (the great
Puerto Rican family), 171n6; proponents
of, 8; racial democracy and, 174n38
racial democracy, Puerto Rican: black-
white spectrum, location on, 67;
diaspora and, 14; diasporic resources
and, 16–17; discrediting of, 9; Eddie Dee
on, 42; female sexuality and, 55; Freyre
and, 171n6; *Generación del 1930s* and, 7–8;
Generación del 1970s and, 8–9; Ivy Queen
and, 114, 118–19; Loíza and, 88–89; race
mixture and, 174n38; racism and, 4, 6;
Ricky Martin as embodiment of, 67;
Tego Calderón on, 94–96; as term,
172n6; underground and, 22, 23; U.S.,
displacement of racism to, 43–44;
whiteness, respectability, and, 58
radio stations, "Hurban," 134–35
Raekwon, 96
raids: on *caseríos*, 36; on record stores, 42;
on schools, 42–43
Raised by the People (Notch), 152–55, 155f
rap: bomba compared to, 62–63; Clemente's
cultural imperialism critique, 44;
gangsta rap, 143–44; as Puerto Rican,
49; reggaetón distinguished from, 176n2;
Reyes on, 45–46. *See also* hip-hop
"Rap: Soy Boricua pa' que Tú lo Sepas"
(Bernabe), 49
"Rapeo sobre el rap en Ciales" (Reyes),
45–46
Rebollo-Gil, Guillermo, 109
reggae en español, 31–33, 176n9
reggaetón: classification of, 1–2, 11–13;
continued resonation in Puerto Rico,
167–68; as "dangerous crossroad," 17;
early U.S. circulation of, 176n72; as
"enemy" of hip-hop, 197n91; gender and
sexuality problematic in, 17; Internet
distribution and globalization of, 167;

mainstreaming of, 49–50, 53, 83–84,
118, 130–33, 147, 166–67; Puerto Rico as
epicenter of, 2; rap distinguished from,
176n2; as transnational and circum-
Caribbean, 15; underground, difference
from, 176n8; underground, shift from,
50–51; urban blackness and, 11. *See also*
specific topics and musicians
Reggaeton Summerfest concert (Madison
Square Garden, 2003), 143
respectability: Anti-Pornography Campaign and racialized female hypersexu-
ality vs., 54–55, 56–59, 70, 73–77; Ivy
Queen and, 108; politics of, 55; white-
ness, association with, 58
Reyes, Edwin, 45–46, 49
Reyes-Santos, Irmary, 103
riddims, 29–30, 33, 178n46, 179n74
Rishi Rich Project, 167
Rivera, Ismael, 84, 91–92, 99
Rivera, Raquel Z., 4, 28, 44, 48, 84, 139,
176n8, 197n91
Rivera, Victor, 60
Rivera Meléndez, Laura, 84
Rodríguez, Chamaco, 99
Rodríguez, Mercedes, 61
Roena, Roberto, 84
romantiqueo, 118, 168, 192n55
roncar, 125
Rosaly, Yolanda, 47
Rose, Tricia, 86
Rosselló, Pedro, 36
Rudolph, Jennifer Domino, 92, 125, 164,
186n4
rumba, 190n62
rumberas, 66

saints and spirit possession, 187n31
salsa, 17, 92, 101, 127
salsa romántica, 127
Santiago, Victor (N.O.R.E.), 147–51,
149f
Santiago-Valles, Kelvin, 35
Santos-Febres, Mayra, 11, 43, 48
Santurce, 82, 91, 92
"Según Tú" (Ivy Queen), 124
Sennah, Kalefa, 1–2
"Señor Oficial" (Eddie Dee), 39–42